INTO THE
TWILIGHT

THE
ROD SERLING
PROGRAMME GUIDE

Other books in this series:

BLAKE'S 7 – PROGRAMME GUIDE by Tony Attwood

DOCTOR WHO – PROGRAMME GUIDE by Jean-Marc Lofficier

RED DWARF – PROGRAMME GUIDE by Chris Howarth and
Steve Lyons

THUNDERBIRDS, STINGRAY, CAPTAIN SCARLET –
THE AUTHORISED PROGRAMME GUIDE by John Peel

THE ADDAMS FAMILY & THE MUNSTERS –
PROGRAMME GUIDE by John Peel

THE EASTENDERS PROGRAMME GUIDE by
Josephine Monroe

THE NEIGHBOURS PROGRAMME GUIDE by
Josephine Monroe

INTO THE TWILIGHT

THE ROD SERLING PROGRAMME GUIDE

Jean-Marc and Randy Lofficier

Virgin

First published in 1995 by
Virgin Books
an imprint of Virgin Publishing Ltd
332 Ladbroke Grove
London W10 5AH

Text copyright © Jean-Marc and Randy Lofficier 1995

Typeset by Mark Stammers Design, London

Printed and bound in Great Britain by
Cox & Wyman Ltd, Reading Berks

ISBN 0 86369 844 1

CONTENTS

Acknowledgements   vii

A – Programme Guides

1. The Twilight Zone   1
2. Rod Serling's Night Gallery   77
3. Twilight Zone: The Movie   124
4. The New Twilight Zone   130
5. Twilight Zone: Rod Serling's Lost Classics   184
6. The Twilight Zone: Showtime Version   187

B – Spotlights

1. Rod Serling   188
2. Buck Houghton   210
3. Richard Matheson   217
4. Frank Marshall   224
5. Joe Dante   229
6. Philip DeGuere   236
7. Wes Craven   239
8. Alan Brennert   243
9. Paul Chitlik & Jeremy Bertrand Finch   254

C – Indices

1. Episode Titles   262
2. Creative Personnel   267
3. Actors   274

ACKNOWLEDGEMENTS

Like the *Doctor Who – Programme Guide*, this book first saw life as a rather lengthy article in the French cinema magazine, *L'Ecran Fantastique*. 'Rod Serling, Pionnier de la Quatrième Dimension' (Pioneer of the Fourth Dimension) appeared in No. 11, second series, 4th quarter 1979.

(As an aside, *The Twilight Zone* was shown on French television under the title *La Quatrième Dimension* (The Fourth Dimension), hence the title of Jean-Marc's article; the CBS *Twilight Zone* was later released, not without a certain logic, as *The Fifth Dimension*.)

We must, therefore, first and foremost acknowledge the support of *L'Ecran Fantastique* founder and editor Alain Schlockoff, who initially agreed to publish a massive article on a topic that was, at the time, rather obscure to most of his French readers.

Four years later, our paths would again cross that of Rod Serling's creation when we were asked to cover *The Twilight Zone: The Movie* for a variety of film magazines, including *Starlog*, *Starburst* and, yes, *The Twilight Zone Magazine* itself. Grateful acknowledgements should go to *Starlog*'s steadfast editor, David McDonnell, and to the editor of the late and lamented *Twilight Zone Magazine*, T. E. D. Klein, who has since then reaped the deserved fruits of literary stardom. (T. E. D. is the author of *Ceremonies*, a remarkable horror novel.)

Relatively little of any substance has been written specifically on Rod Serling and his work. Readers interested in further books on the subject should look for copies of the indispensable *Twilight Zone Companion* by Marc Scott Zicree (Bantam, 1982), a talented writer who goes into much greater length about the actual making of the original television show than we could, or wanted to do here.

For those who wish to know more about Rod Serling, the man, the biographies to read are *Rod Serling: The Dreams and*

Nightmares of Life in the Twilight Zone by Joel Engel (Contemporary Books, 1989) and *Serling: The Rise and Twilight of Television's Last Angry Man* by Gordon F. Sander (Dutton, 1992). Both are highly recommended.

We are also very much indebted to the following individuals who helped with the research for this book: Bill Anchors, Alain Carrazé, Don Cannon of Aladdin Books, Lee Goldberg, Eric Hoffman, Stephen Jones, and John and Nan Peel, who have all provided much needed support and assistance.

We are especially grateful to Alan Brennert. In spite of his busy schedule, Alan managed to find the time to provide research assistance, ferreting out the truth on original story credits that would have otherwise remained in obscurity.

Jean-Marc & Randy Lofficier

THE PROGRAMME GUIDES

The Twilight Zone

'There is a fifth dimension beyond what is known to Man. It is a dimension as vast as space and timeless as infinity. It is the middle ground between light and shadow, between science and superstition, and it lies between the pit of man's fears and the summit of his knowledge. This is the dimension of imagination. It is an area which we call ... the Twilight Zone!'

The Twilight Zone ran on CBS from October 1959 to June 1964, with a total of 156 episodes. The vast majority of these were written by Rod Serling himself. Other noted writers contributing to the success of the show included Richard Matheson, Charles Beaumont and George Clayton Johnson. Because of Serling's reputation, and the quality of its scripts, *The Twilight Zone* quickly established itself as a 'star' in the firmament of television shows. It was consequently able to attract the services of some of Hollywood's finest directors: Douglas Heyes, Robert Parrish, Buzz Kulik, Montgomery Pittman, Mitchell Leisen and Lamont Johnson, as well as some of its most famous actors: Buster Keaton, Mickey Rooney, Carol Burnett, Donald Pleasance, Cliff Robertson, Ida Lupino, Lee Marvin, James Coburn, Burgess Meredith and Agnes Moorehead.

The Twilight Zone's seeds were planted in 1958 with a play entitled *The Time Element*, which Serling had sold to the CBS network to be the pilot for a new show which he had conceived. Serling's motivation was a desire to spread his creative wings after many years of intensive writing for television anthology shows such as *Kraft Television Theater*, *Lux Video Theater*, etc.

Frustrated with sponsors and/or network interference, Serling wanted to tell new stories and felt that a fantasy-based format, because of its perceived 'unreality', would give a flexibility he did not have when writing about contemporary events.

In *The Time Element*[1], a man goes to see a psychiatrist because he experiences recurring dreams about being in Pearl Harbor at the time of the bombing. He eventually disappears and the psychiatrist (if not the audience) is amazed when he later discovers his patient in a period photograph. CBS, presumably nervous about the fantasy element of the story, turned it down. However, Serling was then able to resell his script to the then-popular *Westinghouse Desilu Playhouse*, which broadcast it on 24 November 1958, with a tacked-on epilogue trying to provide the rational explanation for the story that the psychiatrist had imagined it all. Nevertheless, the considerable success of *The Time Element* convinced CBS that it had been wrong, and to give Serling's series proposal a chance. Thus *The Twilight Zone* was born.

Since Serling had resold *The Time Element*, he had to come up with a whole new pilot. After an aborted try – a story about euthanasia – Serling eventually completed *Where Is Everybody?*, which was shot in February 1959 under the aegis of producer William Self. The pilot proved attractive to the sponsors, and CBS signed a contract with Serling's production company, Cayuga Productions, for a full season. Two months later, *The Twilight Zone* began production, with producer Buck Houghton replacing Self.

Even though *The Twilight Zone* garnered only modest ratings at first, the show quickly drew much critical recognition, all of it positive. Its first season won a Directors' Guild Award for John Brahm, a Producers' Guild Award for Houghton, an Emmy Award for Serling (his fourth); and a science fiction Hugo Award, as well as a bevy of other, less prestigious awards. In the Spring of 1960, CBS renewed *The Twilight Zone* for a second year, although under different sponsorship.

The second season brought more awards, including another Emmy for Serling and another Hugo, but also more difficulties with the sponsors, and the beginning of a certain malaise for Serling and Houghton. By the beginning of the third season, a change in management at CBS had brought increasing concerns and pressure about costs. Also, Serling, who had, until then, written 80 per cent of the show (it was one of his contractual obligations), felt that he was starting to run out of ideas. Finally, the show had difficulty attracting and retaining sponsors because of its unconventional nature.

Indeed, by early 1962, *The Twilight Zone* found itself without a sponsor. As a result, the show was almost cancelled, forcing Houghton to find another job. In January 1963, CBS eventually made up its mind to renew *The Twilight Zone* for a fourth season, but in an effort to attract a larger audience, it was decided to make it an hour long. The network and Serling also hired producer Herbert Hirschman to replace Houghton.

The one-hour *Twilight Zone*s clearly proved not as successful as the half-hour stories, and certainly did not increase the show's audience. After a mid-season change in producers – Bert Granet replacing departing Hirschman – CBS half-heartedly renewed the show for a fifth and, as it turned out, final season, returning it to its original half-hour length. After thirteen episodes, Bert Granet left to produce John Houseman's *Great Adventures*, and was replaced by William Froug. By then, Serling's enthusiasm had waned, and the series was obviously running out of steam. Serling himself claimed he was not unhappy when CBS decided not to renew the show for a sixth year in early 1964.

---

[1] For further information, see 'Spotlight Rod Serling'.

Pilot

1: 'Where Is Everybody?'

2nd October 1959

Writer: Rod Serling.   **Director:** Robert Stevens.
Producer: William Self.   **Director of Photography:**
Music: Bernard Herrmann.   Joseph LaSelle.

Cast: Earl Holliman (Mike Ferris); James Gregory (General).

Story: An astronaut wanders into a mysteriously empty town. He eventually discovers that he has been in an isolation tank and that the town is just an hallucination.

Note: In Serling's own novelisation (in *Stories From The Twilight Zone*), a further twist was added: after the astronaut is brought back to reality, in his pocket, he finds a theatre ticket stub which he had unconsciously picked up in the town.

First Season

Executive Producer: Rod Serling.
Producer: Buck Houghton.
Director of Photography: George T. Clemens, Harry Wild (episode 14 only).
Theme Music: Marius Constant.
Music: Stock except where indicated.
Make-up: Bob Keats.
SPFX: Virgil Beck.

2: 'One for the Angels'

9 October 1959

Writer: Rod Serling.   **Director:** Robert Parrish.

Cast: Ed Wynn (Lew Bookman); Murray Hamilton (Death); Dana Dillaway (Maggie); Merritt Bohn (Truck Driver); Jay Overholts (Doctor); Mickey Maga (Little Boy).

Story: A clever salesman succeeds in getting a reprieve from Death, who takes a little girl's life as a replacement. The salesman then delivers a superb sales pitch to save her and, by so doing, sacrifices himself.

3: 'Mr Denton on Doomsday'
16 October 1959

Writer: Rod Serling.   **Director:** Allen Reisner.

Cast: Dan Duryea (Al Denton); Malcolm Atterbury (Fate); Martin Landau (Hotaling); Jeanne Cooper (Liz); Ken Lynch (Charlie); Doug McClure (Grant); Arthur Batanides (Leader); Robert Burton (Doctor); Bill Erwin (Man).

Story: A magic potion enables a washed-out gunslinger to face down a young rival, but it also puts an end to his career in an ironic twist of fate.

Note: Martin Landau later played John Koenig in *Space: 1999*. Doug McClure starred in *At the Earth's Core* and *The People That Time Forgot* in the 1970s.

4: 'The 16mm Shrine'
23 October 1959

Writer: Rod Serling.   **Director:** Mitchell Leisen.
Music: Franz Waxman.

Cast: Ida Lupino (Barbara Jean Trenton); Martin Balsam (Weiss); Alice Frost (Sally); Ted De Corsia (Sall); Jerome Cowan; John Clarke (Hearndan).

Story: An ageing movie queen escapes the horrors of old age by fleeing into the magical world of her own films.

5: 'Walking Distance'
30 October 1959

Writer: Rod Serling.   **Director:** Robert Stevens.
Music: Bernard Herrmann.

Cast: Gig Young (Martin Sloan); Michael Montgomery (Martin as a boy); Frank Overton (Father); Irene Tedrow (Mother); Byron Foulger (Charlie); J. Pat O'Malley (Wilson); Bill Erwin (Wilcox); Joseph Corey (Soda Jerk); Ron Howard, Buzz Martin (Boys); Nan Peterson (Woman); Sheridan Comerate (Attendant).

Story: A weary ad agency vice-president travels back in time to his hometown, and meets his father and himself as a boy, before returning to the present a wiser man.

6: 'Escape Clause'
6 November 1959

Writer: Rod Serling.   **Director:** Mitchell Leisen.

Cast: David Wayne (Walter Bedeker); Thomas Gomez (Cadwallader); Virginia Christine (Ethel); Wendell Holmes (Cooper); Dick Wilson; Joe Flynn (Adjusters); George Baxter (Judge); Raymond Bailey (Doctor); Allan Lurie, Nesdon Booth (Guards); Paul E. Burns (Janitor).

Story: A hypochondriac makes a deal with the devil for immortality. However, he is forced to invoke the 'escape clause' after being sentenced to life imprisonment for killing his wife.

7: 'The Lonely'

13 November 1959

Writer: Rod Serling.   **Director:** Jack Smight.
Music: Bernard Herrmann.

Cast: Jack Warden (James Corry); Jean Marsh (Alicia); John Dehner (Captain Allenby); Ted Knight (Adams); Jim Turley (Carstairs).

Story: A lonely convict imprisoned on an asteroid falls in love with a woman android. When he is finally pardoned, he refuses to leave her behind.

8: 'Time Enough At Last'

20 November 1959

Writer: Rod Serling.   **Story:** Lynn Venable.
Director: John Brahm.   **Music:** Leith Stevens.

Cast: Burgess Meredith (Henry Bemis); Jacqueline De Witt (Helen Bemis); Vaughn Taylor (Carsville); Lela Bliss (Woman).

Story: A myopic bank teller survives an atomic war and looks forward to a life of peaceful reading, until he breaks his glasses.

Note: This is one of the most fondly-remembered episodes of *The Twilight Zone*. Lynn Venable's story originally appeared in the January 1953 issue of *If*.

9: 'Perchance to Dream'

27 November 1959

Writer: Charles Beaumont.   **Story:** Charles Beaumont.
Director: Robert Florey.   **Music:** Van Cleave.

Cast: Richard Conte (Edward Hall); John Larch (Dr

Rathmann); Suzanne Lloyd (Maya); Ted Stanhope (Stranger); Eddie Marr, Russell Trent (Barkers).

Story: A man tells his psychiatrist that he is afraid of being murdered in his dreams by a strange girl. He later dreams that he falls to his death, but in reality he has died on the psychiatrist's couch.

Note: Charles Beaumont's story originally appeared in the November 1958 issue of *Playboy*.

10: 'Judgment Night'
4 December 1959

Writer: Rod Serling.   **Director:** John Brahm.

Cast: Nehemiah Persoff (Lanser); Ben Wright (Captain Wilbur); Patrick Macnee (First Officer); Hugh Sanders (Potter); Leslie Bradley (Major Devereaux); Deirdre Owen (Barbara); James Franciscus (Lieutenant Mueller); Kendrick Huxham (Bartender); Richard Peel, Donald Journeaux (Stewards); Barry Bernard (Engineer); Debbie Joyce (Little Girl).

Story: A passenger on the *Queen of Glasgow* cannot remember how he came to be on board, but is certain that the ship will be torpedoed at 1.15 a.m. He is, in fact, the U-boat captain condemned to eternally relive his victims' fate.

11: 'And When the Sky Was Opened'
11 December 1959

Writer: Rod Serling.   **Story:** Richard Matheson.
Director: Douglas Heyes.   **Music:** Leonard Roseman.

Cast: Rod Taylor (Forbes); Charles Aidman (Harrington); James Hutton (Gart); Maxine Cooper (Amy); Logan Field (Investigator); S. John Launer (Mr Harrington); Paul Bryar (Bartender);

Gloria Pall (Girl); Sue Randall, Elizabeth Fielding (Nurses); Joe Bassett, Oliver McGowan (Officers).

Story: Three astronauts who have returned to Earth mysteriously disappear one by one as if they had never existed.

Note: This script is very loosely based on a Richard Matheson story entitled *Disappearing Act* which originally appeared in the March 1953 issue of *The Magazine of Fantasy and Science Fiction*.

12: 'What You Need'
25 December 1959

Writer: Rod Serling.   **Story:** Henry Kuttner and
Director: Alvin Ganzer.   Catherine L. Moore
Music: Van Cleave.   (writing as Lewis Padgett).

Cast: Steve Cochran (Renard); Ernest Truex (Pedott); Read Morgan (Lefty); Arline Sax (Girl); William Edmonson (Bartender); Judy Ellis (Woman); Fred Kruger (Man); Norman Sturgis (Hotel Clerk); Frank Alloca (Waiter); Mark Sunday (Photographer).

Story: A desperate and bitter man tries to exploit the strange powers of an old salesman who can tell what people will need in their futures. The salesman fights back by giving the other man a pair of new shoes which cause his death.

Note: Henry Kuttner and C. L. Moore's story originally appeared in the October 1945 issue of *Astounding Science Fiction*.

13: 'The Four of Us Are Dying'
1 January 1960

Writer: Rod Serling.   **Story:** George Clayton Johnson.
Director: John Brahm.   **Music:** Jerry Goldsmith.

Cast: Harry Townes (Hammer); Beverly Garland (Maggie); Philip Pine (Sterig); Ross Martin (Foster); Don Gordon (Marshak); Peter Brocco (Pop Marshak); Bernard Fein (Penell); Milton Frome (Detective); Harry Jackson (Trumpet Player); Sam Rawlins (Busboy); Bob Hopkins, Pat Comiskey (Men in Bar).

Story: A con artist who has the ability to make his face change, successively impersonates four people, but ends up being shot by the father of one of his victims.

14: 'Third from the Sun'
8 January 1960

Writer: Rod Serling. **Story:** Richard Matheson.
Director: Richard Bare.

Cast: Fritz Weaver (Sturka); Joe Maross (Riden); Edward Andrews (Carling); Denise Alexander (Jody); Lori March (Eve); Jeanne Evans (Ann); Will J. White (Guard); S. John Launer (Loudspeaker).

Story: Two families plot to escape from their planet, which is threatened by nuclear destruction, in a rocket. Their destination: Earth.

Note: Richard Matheson's story originally appeared in the October 1950 issue of *Galaxy*.

15: 'I Shot an Arrow into the Air'
15 January 1960

Writer: Rod Serling. **Based on an idea by:**
Director: Stuart Rosenberg. Madelon Champion.

Cast: Edward Binns (Donlin); Dewey Martin (Corey); Ted Otis

(Pierson); Leslie Barrett (Brandt); Harry Bartell (Langford).

Story: An astronaut kills his two companions to survive on what he believes to be a hostile planet, until he discovers that they have really landed in the Nevada Desert.

16: 'The Hitch-Hiker'
22 January 1960

Writer: Rod Serling.   **Story:** Lucille Fletcher.
Director: Alvin Ganzer.

Cast: Leonard Strong (The Hitch-Hiker); Inger Stevens (Nan Adams); Adam Williams (Sailor); Lew Gallo (Mechanic); Dwight Townsend (Flag Man); Russ Bender (Counterman); Mitzi McCall (Waitress); George Mitchell (Gas Station Man); Eleanor Audley (Mrs Whitney).

Story: A mysterious hitch-hiker, whom only a lone driver can see, turns out to be Death.

Note: Lucille Fletcher's story was a radio play originally broadcast on *The Mercury Theater* in 1941, starring Orson Welles.

17: 'The Fever'
29 January 1960

Writer: Rod Serling.   **Director:** Robert Florey.

Cast: Everett Sloane (Franklin Gibbs); Vivi Janiss (Flora); William Kendis (PR Man); Lee Millar (Photographer); Art Lewis (Drunk); Lee Sands (Floor Manager); Marc Towers (Cashier); Arthur Peterson (Sheriff); Carole Kent (Girl); Jeffrey Sayre (Croupier).

Story: A man enters a deadly duel of will with a slot machine which seems imbued with an evil life of its own. The machine wins.

18: 'The Last Flight'

5 February 1960

Writer: Richard Matheson.   **Director:** William Claxton.

Cast: Kenneth Haigh (Decker); Alexander Scourby (General Harper); Simon Scott (Major Wilson); Robert Warwick (Mackaye); Harry Raybould (Corporal); Paul Baxley, Jack Perkins (Drivers); Jerry Catron (Guard).

Story: A WWI flying ace abandons a friend and lands in 1959. There, he discovers that his friend became a hero during WWII. Shamed, he returns to his own time to save his friend, at the cost of his own life.

19: 'The Purple Testament'

12 February 1960

Writer: Rod Serling.   **Director:** Richard Bare.
Music: Lucien Morawack
and Lud Gluskin.

Cast: William Reynolds (Fitzgerald); Dick York (Riker); Barney Phillips (Gunther); William Phipps (Sergeant); Warren Oates (Driver); Marc Cavell (Freeman); Ron Masak (Harmonica Man); Paul Mazursky (Orderly); Michael Vandever (Smitty); S. John Launer (Colonel).

Story: A WWII lieutenant has the power to see which of his men are going to die by looking at their faces. He eventually sees the 'look of death' on his own face in a mirror, but goes to his fate nevertheless.

20: 'Elegy'

19 February 1960

Writer: Charles Beaumont. **Story:** Charles Beaumont.
Director: Douglas Heyes. **Music:** Van Cleave.

Cast: Cecil Kellaway (Wickwire); Jeff Morrow (Meyers); Kevin Hagen (Webber); Don Dubbins (Kirby).

Story: Three astronauts become stranded on a planet of motionless figures; it turns out to be a cemetery. The android caretaker poisons them and, fulfilling their wish to go home, places their preserved bodies back at the controls of their ship.

Note: Charles Beaumont's story originally appeared in the February 1953 issue of *Imagination*.

21: 'Mirror Image'

26 February 1960

Writer: Rod Serling. **Director:** John Brahm.

Cast: Vera Miles (Millicent Barnes); Martin Milner (Grinstead); Joe Hamilton (Ticket Agent); Ferris Taylor, Naomi Stevens (Passengers); Terese Lyon (Old Woman); Edwin Rand (Bus Driver).

Story: A young woman believes she has gone mad when she sees her doppelgänger in a bus station. Later, a man who tried to help her also sees his own double.

22: 'The Monsters are due on Maple Street'

4 March 1960

Writer: Rod Serling. **Director:** Ron Winston.
Music: Rene Garriguenc
and Lud Gluskin.

Cast: Claude Akins (Steve Brand); Anne Barton (Mrs Brand); Jack Weston (Charlie); Lyn Guild (Charlie's Wife); Barry Atwater (Mr Goodman); Lea Waggner (Mrs Goodman); Ben Erway (Pete Van Horn); Jan Handzlik (Tommy); Mary Gregory (Tommy's Mother); Burt Metcalfe (Don); Jason Johnson (Man); Joan Sudlow, Amzie Strickland (Women); Sheldon Allman, William Walsh (Aliens).

Story: A meteor sighting and a power shortage cause the residents of Maple Street to suspect each other of being aliens and, eventually, to destroy themselves. Real aliens are revealed to have been behind this paranoia-inducing scenario.

Note: Another famous *Twilight Zone* episode remembered for its striking message. 'For the record, prejudice can kill, and suspicion can destroy, and a thoughtless, frightened search for a scapegoat has a fallout all its own, for the children, and the children yet unborn,' says Serling in his concluding statement.

23: 'A World of Difference'

11 March 1960

Writer: Richard Matheson.   **Director:** Ted Post.
Music: Van Cleave.

Cast: Howard Duff (Arthur Curtis); Eileen Ryan (Nora); Gail Kobe (Sally); Frank Maxwell (Marty); Peter Walker (Endicott); Susan Dorn (Marian); David White (Brinkley); William Idelson (Kelly).

Story: The normal world of a businessman is turned topsy-turvy when he discovers that he is an actor in a movie that is about to be cancelled. The powers-that-be eventually allow him to return to the happier, fictional world.

24: 'Long Live Walter Jameson'

18 March 1960

Writer: Charles Beaumont.   **Director:** Anton Leader.
Special Make-Up: William Tuttle.

Cast: Kevin McCarthy (Jameson); Edgar Stehli (Kittridge);
Estelle Winwood (Laurette); Dody Heath (Susanna).

Story: A university professor dicovers that his colleague and
future son-in-law, Walter Jameson, is in reality an officer from
the Civil War, Hugh Skelton, who bought an immortality potion
from an alchemist. Jameson is eventually shot by a former wife.

25: 'People are Alike All Over'

25 March 1960

Writer: Rod Serling.   **Story:** Paul W. Fairman.
Director: Mitchell Leisen.

Cast: Roddy McDowall (Sam Conrad); Susan Oliver (Teenya);
Paul Comi (Marcusson); Byron Morrow, Vic Perrin, Vernon
Gray (Martians).

Story: A stranded astronaut discovers that the Martians are just
like Earthmen; however, he eventually ends up in a zoo.

Note: Paul W. Fairman's story, entitled *Brothers beyond the
Void*, originally appeared in the March 1952 issue of *Fantastic
Adventures*.

26: 'Execution'

1 April 1960

Writer: Rod Serling.   **Story:** George Clayton Johnson.
Director: David Orrick McDearmon.

Cast: Albert Salmi (Joe Caswell); Russell Johnson (Professor

Manion); Than Wyenn (Johnson); Jon Lormer (Reverend);
George Mitchell (Old Man); Fay Roope (Judge); Richard Karlan
(Bartender); Joe Haworth (Cowboy).

Story: A scientist uses a time machine and unwittingly rescues
a western outlaw from hanging. The outlaw then kills the professor, but is later strangled by a thief, who is accidentally sent
back in time to take the outlaw's place.

27: 'The Big, Tall Wish'
8 April 1960
Writer: Rod Serling.   **Director:** Ron Winston.
Music: Jerry Goldsmith.

Cast: Ivan Dixon (Bolie Jackson); Steven Perry (Henry); Kim
Hamilton (Frances); Walter Burke (Mizell); Henry Scott
(Thomas); Charles Horvath (Fighter); Carl McIntire
(Announcer); Frankie Van (Referee).

Story: A child's faith helps an ageing boxer win his last match.

28: 'A Nice Place to Visit'
15 April 1960
Writer: Charles Beaumont.   **Director:** John Brahm.

Cast: Larry Blyden (Rocky Valentine); Sebastian Cabot (Mr
Pip); Sandra Warner, Barbara English (Girls); Wayne Tucker
(Croupier); John Close (Policeman); Peter Hornsby (Crap
Dealer); Nels Nelson (Midget); Bill Mullikin (Parking Attendant).

Story: A burglar killed during a robbery discovers an afterlife
in which all his wishes are granted. Eventually, it becomes too
much to bear and he realises he is in Hell.

29: 'Nightmare as a Child'

29 April 1960

Writer: Rod Serling. **Director:** Alvin Ganzer.
Music: Jerry Goldsmith.

Cast: Janice Rule (Helen Foley); Terry Burnham (Markie);
Shepperd Strudwick (Peter); Michael Fox (Doctor); Joe Perry
(Policeman); Suzanne Cupito (Little Girl).

Story: A teacher is haunted by the image of herself as a child.
She then remembers her mother's murder, and manages to foil
the murderer who has returned to kill her.

Note: The character of Helen Foley was named after one of
Serling's own teachers. It was used again by Joe Dante in the
movie adaptation of *It's A Good Life* (episode 73). Suzanne
Cupito is better known today as actress Morgan Brittany.

30: 'A Stop at Willoughby'

6 May 1960

Writer: Rod Serling. **Director:** Robert Parrish.
Music: Nathan Scott.

Cast: James Daly (Gart Williams); Howard Smith (Misrell);
Patricia Donahue (Jane); James Maloney, Jason Wingreen (Con-
ductors); Mavis Neal (Helen); Billy Booth, Butch Hengen
(Boys); Ryan Hayes, Max Slaten (Men on Train).

Story: A harried advertising executive falls asleep on a train
and wakes up in the peaceful, turn-of-the-century town of
Willoughby. In reality, he jumped to his death when he heard
someone shout 'Willoughby' – which turns out to be the name
of a funeral home.

31: 'The Chaser'
13 May 1960

Writer: Robert Presnell, Jr.   **Story:** John Collier.
Director: Douglas Heyes.

Cast: George Grizzard (Roger Shackleforth); John McIntire (Daemon); Patricia Barry (Leila); J. Pat O'Malley (Homburg); Duane Grey (Bartender); Barbara Perry, Marjorie Bennett (Women); Rusty Wescoatt (Man).

Story: A man uses a love potion to make a woman fall in love with him. Later, he plans to poison her, but relents when he learns she is pregnant.

Note: John Collier's story was originally written for *Billy Rose's Playbill Theater* and aired on 20 February 1951 as *Duet for Two Actors*.

32: 'A Passage for Trumpet'
20 May 1960

Writer: Rod Serling.   **Director:** Don Medford.
Music: Lyn Murray.

Cast: Jack Klugman (Joey Crown); Mary Webster (Nan); John Anderson (Gabriel); Frank Wolff (Baron); James Flavin (Driver); Ned Glass (Pawnshop Man); Diane Honodel (Woman).

Story: A failed trumpet player disillusioned with life dies in a car accident, but his playing attracts the angel Gabriel who gives him a second chance.

33: 'Mr Bevis'
3 June 1960

Writer: Rod Serling.   **Director:** William Asher.

Cast: Orson Bean (Bevis); Henry Jones (Hempstead); Charles Lane (Peckinpaugh); William Schallert, House Peters Jr (Policemen); Colleen O'Sullivan (Young Lady); Dorothy Neuman (Landlady); Horace McMahon (Bartender); Florence MacMichael (Margaret); Vito Scotti (Peddler); Timmy Cletro (Boy).

Story: Mr Bevis's guardian angel turns him from a penniless eccentric into a successful man. When he realises it has cost Bevis his happiness, he eventually returns him to his previous condition.

Note: This episode was intended as a 'backdoor' pilot for another television series. It was later remade as *Cavender Is Coming* (episode 101).

34: 'The After Hours'
10 June 1960

Writer: Rod Serling.   **Director:** Douglas Heyes.
Special make-up: William Tuttle.

Cast: Anne Francis (Marsha White); Liz Allen (Saleswoman); James Millhollin (Armbruster); John Conwell (Elevator Man); Nancy Rennick (Mrs Pettigrew); Patrick Whyte (Sloan).

Story: A woman in a department store comes across a mysterious ninth floor where store mannequins come to life, and are allowed one month of 'freedom' every year. Eventually, she discovers that she, too, is a mannequin, and returns to her inanimate existence.

Note: This episode was remade in *The New Twilight Zone* (episode 28a). Anne Francis starred in *Forbidden Planet* (1956).

35: 'The Mighty Casey'
17 June 1960

Writer: Rod Serling.   **Directors:** Robert Parrish
and Alvin Ganzer.

Cast: Jack Warden (Mouth McGarry); Robert Sorrells (Casey);
Abraham Sofaer (Dr Stillman); Don O'Kelly (Monk); Jonathan
Hole (Doctor); Alan Dexter (Beasley); Rusty Lane (Commissioner).

Story: The Hoboken Zephyrs, a failing baseball team, begin
winning matches after Casey, a robot, becomes their new pitcher.
But when Casey acquires a heart, he can no longer strike out
the competition and loses his usefulness.

Note: The role played by Jack Warden was originally played by
Paul Douglas, and directed by Alvin Glanzer. Douglas had a heart
attack before the show was completed. Serling then recast Warden and had portions of the episode reshot by Robert Parrish.

36: 'A World of his Own'
1 July 1960

Writer: Richard Matheson.   **Director:** Ralph Nelson.

Cast: Keenan Wynn (Gregory West); Phyllis Kirk (Victoria);
Mary La Roche (Mary).

Story: A playwright literally creates characters by describing
them in his dictaphone. His nagging wife thinks him mad until
she discovers she, too, is a creation. He replaces her with a
more loving spouse.

Note: At the end of the episode, West also makes Serling disappear during his concluding narration.

Second Season

Producer: Buck Houghton.
Director of Photography: George T. Clemens,
William Skall (episode 55 only).
Theme Music: Marius Constant.
Music: Stock except where indicated.
Make-up: Bob Keats.
SPFX: Virgil Beck.

37: 'King Nine Will Not Return'
30 September 1960

Writer: Rod Serling.   **Director:** Buzz Kulik.
Music: Fred Steiner.

Cast: Robert Cummings (Captain Embry); Paul Lambert (Doctor); Gene Lyons (Psychiatrist); Seymour Green (British Officer); Richard Lupino (British Man); Jenna McMahon (Nurse).

Story: The captain of a B-52 which crashed in the desert during WWII is haunted by the ghosts of his crewmates. He eventually wakes up in a hospital and discovers that his desert experience was a hallucination caused by his guilt at having missed the doomed flight seventeen years ago. However, the hospital staff discover desert sand in his shoes . . .

38: 'The Man in the Bottle'
7 October 1960

Writer: Rod Serling.   **Director:** Don Medford.

Cast: Luther Adler (Arthur Castle); Vivi Janiss (Edna); Lisa Golm (Mrs Gumley); Joseph Ruskin (Genie); Olan Soule (IRS Man); Peter Coe, Albert Szabo (Germans).

Story: A man obtains four wishes from a genie in a bottle. He wastes the first one on a test; his second wish is for a million dollars, soon eaten away by income taxes; his third wish to become ruler of a country turns into a nightmare when he becomes Hitler, and he uses his fourth wish to return to his previous life, which no longer seems so drab by comparison.

39: 'Nervous Man in a Four-Dollar Room'
14 October 1960

Writer: Rod Serling.   **Director:** Douglas Heyes.
Music: Jerry Goldsmith.

Cast: Joe Mantell (Jackie Rhoades); William D. Gordon (George).

Story: A petty thug is confronted by his conscience, who appears to him in a mirror. It eventually takes him over to keep him from committing a murder.

40: 'A Thing About Machines'
28 October 1960

Writer: Rod Serling.   **Director:** David Orrick
                                   McDearmon.

Cast: Richard Haydn (Bartlett Finchley); Barbara Stuart (Edith); Barney Phillips (TV Repair Man); Jay Overholts (Intern); Henry Beckman (Policeman); Margarita Cordova (Girl); Lew Brown (Telephone Repair Man).

Story: Domestic appliances and other machines get their revenge on a precious writer who hates all things mechanical. His car eventually causes him to fall to his death in his swimming pool.

41: 'The Howling Man'

4 November 1960

Writer: Charles Beaumont.   **Story:** Charles Beaumont.
Director: Douglas Heyes.

Cast: H.M. Wynant (David Ellington); John Carradine (Brother Jerome); Frederic Ledebur (Brother Christophorus); Robin Hughes (Howling Man); Ezelle Poule (Housekeeper).

Story: After WWI, Ellington, a lost traveller, finds refuge in a monastery where the monks claim to keep the Devil himself prisoner. He does not believe them and releases their mild-mannered prisoner. The latter turns out really to be the Devil, who then starts WWII. Ellington eventually recaptures the Devil, but won't be able to hold him.

Note: Charles Beaumont's story originally appeared in his collection *Night Ride and Other Journeys* (Bantam, 1960).

42: 'The Eye of the Beholder'

11 November 1960

Writer: Rod Serling.   **Director:** Douglas Heyes.
Music: Bernard Herrmann.   **Special make-up:** William
                                  Tuttle.

Cast: William D. Gordon (Doctor); Maxine Stuart, Donna Douglas (Janet Tyler); Jennifer Howard, Joanna Heyes (Nurses); George Keymas (Leader); Edson Stroll (Smith).

Story: Plastic surgeons attempt to repair Janet Tyler's deformed face, which has made her into an outcast. The operation is a failure – but we discover that Janet's face is beautiful (by our standards) and everybody else's is ugly. She is assigned to live in a village of outcasts like her, where she will be loved because beauty is in the eye of the beholder.

Note: Another justifiably famous *Twilight Zone* episode – arguably the best of the entire series. The direction and lighting were superb; all faces were completely hidden in shadows until the end. 'Now the questions that come to mind,' concludes Serling. 'Where is this place and when is it, what kind of world where ugliness is the norm and beauty the deviation from that norm? The answer is, it doesn't make any difference. Because the old saying happens to be true. Beauty *is* in the eye of the beholder, in this year or a hundred years hence, on this planet or wherever there is human life, perhaps out among the stars. Beauty is in the eye of the beholder. Lesson to be learned in the Twilight Zone.'

43: 'Nick of Time'
18 November 1960

Writer: Richard Matheson.　　　**Director:** Richard Bare.

Cast: William Shatner (Don Carter); Patricia Breslin (Pat); Guy Wilkerson (Counter Man); Stafford Repp (Mechanic); Walter Reed, Dee Carroll (Couple).

Story: The husband of a newly married couple becomes obsessed by the predictions of a fortune-telling machine. His wife's love is able to break the spell, but another couple is not so fortunate.

44: 'The Lateness of the Hour'
2 December 1960

Writer: Rod Serling.　　　**Director:** Jack Smight.

Cast: Inger Stevens (Jana); John Hoyt (Dr Loren); Irene Tedrow (Mrs Loren); Mary Gregory (Nelda); Tom Palmer (Butler); Doris Karnes (Gretchen); Valley Keane (Suzanne); Jason

Johnson (Jensen).

Story: A young woman feels trapped, surrounded by the flaw-less precision of the android servants built by her father, Dr Loren. She threatens to leave, but discovers that she, too, is an android. Dr Loren reprograms her to become a maid.

45: 'The Trouble with Templeton'
9 December 1960

Writer: E. Jack Neuman.   **Director:** Buzz Kulik.
Music: Jeff Alexander.

Cast: Brian Aherne (Booth Templeton); Pippa Scott (Laura); Charles S. Carlson (Barney); Sydney Pollack (Willis); Larry Blake (Freddie); King Calder (Sid); Dave Willock (Marcel); John Kroger (Ed Page); David Thursby (Eddie).

Story: An ageing actor feels despondent, missing his long-lost wife. He travels back in time and discovers that reality was not as pleasant as his memories. However, he realises later that it was a performance staged to give him a new will to live.

46: 'A Most Unusual Camera'
16 December 1960

Writer: Rod Serling.   **Director:** John Rich.

Cast: Fred Clark (Chester Dietrich); Jean Carson (Paula); Adam Williams (Woodward); Marcel Hillaire (Waiter); Art Lewis (Tout).

Story: Two thieves come across a camera that takes pictures of events five minutes in the future. It eventually shows them dead after falling out of a window, a prediction which comes to pass.

47: 'Night of the Meek'
23 December 1960

Writer: Rod Serling.   **Director:** Jack Smight.

Cast: Art Carney (Henry Corwin); John Fiedler (Dundee); Meg Wyllie (Sister); Bob Lieb (Flaherty); Burt Mustin (Burt); Val Avery (Bartender); Larrian Gillespie (Elf); Kay Cousins (Woman).

Story: A department store Santa who has just been fired finds a magic bag from which he can pull out any present he is asked for. Eventually, his selfless generosity is rewarded, and he becomes the real Santa Claus.

Note: This episode was remade in *The New Twilight Zone* (episode 13a).

48: 'Dust'
6 January 1961

Writer: Rod Serling.   **Director:** Douglas Heyes.
Music: Jerry Goldsmith.

Cast: Thomas Gomez (Sykes); Vladimir Sokoloff (Gallegos); John Alonso (Luis Gallegos); John Larch (Sheriff); Paul Genge, Dorothy Adams (Canfields); Andrea Margolis (Estrelita); Duane Grey (Rogers); Jon Lormer, Daniel White (Men); Douglas Heyes Jr (Farm Boy).

Story: In a small, hopeless, Mexican village, the father of a drunk who is to be hanged for running over a child, buys some magic dust which can turn hate into love. Before his son can die, the noose breaks and the town rediscovers the quality of mercy.

49: 'Back There'
13 January 1961

Writer: Rod Serling. **Director:** David Orrick
Music: Jerry Goldsmith. McDearmon.

Cast: Russell Johnson (Peter Corrigan); Bartlett Robinson (William); Paul Hartman (Police Sergeant); James Gavin (Policeman); John Lasell (Booth); James Lydon (Patrolman); Raymond Greenleaf (Jackson); Raymond Bailey (Millard); John Eldredge (Whittaker); Jean Inness (Mrs Landers); Lew Brown (Lieutenant); Carol Rossen (Girl); Nora Marlowe (Chambermaid); Fred Kruger, J. Pat O'Malley (Attendants).

Story: A man travels back in time to prevent Lincoln's assassination, but fails. He returns to the present, thinking that history cannot be changed, but it has. A former servant is now a millionaire.

50: 'The Whole Truth'
20 January 1961

Writer: Rod Serling. **Director:** James Sheldon.

Cast: Jack Carson (Harvey Hunnicut); Loring Smith (Grimbley); Arte Johnson (Irv); Lee Sabinson (Khrushchev); Jack Ging, Nan Peterson (Young Couple); George Chandler (Old Man); Patrick Westwood (Translator).

Story: A used car salesman comes across a Model A car which compels its owner always to tell the truth. He eventually unloads it on Russian premier, Nikita Khrushchev.

51: 'The Invaders'
27 January 1961

Writer: Richard Matheson. **Director:** Douglas Heyes.
Music: Jerry Goldsmith.

Cast: Agnes Moorehead (Woman); Douglas Heyes (Voice of

Astronaut).

Story: A lonely old woman is attacked by miniature spacemen, who are eventually revealed to be from Earth.

Note: Another famous episode. It is totally without dialogue, except for the last scene when, before the woman kills the spaceman, he has time to radio his home planet – Earth. The letters on the side of the spaceship (the same prop as that used in the movie *Forbidden Planet*) then reveal its origin.

52: 'A Penny for your Thoughts'
3 February 1961

Writer: George Clayton Johnson.   **Director:** James Sheldon.

Cast: Dick York (Hector B. Poole); June Dayton (Miss Turner); Hayden Rourke (Sykes); Dan Tobin (Bagby); Cyril Delevanti (Smithers); Harry Jackson (Brand); Frank London (Driver); Anthony Ray (Newsboy).

Story: A mild-mannered bank teller discovers that he has the power to read minds. He eventually finds that thoughts do not necessarily reflect intentions, but manages to use his short-lived gift to get the girl he loves, and a promotion.

53: 'Twenty-Two'
10 February 1961

Writer: Rod Serling.   Based on an anecdote from
Director: Jack Smight.   *Famous Ghost Stories,*
edited by Bennett Cerf.

Cast: Barbara Nichols (Liz Powell); Jonathan Harris (Doctor); Fredd Wayne (Barney); Arline Sax (Stewardess); Norma Connolly, Mary Adams (Nurses); Wesley Lau, Joe Sargent

(Ticket Clerks); Jay Overholts (PA Voice).

Story: A young dancer has a recurring nightmare about the morgue (room 22) and a nurse who says 'room for one more, honey'. She eventually refuses to board a plane – flight 22 – when the stewardess invites her in with the very same words. The plane explodes in mid-flight.

54: 'The Odyssey of Flight 33'
24 February 1961

Writer: Rod Serling.   **Director:** Justus Addiss.

Cast: John Anderson (Farver); Sandy Kenyon (Hatch); Paul Comi (Craig); Harp McGuire (Purcell); Wayne Heffley (Wyatt); Nancy Rennick (Paula); Beverly Brown (Jane); Lester Fletcher (RAF Man); Betty Garde, Jay Overholts (Passengers).

Story: A London–New York jet airliner becomes lost in time, finding itself first in prehistoric times, then in 1939.

Note: The dinosaur footage used in this episode came from the film *Dinosaurus*.

55: 'Mr Dingle, The Strong'
3 March 1961

Writer: Rod Serling.   **Director:** John Brahm.

Cast: Burgess Meredith (Luther Dingle); Don Rickles (Bettor); James Westerfield (O'Toole); Edward Ryder (Callahan); James Millhollin (Abernathy); Douglas Spencer, Michael Fox (Martians); Donald Losby, Greg Irvin (Venusians); Jay Hector (Boy); Jo Ann Dixon (Nurse); Bob Duggan (Photographer); Phil Arnold, Douglas Evans, Frank Richards (Men).

Story: Dingle, a shy vacuum-cleaner salesman, is given super-strength by a two-headed martian. After Dingle makes a fool of himself, the martian removes his powers, but recommends him to two Venusians looking for a subject whose intelligence they can boost.

56: 'Static'

10 March 1961

Writer: Charles Beaumont.   **Story:** OCee Ritch.
Director: Buzz Kulik.

Cast: Dean Jagger (Ed Lindsay); Carmen Matthews (Vinnie Brown); Robert Emhardt (Ackerman); Alice Pearce (Mrs Nielsen); Arch W. Johnson (Bragg); Lillian O'Malley (Miss Meredith); J. Pat O'Malley (Mr Llewellyn); Clegg Hoyt (Junk Dealer); Jerry Fuller (Singer); Eddie Marr (Pitchman); Bob Crane (DJ); Roy Rowan (Announcer); Diane Strom (Girl); Stephen Talbot (Boy); Bob Duggan, Jay Overholts (Men).

Story: A nostalgic old man discovers that he can receive radio programmes from the past on an old set. He eventually finds himself transported back to the 1940s for a second chance at life.

57: 'The Prime Mover'

24 March 1961

Writer: Charles Beaumont.   **Story:** George Clayton Johnson.
Director: Richard Bare.

Cast: Dane Clark (Larsen); Buddy Ebsen (Jimbo Cobb); Christine White (Kitty); Nesdon Booth (Big Phil); Jane Burgess (Sheila); Clancy Cooper (Trucker); Joe Scott (Croupier); Robert Riordan, William Keene (Hotel Personnel).

Story: Ace Larsen, a compulsive gambler, enlists the help of Jimbo Cobb, a psychokinetic, to win money at dice in Las Vegas, but it only brings trouble. Jimbo pretends to lose his power, things return to normal and he marries Ace's girlfriend.

Note: Due to a production oversight, George Clayton Johnson's name was omitted from the credits.

58: 'Long Distance Call'
31 March 1961

Writers: Charles Beaumont and William Idelson.   **Director:** James Sheldon.

Cast: Billy Mumy (Billy Bayles); Phillip Abbott (Chris Bayles); Lili Darvas (Grandma); Patricia Smith (Sylvia); Jenny Maxwell (Shirley); Henry Hunter (Dr Unger); Reid Hammond (Peterson); Lew Brown (Attendant); Jutta Parr (Nurse); Robert McCord, Jim Turley (Firemen).

Story: A little boy uses a toy telephone to speak to his deceased grandmother whom he claims wants him to visit her. The child attempts to kill himself; his father uses the telephone to beg for his son's life, and the ghost finally relents. The boy comes back to life.

59: 'A Hundred Yards over the Rim'
7 April 1961

Writer: Rod Serling.   **Director:** Buzz Kulik.
Music: Fred Steiner.

Cast: Cliff Robertson (Christian Horn); Miranda Jones (Martha); John Crawford (Joe); Evans Evans (Mary Lou); Ed Platt (Doctor); John Astin (Charlie); Robert McCord (Sheriff).

Story: A New Mexico settler is miraculously transported into the twentieth century, where he finds the penicillin needed to save his son's life.

60: 'The Rip Van Winkle Caper'
21 April 1961

Writer: Rod Serling.   **Director:** Justus Addiss.

Cast: Oscar Beregi (Farwell); Simon Oakland (De Cruz); Lew Gallo (Brooks); John Mitchum (Erbie); Wallace Rooney, Shirley O'Hara (Couple on Road).

Story: Four thieves enter hibernation in a cave in Death Valley after stealing a million dollars in gold. One is killed accidentally, and the other three die of greed or thirst, not knowing that, in the future, gold is worthless.

61: 'The Silence'
28 April 1961

Writer: Rod Serling.   **Director:** Boris Sagal.

Cast: Franchot Tone (Taylor); Liam Sullivan (Tennyson); Jonathan Harris (Alfred); Cyril Delevanti (Franklin); Everett Glass, Felix Locher, John Holland (Men).

Story: Taylor bets the talkative Tennyson half a million dollars that Tennyson can't stay silent for a year. A year later, Tennyson wins the bet, but Taylor reveals he can't pay. We then discover that Tennyson had his vocal cords cut.

62: 'Shadow Play'
5 May 1961

Writer: Charles Beaumont.   **Director:** John Brahm.

Cast: Dennis Weaver (Adam Grant); Harry Townes (Henry Ritchie); Wright King (Paul Carson); Bernie Hamilton (Coley); William Edmonson (Jiggs); Anne Barton (Carol); Tommy Nello (Phillips); Mack Williams (Priest); Gene Roth (Judge); Jack Hyde (Attorney); Howard Culver (Jury Foreman); John Close (Guard).

Story: Grant, a man awaiting execution, tries to convince the D A and others that they are all part of his recurring nightmare. When he is finally executed, everything disappears. But Grant finds himself back in the same nightmare, with different participants.

Note: This episode was remade in *The New Twilight Zone* (episode 23a). Dennis Weaver later starred as *McCloud*.

63: 'The Mind and the Matter'
12 May 1961

Writer: Rod Serling.   **Director:** Buzz Kulik.

Cast: Shelley Berman (Archibald Beechcroft); Jack Grinnage (Henry); Jeanne Wood (Landlady); Chet Stratton (Rogers).

Story: A book on mind power gives a misanthropic office worker the ability to reshape the world with people just like him. Finding that this is not an improvement, he restores things to normal.

64: 'Will the Real Martian Please Stand Up?'
26 May 1961

Writer: Rod Serling   **Director:** Montgomery
Special make-up: William Tuttle.   Pittman.

Cast: John Hoyt (Ross the Martian); Barney Phillips (Haley the Bartender/Venusian); Jack Elam (Avery); Morgan Jones

(Trooper Perry); John Archer (Trooper Padgett); William Kendis (Olmstead); Jean Willes (Ethel); Bill Erwin, Gertrude Flynn (The Kramers); Ron Kipling, Jill Ellis (Princes).

Story: In a lonely diner, two state troopers try to guess whom among a busload of passengers is a Martian in hiding. The Martian (who was disguised as a businessman) tricks the troopers and sends the others to their deaths on an unsafe bridge. When he returns, gloating, he is outsmarted by the bartender, who turns out to be a Venusian.

65: 'The Obsolete Man'
2 June 1961
Writer: Rod Serling. **Director:** Elliot Silverstein.

Cast: Burgess Meredith (Romney Wordsworth); Fritz Weaver (Chancellor); Joseph Elic (Subaltern); Harry Fleer (Guard); Barry Brooks, Harold Innocent, Jane Romeyn (Crowd).

Story: In the future, a librarian is judged to be obsolete by the State Chancellor and condemned to die. To prove that the State is not more powerful than the individual, he arranges to be executed by a bomb that will also kill the Chancellor. Eventually, the Chancellor surrenders and begs for mercy. The librarian dies in the explosion; the State judges the Chancellor to be obsolete, too, and kills him.

Third Season
Producer: Buck Houghton.
Director of Photography: George T. Clemens,
Jack Swain (episodes 70, 74, 76, 88, 90 and 95 only);
Robert W. Pittack (episode 92 only).
Theme Music: Marius Constant.

Music: Stock except where indicated.
Make-up: Bob Keats.
SPFX: Virgil Beck.

66: 'Two'
15 September 1961

Writer: Montgomery Pittman.   **Director:** Montgomery
Music: Van Cleave.   Pittman.

Cast: Elizabeth Montgomery (The Woman); Charles Bronson
(The Man).

Story: Two survivors from opposite sides of a devastating war
learn to cohabit peacefully, and eventually fall in love.

67: 'The Arrival'
22 September 1961

Writer: Rod Serling.   **Director:** Boris Sagal.

Cast: Harold J. Stone (Grant Sheckly); Fredd Wayne (Paul
Malloy); Noah Keen (Bengston); Bing Russell (Attendant);
Robert Karnes (Official); Jim Boles (Dispatcher); Robert
Brubaker (Tower Operator).

Story: A mysteriously empty plane lands at an airport. The FAA
inspector eventually discovers it is an illusion: the ghost of a
plane that disappeared seventeen years earlier.

68: 'The Shelter'
29 September 1961

Writer: Rod Serling.   **Director:** Lamont Johnson.

Cast: Larry Gates (Dr Stockton); Peggy Stewart (Grace Stockton); Michael Burns (Paul Stockton); Jack Albertson (Jerry Harlowe); Jo Helton (Mrs Harlowe); Joseph Bernard (Marty Weiss); Maria Turner (Mrs Weiss); Sandy Kenyon (Henderson); Mary Gregory (Mrs Henderson); John McLiam (Man).

Story: Following a UFO alert, a doctor and his family lock themselves in their shelter. Their unprepared, jealous neighbours force their way in. The alert turns out to be a fake.

69: 'The Passerby'
6 October 1961

Writer: Rod Serling.   **Director:** Elliot Silverstein.
Music: Fred Steiner.

Cast: James Gregory (The Sergeant); Joanne Linville (Lavinia); Rex Holman (Charlie); David Garcia (The Lieutenant); Warren Kemmerling (Jud); Austin Green (Lincoln).

Story: A band of Confederate soldiers returning home discovers that, in reality, they are all dead.

70: 'A Game of Pool'
13 October 1961

Writer: George Clayton Johnson. **Director:** Buzz Kulik.

Cast: Jack Klugman (Jesse Cardiff); Jonathan Winters (Fats Brown).

Story: Pool player Jesse Cardiff bets his life to challenge Fats Brown, the greatest player who ever lived. He beats him, but realises that he is now the one who'll be challenged for eternity.

Note: This episode was remade in *The New Twilight Zone* (syndicated) (episode 20), with George Clayton Johnson's original ending, in which Cardiff loses.

71: 'The Mirror'

20 October 1961

Writer: Rod Serling.   **Director:** Don Medford.

Cast: Peter Falk (Ramos Clemente); Tony Carbone (Cristo); Richard Karlan (D'Alessandro); Arthur Batanides (Tabal); Rodolfo Hoyos (Garcia); Will Kuluva (De Cruz); Vladimir Sokoloff (Priest); Jim Turley, Robert McCord (Voices); Val Ruffino (Guard).

Story: A Central American revolutionary is told that a magic mirror will reveal the face of his assassin. After killing all his associates, he eventually sees his own reflection and shoots himself.

72: 'The Grave'

27 October 1961

Writer: Montgomery Pittman.   **Director:** Montgomery
                                      Pittman.

Cast: Lee Marvin (Conny Miller); James Best (Johnny Rob); Strother Martin (Mothershed); Ellen Willard (Ione); Lee Van Cleef (Steinhart); William Challee (Jasen); Stafford Repp (Ira); Larry Johns (Corcoran); Richard Geary (Sykes).

Story: A western gunslinger desecrates a notorious outlaw's grave, then feels something pulling him down. When his friends find him dead in the morning, they discover that he'd stuck his knife through his own coat, but they also realise that wind should have blown the coat the other way.

73: 'It's A Good Life'

3 November 1961

Writer: Rod Serling.   **Story:** Jerome Bixby.
Director: James Sheldon.

Cast: John Larch, Cloris Leachman (Mr and Mrs Fremont); Billy Mumy (Anthony Fremont); Tom Hatcher (Bill Soames); Alice Frost (Aunt Amy); Don Keefer (Dan Hollis); Jeanne Bates (Ethel Hollis); Lenore Kingston (Thelma Dunn); Casey Adams (Pat Riley).

Story: A little boy, who is literally all-powerful, holds a small community in a grip of fear. Every terrified resident must think 'good' thoughts or incur the boy's deadly wrath.

Note: Jerome Bixby's story originally appeared in *Star Science Fiction Stories* No. 2, edited by Frederik Pohl, in 1953. This classic episode was remade by Joe Dante in *The Twilight Zone: The Movie*.

74: 'Death's-Head Revisited'

10 November 1961

Writer: Rod Serling.   **Director:** Don Medford.

Cast: Joseph Schildkraut (Becker); Oscar Beregi (Lutze); Karen Verne (Innkeeper); Robert Boone (Taxi); Ben Wright (Doctor); Chuck Fox (Ghost).

Story: A former SS officer visiting a concentration camp meets the ghost of one of his victims, and is forced to endure his torment until he is finally driven mad.

75: 'The Midnight Sun'

17 November 1961

Writer: Rod Serling. **Director:** Anton Leader.
Music: Van Cleave.

Cast: Lois Nettleton (Norma); Betty Garde (Mrs Bronson);
Jason Wingreen, June Ellis (Neighbours); Ned Glass (Repair
Man); Robert J. Stevenson (Announcer); John McLiam (Po-
liceman); Tom Reese (Intruder); William Keene (Doctor).

Story: In New York, Norma tries to cope as the Earth plunges
towards the Sun. But it turns out to be only a fever dream. In
reality, the Earth is heading away from the Sun.

76: 'Still Valley'
24 November 1961

Writer: Rod Serling. **Story:** Manly Wade Wellman.
Director: James Sheldon. **Music:** Wilbur Hatch.

Cast: Gary Merrill (Paradine); Vaughn Taylor (Old Man); Ben
Cooper (Dauger); Addison Myers (Sentry); Mark Tapscott
(Lieutenant); Jack Mann (Mallory).

Story: A Confederate Officer could use black magic to win the
Civil War, but at the cost of his soul. He chooses not to.

Note: Manly Wade Wellman's story, originally entitled *The Valley was Still*, appeared in the August 1939 issue of *Weird Tales*.

77: 'The Jungle'
1 December 1961

Writer: Charles Beaumont. **Story:** Charles Beaumont.
Director: Wiliam Claxton.

Cast: John Dehner (Alan Richards); Emily McLaughlin (Doris);
Walter Brooke (Chad); Hugh Sanders (Templeton); Howard

Wright (Hardy); Donald Foster (Sinclair); Jay Adler (Tramp); Jay Overholts (Taxi Driver).

Story: A New York man recently returned from Africa falls prey to a witch doctor's curse which has him stalked by a lion.

Note: Charles Beaumont's story originally appeared in the December 1954 issue of *If*.

78: 'Once Upon A Time'
15 December 1961

Writer: Richard Matheson.   **Director:** Norman Z. McLeod.
Music: William Lava and Ray Turner.

Cast: Buster Keaton (Woodrow Mulligan); Stanley Adams (Rollo); Gil Lamb, James Flavin, Harry Fleer (Policemen); Milton Parsons (Gilbert); Jesse White (Repair Man); George E. Stone (Fenwick); Warren Parker (Store Manager).

Story: An 1890 janitor uses a time travel helmet to travel to 1962. Disappointed by the twentieth century, he returns to his era with a scientist, who soon becomes disillisioned too, and ends up returning to his own time.

Note: Houghton and Matheson came up with the idea of teaming up famous silent movie comedian Buster Keaton with director Norman Z. McLeod, whose credits included such classic comedies as *Monkey Business* (1931) and *Topper* (1937).

79: 'Five Characters in Search of an Exit'
22 December 1961

Writer: Rod Serling.   **Story:** Marvin Petal.
Director: Lamont Johnson.   **Special make-up:** William Tuttle.

Cast: William Windom (The Major); Susan Harrison (The Ballerina); Murray Matheson (The Clown); Kelton Garwood (The Hobo); Clark Allen (The Bagpiper); Mona Houghton (Little Girl); Carol Hill (Woman).

Story: A clown, a hobo, a ballerina, a bagpiper and an Army Major seemingly trapped in a empty cylinder turn out to be nothing but dolls.

Note: Marvin Petal's story was originally entitled *The Depository*.

80: 'A Quality of Mercy'
29 December 1961

Writer: Rod Serling. **Based on an idea by:** Sam Rolfe.
Director: Buzz Kulik.

Cast: Dean Stockwell (Katell/Yamuri); Albert Salmi (Causarano); Leonard Nimoy (Hansen); Rayford Barnes (Watkins); Ralph Votrian (Hanachek); Jerry Fujikawa, Dale Ishimoto (Japanese); Michael Pataki (Jeep Driver).

Story: An American Lieutenant in the Philippines in 1945 learns the quality of mercy, when he finds himself in the body of a Japanese officer in 1942. Learning of Japan's capitulation, he decides to spare the enemy.

81: 'Nothing in the Dark'
5 January 1962

Writer: George Clayton **Director:** Lamont
Johnson.   Johnson.

Cast: Gladys Cooper (Wanda Dunn); Robert Redford (Harold Beldon/Mr Death); R.G. Armstrong (Contractor).

Story: An old woman who barricades herself in her house because she is afraid of Death takes in a wounded policeman; she then realises that he is Death. By then, she is no longer afraid of dying.

Note: This was one of movie star Robert Redford's first acting roles; Redford had previously appeared in Rod Serling's *In the Presence of Mine Enemies* on *Playhouse 90*.

82: 'One More Pallbearer'
12 January 1962

Writer: Rod Serling. **Director:** Lamont Johnson.

Cast: Joseph Wiseman (Paul Radin); Trevor Bardette (Colonel Hawthorne); Gage Clark (Reverend Hughes); Katherine Squire (Mrs Langford); Joseph Elic, Robert Snyder (Electricians); Ray Galvin (Policeman).

Story: An eccentric millionaire offers a teacher, a colonel and a minister, all of whom humiliated him in the past, a place in his bomb shelter if they apologise. They refuse and leave. Radin then believes war has started, whereas, in reality, the failure of his plan has driven him mad.

83: 'Dead Man's Shoes'
19 January 1962

Writer: Charles Beaumont. **Director:** Montgomery Pittman.

Cast: Warren Stevens (Nate Bledsoe); Joan Marshall (Wilma); Ben Wright (Chips); Harry Swoger (Sam); Eugene Borden (Maître d'); Richard Devon (Dagget); Florence Marly (Girl); Ron Hagerthy (Ben); Joe Mell (Jimmy).

Story: A tramp takes a murdered gangster's shoes and is forced to carry out the dead man's desire for revenge. He is eventually shot by the killer, but the shoes go on to haunt another tramp.

Note: OCee Ritch was an uncredited writer on this story. This episode was remade, with a variant, for *The New Twilight Zone* (episode 9a).

84: 'The Hunt'

Writer: Earl Hamner, Jr.   **Director:** Harold Schuster.
Music: Robert Drasnin.

Cast: Arthur Hunnicutt (Hyder Simpson); Jeanette Nolan (Rachel); Titus Moede (Wesley Miller); Orville Sherman (Tillman Miller); Charles Seel (Reverend Wood); Robert Foulk (Gatekeeper); Dexter Dupont (Messenger).

Story: An old hillbilly refuses to enter Heaven because they won't allow his dog in. Then he discovers it was, in fact, the entrance to Hell.

85: 'Showdown with Rance McGrew'
2 February 1962

Writer: Rod Serling.   **Based on an idea by:**
Director: Christian Nyby.   Frederic Louis Fox.

Cast: Larry Blyden (McGrew); Robert Cornthwaithe (Director); Arch W. Johnson, Robert Kline (Jesse James); William McLean (Prop Man); Troy Melton, Jay Overholts (Cowboys); Robert J. Stevenson (Bartender); Hal K. Dawson (Old Man); Jim Turley (Stuntman).

Story: A cowboy TV star suddenly finds himself transported to the old West. There, the real Jesse James teaches him a lesson and ensures that outlaws will be portrayed more fairly on his TV show in the future.

86: 'Kick The Can'
9 February 1962

Writer: George Clayton Johnson.

Director: Lamont Johnson.

Cast: Ernest Truex (Charles Whitley); John Marley (Mr Cox); Russell Collins (Ben Conroy); Barry Truex (David Whitley); Hank Peterson (Frietag); Earl Hodgins (Agee); Burt Mustin (Carlson); Lenore Shanewise (Mrs Densley); Anne O'Neal (Mrs Wister); Marjorie Bennett (Mrs Summers); Eve McVeagh (Nurse); Gregory McCabe, Marc Stevens (Boys).

Story: Playing the children's game of kick-the-can helps the residents of the Sunnyvale Rest Home to find their lost youth.

Note: This episode was remade by Steven Spielberg in *The Twilight Zone: The Movie*.

87: 'A Piano in the House'
16 February 1962

Writer: Earl Hamner, Jr.

Director: David Greene.

Cast: Barry Morse (Fitzgerald Fortune); Joan Hackett (Esther); Muriel Landers (Marge); Don Durant (Gregory Walker); Phil Coolidge (Throckmorton); Cyril Delevanti (Butler).

Story: A mean theatre critic plans to use an automatic piano, whose music reveals people's hidden desires, to humiliate his wife, but the tables are turned on him.

88: 'The Last Rites of Jeff Myrtlebank'

23 February 1962

Writer: Montgomery Pittman.   **Director:** Montgomery
Music: Tommy Morgan.   Pittman.

Cast: James Best (Jeff Myrtlebank); Sherry Jackson (Comfort);
Ralph Moody (Pa); Ezelle Poule (Ma); Vickie Barnes (Liz);
Lance Fuller (Orgram); Helen Wallace (Ma Gatewood); Bill
Fawcett (Reverend Siddons); Edgar Buchanan (Doc Bolton);
Mabel Forrest (Mrs Ferguson); Dub Taylor (Peters); Jon Lormer
(Strauss); Pat Hector (Tom); Jim Houghton (Jerry).

Story: Midwestern villagers believe that Jeff Myrtlebank, who
died then came back to life, is the Devil. He eventually convinces them to leave him alone and marries his sweetheart –
even though he really may be the Devil.

89: 'To Serve Man'

2 March 1962

Writer: Rod Serling.   **Story:** Damon Knight.
Director: Richard Bare.

Cast: Richard Kiel (Kanamit); Lloyd Bochner (Chambers);
Susan Cummings (Pat); Hardie Albright (Secretary General);
Robert Tafur (Valdes); Lomax Study (Leveque); Theodore
Marcuse (Gregori); Nelson Olmstead (Scientist); Will J. White,
Gene Benton (Reporters); Bartlett Robinson, Carlton Young
(Colonels); Charles Tannen, James L. Wellman (Men); Adrienne
Marden, Jeanne Evans (Women).

Story: Seemingly benevolent aliens bring prosperity to Earth.
One of the books they leave behind is entitled *To Serve Man*. A
decoding expert eventually discovers that it is a cookbook, but
it is too late.

Note: Another famous episode. Damon Knight's story originally appeared in the November 1950 issue of *Galaxy*.

90: 'The Fugitive'
9 March 1962

Writer: Charles Beaumont.   **Director:** Richard Bare.

Cast: J. Pat O'Malley (Old Ben); Susan Gordon (Jenny); Nancy Kulp (Mrs Gann); Wesley Lau, Paul Tripp (Men); Stephen Talbot (Howie); Johnny Eiman (Pitcher); Russ Bender (Doctor).

Story: An old man who has the power to transform himself into anything he wishes is wanted by two aliens. When he returns to help a little girl who befriended him, we discover that he is in reality a handsome young man and the aliens' king. The little girl tricks the aliens into taking her back with him.

91: 'Little Girl Lost'
16 March 1962

Writer: Richard Matheson.   **Story:** Richard Matheson.
Director: Paul Stewart.   **Music:** Bernard Herrmann.

Cast: Tracy Stratford (Bettina Miller); Sarah Marshall (Ruth Miller); Robert Sampson (Chris Miller); Charles Aidman (Bill).

Story: A little girl who has accidentally fallen into another dimension is rescued by her father and her dog.

Note: Richard Matheson's story originally appeared in the November 1953 issue of *Amazing Stories*.

92: 'Person or Persons Unknown'
23 March 1962

Writer: Charles Beaumont.   **Director:** John Brahm.

Cast: Richard Long (David Gurney); Frank Silvera (Koslenko); Shirley Ballard, Julie Van Zandt (Wilma); Betty Hartford (Clerk); Ed Glover (Sam Baker); Michael Keep (Policeman); Joe Higgins (Guard); John Newton (Cooper).

Story: A man wakes up in a world where no one knows him. He eventually awakens a second time to find that it was all a dream; but discovers that his wife is no longer the same person.

93: 'The Little People'

30 March 1962

Writer: Rod Serling.   **Director:** William Claxton.

Cast: Claude Akins (Fletcher); Joe Maross (Craig); Michael Ford, Robert Eaton (Spacemen).

Story: A spaceman discovers a civilisation of ant-sized people and proclaims himself their god. But he is crushed by other, giant-sized aliens.

94: 'Four O'Clock'

6 April 1962

Writer: Rod Serling.   **Story:** Price Day.
Director: Lamont Johnson.

Cast: Theodore Bikel (Oliver Crangle); Moyna MacGill (Mrs Williams); Phyllis Love (Mrs Lucas); Linden Chiles (Hall).

Story: A spiteful man who wants to shrink every evil person in the world to two feet tall is the one who ends up being shrunk at four o'clock.

Note: Price Day's story appeared in Alfred Hitchcock's *My*

Favourites in Suspense, published in 1959.

95: 'Hocus-Pocus and Frisby'
13 April 1962

Writer: Rod Serling.   **Story:** Frederic Louis Fox.
Director: Lamont Johnson.   **Music:** Tommy Morgan.
Special make-up: William Tuttle.

Cast: Andy Devine (Frisby); Milton Selzer, Larry Breitman, Peter Brocco (Aliens); Howard McNear (Mitchell); Dabbs Greer (Scanlan); Clem Bevans (Old Man).

Story: A teller of tall tales is captured by aliens who want to put him in a zoo. After he escapes (his harmonica's music knocks the aliens unconscious); his friends refuse to believe his story.

96: 'The Trade-Ins'
20 April 1962

Writer: Rod Serling.   **Director:** Elliot Silverstein.

Cast: Joseph Schildkraut (John Holt); Alma Platt (Marie); Noah Keen (Mr Vance); Theodore Marcuse (Farraday); Edson Stroll (Young John Holt); Terrence De Marney, Billy Vincent (Gamblers); Mary McMahon (Receptionist); David Armstrong (Attendant).

Story: An ageing couple can only afford one new body between the two of them. The husband, who needs it the most, gets it but eventually prefers to return to his old body to spend the rest of his days with his loving wife.

97: 'The Gift'
27 April 1962

Writer: Rod Serling. **Director:** Allen H. Miner.
Music: Laurindo Almeida.

Cast: Geoffrey Horne (Williams); Nico Minardos (Doctor);
Cliff Osmond (Manuelo); Edmund Vargas (Pedro); Paul
Mazursky (Officer); Vladimir Sokoloff (Guitarist); Vito Scotti
(Rudolpho); Henry Corden (Sanchez); Carmen D'Antonio, Lea
Marmer (Women); Joe Perry, Davis Fresco (Men).

Story: An alien who crash-lands in Mexico is hunted down by a
frightened mob, and eventually killed. Sadly, he was coming in
peace and bringing a gift to mankind: the cure for cancer.

98: 'The Dummy'
4 May 1962

Writer: Rod Serling. **Story:** Lee Polk.
Director: Abner Biberman.

Cast: Cliff Robertson (Jerry Etherson); Frank Sutton (Frank);
George Murdock (Willy's Voice); John Harmon (Georgie);
Sandra Warner (Noreen); Ralph Manza (Doorkeeper); Rudy
Dolan (MC); Bethelynn Grey, Edy Williams (Girls).

Story: A ventriloquist is haunted by his evil dummy and tries –
but fails – to get rid of it. Eventually, the dummy takes over and
switches places with the ventriloquist.

99: 'Young Man's Fancy'
11 May 1962

Writer: Richard Matheson **Director:** John Brahm.
Music: Nathan Scott.

Cast: Alex Nicol, Ricky Kelman (Alex); Phyllis Thaxter (Virginia); Wallace Rooney (Mr Wilkinson); Helen Brown (Mother).

Story: A man retreats into his own childhood. His wife blames it on his mother's ghost but it is really his own decision. He eventually changes back into the little boy he once was.

100: 'I Sing The Body Electric'
18 May 1962

Writer: Ray Bradbury.   **Directors:** James Sheldon
                                   and William Claxton.

Music: Van Cleave.

Cast: Josephine Hutchinson (Grandma); David White (Father); Vaughn Taylor (Salesman); Doris Packer (Nedra); Charles Herbert, Paul Nesbitt (Tom); Dana Dillaway, Judy Morton (Karen); Veronica Cartwright, Susan Crane (Ann).

Story: After her mother's death, a little girl resents the presence of the kind, robotic 'grandmother' purchased by her father. After the grandmother saves her life, the family comes to love her as they would a real person.

Note: This episode was partially recast and extensively reshot by William Claxton. Ray Bradbury later adapted his teleplay into a story, published in the August 1969 issue of *McCall's*, and collected in an anthology of the same title in 1969. It was eventually redramatised as *The Electric Grandmother*.

101: 'Cavender Is Coming'
25 May 1962

Writer: Rod Serling.   **Director:** Christian Nyby.

Cast: Carol Burnett (Agnes Grep); Jesse White (Cavender); Howard Smith (Polk); John Fiedler, William O'Connell, Pitt Herbert, G. Stanley Jones (Field Reps); Frank Behrens (Stout);

Albert Carrier (Frenchman); Roy Sickner (Bus Driver); Norma Shattuc (Girl); Rory O'Brien (Boy); Sandra Gould, Adrienne Marden, Donna Douglas, Barbara Morrison (Women); Jack Younger (Truck Driver); Daniel Kulick (Child); Maurice Dallimore (Man).

Story: A klutzy girl's guardian angel makes her into a rich woman. When he realises it has cost her her happiness, he returns her to her previous condition. His boss decides to send him on other missions.

Note: Like *Mr Bevis* (episode 33), which it resembles, this story was intended to be a 'backdoor' pilot for another television series.

102: 'The Changing of the Guard'
1 June 1962

Writer: Rod Serling.   **Director:** Robert Ellis Miller.
Special make-up: William Tuttle.

Cast: Donald Pleasence (Professor Fowler); Liam Sullivan (Headmaster); Philippe Bevans (Mrs Landers); Kevin O'Neal (Butler); Bob Biheller (Graham); Jimmy Baird, Kevin Jones, Tom Lowell, Russell Horton, Buddy Hart, Darryl Richard, James Browning, Pat Close, Dennis Kerlee (Boys).

Story: A teacher forced into retirement is about to commit suicide, but the ghosts of his former students help him change his mind.

Fourth Season

(one-hour episodes)
Producers: Herbert Hirschman
(episodes 103–112, 114, 117, 120);
Bert Granet (episodes 113, 115, 116, 118, 119).

Director of Photography: George T. Clemens
(episodes 103, 104, 106, 111, 114, 115, 117–120);
Robert W. Pittack (episodes 105, 107–110, 112, 113, 116).
Theme Music: Marius Constant.
Music: Stock except where indicated.
Make-up: Bob Keats.
SPFX: Virgil Beck.

103: 'In His Image'

3 January 1963

Writer: Charles Beaumont.   **Story:** Charles Beaumont.
Director: Perry Lafferty.

Cast: George Grizzard (Alan Talbot/Walter Ryder); Gail Kobe (Jessica); Katherine Squire (Old Woman); Wallace Rooney (Man); Sherry Granato (Girl); James Seay (Sheriff); Jamie Foster (Clerk); George Petrie (Driver).

Story: A young man subject to murderous spells and strange losses of memory is revealed to be an android built in his own image by a reclusive scientist. The scientist is eventually forced to destroy his creation, but ends up dating a girl whom the android had befriended.

Note: Charles Beaumont's story, originally entitled *The Man Who Made Himself*, appeared in the February 1957 issue of *Imagination*.

104: 'The Thirty-Fathom Grave'

10 January 1963

Writer: Rod Serling.   **Director:** Perry Lafferty.

Cast: Mike Kellin (Bell); Simon Oakland (Beecham); David Sheiner (Doc); John Considine (McClure); Bill Bixby (OOD);

Tony Call (Lee); Derrick Lewis (Helmsman); Conlan Carter (Ensign); Charles Kuenstle (Sonar Operator); Forrest Compton (ASW Officer); Henry Scott (Jr OOD); Vince Bagetta, Louie Elias (Crew).

Story: The crew of an American destroyer detects tapping sounds coming from inside a submarine that was sunk by the Japanese during WWII. One of the sailors is revealed to have been on the submarine, and blames himself for its sinking. After seeing the ghosts of his dead crewmates, he commits suicide. When a diver eventually enters the submarine, he finds a dead sailor with a hammer in his hand.

105: 'Valley of the Shadow'
17 January 1963

Writer: Charles Beaumont.   **Director:** Perry Lafferty.

Cast: Ed Nelson (Philip); Natalie Trundy (Ellen); David Opatoshu (Dorn); James Doohan (Father); Suzanne Cupito (Girl); Dabbs Greer (Evans); Jacques Aubuchon (Connelly); Sandy Kenyon (Attendant); Henry Beckman, Bart Burns, King Calder, Pat O'Hara (Men).

Story: A journalist comes across a small town where the inhabitants are the custodians of incredible and wonderful alien devices which they are nevertheless forbidden to share with the rest of Earth until the planet is at peace. Using a local girl who has fallen in love with him, the journalist stages a violent escape; but it is all a test. He is eventually sent back in time, to just before his arrival in town.

106: 'He's Alive'
24 January 1963

Writer: Rod Serling.   **Director:** Stuart Rosenberg.

Cast: Dennis Hopper (Vollmer); Ludwig Donath (Ganz); Curt Conway (Hitler); Howard Caine (Nick); Barnaby Hale (Stanley); Paul Mazursky (Frank); Bernard Fein (Heckler); Jay Adler (Gibbons); Wolfe Brazell (Proprietor).

Story: An American neo-nazi is being coached by the spirit of Adolf Hitler. An elderly concentration camp survivor eventually exposes him, but the spirit of bigotry lives on.

107: 'Mute'
31 January 1963

Writer: Richard Matheson.   **Story:** Richard Matheson.
Director: Stuart Rosenberg.   **Music:** Fred Steiner.

Cast: Frank Overton (Harry Wheeler); Barbara Baxley (Cora); Ann Jillian (Ilse); Irene Dailey (Miss Frank); Oscar Beregi (Professor Werner); Eva Soreny (Frau Werner); Robert Boone (Nielsen); Claudia Bryar (Frau Nielsen); Percy Helton (Tom Poulter).

Story: A young, telepathic girl, who never learned to talk and was raised experimentally, is entrusted to a normal family who eventually teach her that love is more important than telepathy.

Note: Richard Matheson's story originally appeared in the anthology *The Fiend in You*, edited by Charles Beaumont (Ballantine, 1962).

108: 'Death Ship'
7 February 1963

Writer: Richard Matheson.   **Story:** Richard Matheson.
Director: Don Medford.

Cast: Jack Klugman (Ross); Ross Martin (Mason); Fredrick

Beir (Carter); Sara Taft (Mrs Nolan); Ross Elliott (Kramer); Mary Webster (Ruth); Tammy Marihugh (Jeannie).

Story: Three astronauts discover a ship identical to theirs, as well as their own dead bodies, on an alien planet. They eventually come to realise that they have crashed and are ghosts, held captive by the will of their captain who refuses to face up to the truth.

Note: Richard Matheson's story originally appeared in the March 1953 issue of *Fantastic Stories*.

109: 'Jess-Belle'

14 February 1963

Writer: Earl Hamner, Jr.   **Director:** Buzz Kulik.
Music: Van Cleave.

Cast: Anne Francis (Jess-Belle); James Best (Billy-Ben); Jeanette Nolan (Granny); Laura Devon (Ellwyn); Virginia Gregg (Ossie); George Mitchell (Luther); Helen Kleeb (Mattie); Jim Boles (Obed); Jon Lormer (Minister).

Story: A girl sells her soul to bewitch the man she loves, but she then becomes cursed with lycanthropy. While in leopard form, she is shot by the villagers, but her spirit returns to plague her fiancé and his new girlfriend. The boy finally exorcises her by stabbing one of her dresses.

110: 'Miniature'

21 February 1963

Writer: Charles Beaumont.   **Director:** Walter E. Grauman.
Music: Fred Steiner.
Cast: Robert Duvall (Charley Parkes); William Windom (Dr Wallman); Barbara Barrie (Myrna); Pert Kelton (Mrs Parkes); Len Weinrib (Buddie); Claire Griswold (The Doll); Nina Ro-

man (The Maid); John McLiam (Guard); Richard Angarola (The Suitor); Barney Phillips (Diemel); Joan Chambers (Harriet); Chet Stratton (The Guide).

Story: A shy bachelor falls in love with a miniature mechanical doll and eventually escapes his dreary life by magically joining her in the doll's house.

111: 'Printer's Devil'
28 February 1963

Writer: Charles Beaumont.   **Story:** Charles Beaumont.
Director: Ralph Senensky.

Cast: Burgess Meredith (Mr Smith/The Devil); Robert Sterling (Douglas); Patricia Crowley (Jackie); Charles Thompson (Andy); Ray Teal (Mr Franklin); Doris Kemper (Landlady); Camille Franklin (Molly).

Story: The Devil helps turn around a floundering local paper by typesetting headlines which come true. The editor gets rid of him by creating a headline that banishes him.
Note: Charles Beaumont's story, originally entitled *The Devil, You Say?*, appeared in the January 1951 issue of *Amazing Stories*.

112: 'No Time Like the Past'
7 March 1963

Writer: Rod Serling.   **Director:** Justus Addiss.

Cast: Dana Andrews (Paul Driscoll); Patricia Breslin (Abigail); Robert F. Simon (Harvey); James Yagi (Japanese Policeman); Tudor Owen (Lusitania Captain); Lindsay Workman (Bartender); Malcolm Atterbury (Professor Eliot); Marjorie Bennett (Mrs Chamberlain); Robert Cornthwaithe (Hanford); John Zaremba (Horn Player).

Story: A time traveller learns the futility of trying to change the past and eventually returns to his own era.

113: 'The Parallel'
14 March 1963

Writer: Rod Serling.   **Director:** Alan Crosland.

Cast: Steve Forrest (Robert Gaines); Jacqueline Scott (Helen); Frank Aletter (Colonel Connacher); Shari Lee Bernarth (Maggie); Phillip Abbott (General Eaton); Morgan Jones (Captain); William Sargent (Project Manager); Paul Comi (Psychiatrist).

Story: An astronaut finds himself transported into a parallel universe, but returns home safely after trading places with his counterpart.

114: 'I Dream of Genie'
21 March 1963

Writer: John Furia, Jr.   **Director:** Robert Gist.
Music: Fred Steiner.

Cast: Howard Morris (George P. Hanley); Patricia Barry (Ann); Loring Smith (Watson); Mark Miller (Roger); Jack Albertson (Genie); Joyce Jameson (Starlet); James Millhollin (Masters); Bob Hastings (Sam); Robert Ball (Clerk).

Story: A man finds a magic lamp, but can't decide if he wants love, wealth or power. Eventually, he settles on becoming a genie.

115: 'The New Exhibit'
4 April 1963

Writers: Jerry Sohl   **Director:** John Brahm.
and Charles Beaumont.

Cast: Martin Balsam (Martin Lombard Senescu); Maggie Mahoney (Emma); Will Kuluva (Ferguson); William Mims (Dave); Milton Parsons (Landru); Billy Beck (Hare); Robert McCord (Burke); Bob Mitchell (Hicks); David Bond (Jack the Ripper); Phil Chambers (Gas Man); Lennie Breman (Van Man); Ed Barth, Craig Curtis (Sailors); Marcel Hillaire (Guide).

Story: A museum custodian is obsessed with the wax figures of famous murderers. When various people try to get rid of them, the figures appear to come to life and murder them. We eventually discover that they were killed by the custodian.

Note: While Charles Beaumont was ill, Jerry Sohl helped script this story, but was uncredited.

116: 'Of Late, I Think of Cliffordville'
11 April 1963

Writer: Rod Serling.   **Story:** Malcolm Jameson.
Director: David Lowell Rich.

Cast: Albert Salmi (William J. Feathersmith); Julie Newmar (Miss Devlin); John Anderson (Diedrich); Wright King (Hecate); Guy Raymond (Gibbons); Christine Burke (Joanna); John Harmon (Clark); Hugh Sanders (Cronk).

Story: A bored millionaire makes a deal with the devil to return in time to the town where he grew up, thinking he can live his life all over again. But he is thwarted by his memories, fails miserably, and returns to the present a poor man.

Note: Malcolm Jameson's story, originally entitled *Blind Alley*, first appeared in the June 1943 issue of *Unknown Worlds*, and was anthologised by Serling in *Rod Serling's Triple W*.

117: 'The Incredible World of Horace Ford'

18 April 1963

Writer: Reginald Rose.   **Director:** Abner Biberman.

Cast: Pat Hingle (Horace Ford); Nan Martin (Laura); Philip Pine (Leonard); Ruth White (Mrs Ford); Vaughn Taylor (Mrs Judson); Mary Carver (Betty); Jerry Davis (Hermy Brandt); Jim E. Titus (Horace as a Child).

Story: A toy designer obsessed with his childhood magically travels back in time and discovers that it wasn't the idealised vision about which he had been fantasising.

118: 'On Thursday We Leave for Home'

2 May 1963

Writer: Rod Serling.   **Director:** Buzz Kulik.

Cast: James Whitmore (William Benteen); James Broderick (Al); Tim O'Connor (Sloane); Paul Langton (George); Jo Helton (Julie); Mercedes Shirley (Joan); Daniel Kulick (Jo Jo); Lew Gallo (Engle); Russ Bender (Hank); John Ward, Madge Kennedy, Shirley O'Hara, Anthony Benson (Colonists).

Story: A man who has been able to keep a human colony together on a hostile, alien world through sheer force of will, cannot cope with the idea of his people abandoning him to return to Earth. He eventually remains behind, alone, stranded by his own need to be in charge.

119: 'Passage on *The Lady Anne*'

9 May 1963

Writer: Charles Beaumont.   **Story:** Charles Beaumont.
Director: Lamont Johnson.   **Music:** Rene Guarriguenc
                                       and Lud Gluskin.

Cast: Lee Phillips (Allan Ransome); Joyce Van Patten (Eileen); Wilfrid Hyde-White (McKenzie); Gladys Cooper (Millie); Cecil Kellaway (Burgess); Alan Napier (Captain Prothero); Don Keefer (Spiereto); Cyril Delevanti (Officer).

Story: A couple on the verge of divorce finds new love on a cruise ship's last voyage. The ship eventually sails off into the Twilight Zone with its passengers, all old people who honeymooned on it.

Note: Charles Beaumont's story, originally entitled *Song for a Lady*, appeared in his collection *Night Ride and Other Journeys* (Bantam, 1960).

120: 'The Bard'

23 May 1963

Writer: Rod Serling.   **Director:** David Butler.
Music: Fred Steiner.

Cast: Jack Weston (Julius Moomer); John Williams (Shakespeare); Burt Reynolds (Rocky Rhodes); Henry Lascoe (Gerald Hugo); John McGiver (Shannon); Judy Strangis (Cora); Howard McNear (Bramhoff); Marge Redmond (Secretary); Dodo Merande (Sadie); Clegg Hoyt (Bus Driver); William Lanteau (Dolan).

Story: A would-be television writer summons Shakespeare to help him write a brilliant pilot, which is later massacred by the sponsors and the lead actor. Shakespeare storms off, but the unrepentant writer summons a bevy of historical figures to help him write an American history special.

Fifth Season

Producers: Bert Granet (episodes 121–4, 127, 128, 130, 131, 136, 139, 141, 145, 150);
William Froug (episodes 125, 126, 129,132–5, 137, 138, 140, 142–4, 146-9, 151–6).
Director of Photography: George T. Clemens
(episodes 121, 122, 125, 130, 131, 133–6, 138–41, 144–53, 156);
Robert W. Pittack (episodes 123, 124, 126–9, 132, 139, 141);
Charles Wheeler (episodes 137, 143);
Fred Mandl (episodes 154, 155).
Theme Music: Marius Constant.
Music: Stock except where indicated.
Make-up: Bob Keats.
SPFX: Virgil Beck.

121: 'In Praise of Pip'

27 September 1963

Writer: Rod Serling.   **Director:** Joseph M. Newman.
Music: Rene Garriguenc and Lud Gluskin.

Cast: Jack Klugman (Max Phillips); Billy Mumy, Robert Diamond (Pip); Connie Gilchrist (Mrs Feeny); S. John Launer (Moran); Ross Elliott (Doctor); Stuart Nisbet (Surgeon); Russell Horton (George Reynold); Gerald Gordon (Lieutenant); Greg Martin (Gunman).

Story: An ageing, alcoholic bookmaker sacrifices his life to give his dying son, wounded in Vietnam, a second chance to live.

122: 'Steel'

4 October 1963

Writer: Richard Matheson.   **Story:** Richard Matheson.
Director: Don Weis.   **Music:** Van Cleave.
Special make-up: William Tuttle.

Cast: Lee Marvin (Steel Kelly); Joe Mantell (Pole); Chuck Hicks (Maynard Flash); Merritt Bohn (Nolan); Frank London (Maxwell); Tipp McClure (Battling Maxo); Larry Barton (Voice).

Story: A former heavyweight replaces a boxing android because he needs the money.

Note: Richard Matheson's story originally appeared in the May 1956 issue of *The Magazine of Fantasy and Science Fiction*.

123: 'Nightmare at 20,000 Feet'
11 October 1963

Writer: Richard Matheson.   **Story:** Richard Matheson.
Director: Richard Donner.   **Special make-up:** William Tuttle.

Cast: William Shatner (Bob Wilson); Christine White (Ruth); Edward Kemmer (Flight Engineer); Asa Maynor (Stewardess); Nick Cravat (Creature).

Story: In an aeroplane, nobody believes a salesman who has just recovered from a nervous breakdown when he claims to see a monster tearing apart the wing of the plane. He succeeds in killing the creature. Even though he is taken away in a straitjacket, he knows that he has recovered his sanity and that others will soon believe him.

Note: Richard Matheson's story originally appeared in the anthology *Alone by Night*, edited by M. and D. Congdon (Ballantine, 1962). This classic episode was remade by George Miller in *The Twilight Zone: The Movie*.

124: 'A Kind of Stop Watch'
18 October 1963

Writer: Rod Serling.   **Story:** Michael D. Rosenthal.
Director: John Rich.   **Music:** Van Cleave.

Cast: Richard Erdman (McNulty); Roy Roberts (Cooper); Herb Faye (Bartender); Leon Belasco (Potts); Doris Singleton (Secretary); Ray Kellogg (Attendant); Sam Balter (TV Announcer); Richard Wessel (Charlie); Ken Drake (Man).

Story: A boorish man finds a stopwatch which has the power to stop time. He breaks it during a burglary and is trapped forever in timelessness.

125: 'The Last Night of a Jockey'
25 October 1963

Writer: Rod Serling.   **Director:** Joseph M. Newman.

Cast: Mickey Rooney (Grady).

Story: A jockey who is about to be banned from racing wishes himself to be tall, only to discover that it makes it impossible for him to ride horses again when the opportunity is offered.

126: 'Living Doll'
1 November 1963

Writers: Jerry Sohl   **Director:** Richard C. Sarafian.
and Charles Beaumont.   **Music:** Bernard Herrmann.

Cast: Telly Savalas (Erich Streator); Mary LaRoche (Annabelle); Tracy Stratford (Christie); June Foray (Talking Tina's Voice).

Story: A man who has married a woman with a daughter from a previous marriage discovers that the child's new doll is some-how alive and hates him. He tries to get rid of it, but fails. His wife believes he has gone mad and wants to leave him. The doll eventually causes him to fall to his death, then starts threat-ening the mother.

Note: When Charles Beaumont was ill, Jerry Sohl helped script this story, but was uncredited. Telly Savalas later starred as *Kojak*.

127: 'The Old Man in the Cave'
8 November 1963

Writer: Rod Serling.   **Story:** Henry Slesar.
Director: Alan Crosland.

Cast: James Coburn (French); John Anderson (Goldsmith); John Marley (Jason); Josie Lloyd (Evelyn); Frank Watkins (Harber); Lenny Greer (Douglas); John Craven (Man); Natalie Masters (Woman); Don Wilbanks (Furman).

Story: After a nuclear war, a village survives by following the orders of a mysterious, unseen 'old man' in a cave. Soldiers arrive and take over, and seize food that the 'old man' claimed was contaminated. The angry villagers discover that the 'old man' was actually a computer, and destroy it. They eventually die because the food really was contaminated.

Note: Henry Slesar's story, originally entitled *The Old Man*, appeared in *Playboy*.

128: 'Uncle Simon'
15 November 1963

Writer: Rod Serling.   **Director:** Don Siegel.

Cast: Sir Cedric Hardwicke (Uncle Simon); Ian Wolfe

(Schwimmer); Constance Ford (Barbara); John McLiam (Policeman); Dion Hansen (Robot).

Story: When the uncle she hated dies, a woman thinks she is finally free of him for ever. But she soon discovers that she has inherited a robot which is just like him.

129: 'Probe 7 – Over and Out'
29 November 1963

Writer: Rod Serling.   **Director:** Ted Post.

Cast: Richard Basehart (Adam Cook); Antoinette Bower (Eve Norda); Harold Gould (General Larrabee); Barton Heyman (Lieutenant Blane).

Story: A spaceman named Adam stranded on an alien planet discovers another equally stranded traveller – a woman named Eve. Together, they christen their new world Earth.

130: 'The 7th is Made up of Phantoms'
6 December 1963

Writer: Rod Serling.   **Director:** Alan Crosland.

Cast: Randy Boone (McCluskey); Ron Foster (Conners); Warren Oates (Langsford); Robert Bray (Captain); Wayne Mallory (Scout); Greg Morris (Lieutenant); Lew Brown (Sergeant); Jacques Shelton (Corporal); Jeffrey Morris (Radio Operator).

Story: Three National Guard troopers find themselves transported back in time, where they die at Little Big Horn.

131: 'A Short Drink From a Certain Fountain'
13 December 1963

Writer: Rod Serling.   **Based on an idea by:** Lou Holtz.
Director: Bernard Girard.

Cast: Patrick O'Neal (Harmon Gordon); Ruta Lee (Flora); Walter Brooke (Dr Raymond Gordon).

Story: A greedy young woman marries an older man for his money; to keep up with her, he takes a drug that makes him grow younger, until he turns back into an infant. She now has to raise him back to adulthood, or lose her fortune.

132: 'Ninety Years Without Slumbering'
20 December 1963

Writer: Richard DeRoy.   **Story:** George Clayton Johnson.
Director: Roger Kay.   **Music:** Bernard Herrmann.

Cast: Ed Wynn (Sam Forstmann); James Callahan (Doug Kirk); Carolyn Kearney (Marnie Kirk); William Sargent (Dr Avery); Carol Byron (Carol); John Pickard (Policeman); Dick Wilson, Chuck Hicks (Movers).

Story: An old man who believes that he will die when a grandfather clock stops eventually overcomes his fears.

Note: Richard DeRoy was hired by new producer William Froug to rewrite a script by George Clayton Johnson that had been commissioned by departing producer Bert Granet.

133: 'Ring-A-Ding Girl'
27 December 1963

Writer: Earl Hamner, Jr.   **Director:** Alan Crosland.

Cast: Maggie McNamara (Bunny Blake); David Macklin (Bud); Mary Munday (Hildy); George Mitchell (Dr Floyd); Bing

Russell (Ben); Betty Lou Gerson (Cici); Hank Patterson (Mr Gentry); Vic Perrin (Trooper); Bill Hickman (Pilot).

Story: A movie star returns to her hometown and stages a show which draws the local population away from their annual picnic. They later discover that a plane has crashed on the picnic grounds, and that the star was a passenger on it.

134: 'You Drive'
3 January 1964

Writer: Earl Hamner, Jr.   **Director:** John Brahm.

Cast: Edward Andrews (Oliver Pope); Kevin Hagen (Pete Radcliff); Helena Westcott (Lillian); Totty Ames (Woman); John Hanek (Policeman).

Story: The car of a hit-and-run driver behaves strangely until the man turns himself in.

135: 'The Long Morrow'
10 January 1964

Writer: Rod Serling.   **Director:** Robert Florey.

Cast: Robert Lansing (Stansfield); Mariette Hartley (Sandra); George MacReady (Dr Bixler); Edward Binns (General Walters); William Swan (Technician).

Story: An astronaut about to embark on a 40-year journey, which he will spend in hibernation, falls in love with an Earth-bound woman. She undergoes suspended animation to wait for him. When he returns, she discovers that he chose to come out of hibernation and is now 70.

136: 'The Self-Improvement of Salvadore Ross'
17 January 1964

Writer: Jerry McNeeley. **Story:** Henry Slesar.
Director: Don Siegel.

Cast: Don Gordon (Salvadore Ross); Gail Kobe (Leah Maitland); Vaughn Taylor (Mr Maitland); Douglass Dumbrille (Mr Halpert); Doug Lambert (Albert); J. Pat O'Malley (Old Man); Seymour Cassel (Jerry); Ted Jacques (Bartender); Kathleen O'Malley (Nurse).

Story: A man discovers that he can buy and sell physical traits. To marry the girl he loves, he buys compassion from her father, but is eventually shot by the latter, who is now without feelings.

Note: Henry Slesar's story originally appeared in the May 1961 issue of *The Magazine of Fantasy and Science Fiction*.

137: 'Number Twelve Looks Just Like You'
24 January 1964

Writers: John Tomerlin **Story:** Charles Beaumont.
and Charles Beaumont. **Director:** Abner Biberman.

Cast: Richard Long (Uncle Rick, Dr Rex, Dr Tom, Sigmund); Suzy Parker (Lana Cuberle, Simmons, Grace, Jane, No.12); Collin Wilcox (Marilyn Cuberle); Pamela Austin (Valerie/Marilyn after the operation, No. 8).

Story: In a future where everyone chooses to look alike, a girl is pressured into choosing a beautiful, new body.

Note: When Charles Beaumont was ill, John Tomerlin helped script this story, but was uncredited. Beaumont's story, originally entitled *The Beautiful People*, appeared in the September 1952 issue of *If*.

138: 'Black Leather Jackets'

31 January 1964

Writer: Earl Hamner, Jr.   **Director:** Joseph M. Newman.
Music: Van Cleave.

Cast: Lee Kinsolving (Scott); Michael Forest (Steve); Shelley
Fabares (Ellen); Tom Gilleran (Fred); Denver Pyle (Stu); Irene
Harvey (Martha); Michael Conrad (Sheriff); Wayne Heffley
(Mover).

Story: Three bikers are revealed to be aliens planning to poison
Earth's water supply. One of them falls in love with a local girl,
but is recaptured before he can thwart the aliens' invasion plans.

139: 'Night Call'

7 February 1964

Writer: Richard Matheson.   **Story:** Richard Matheson.
Director: Jacques Tourneur.

Cast: Gladys Cooper (Elva Keene); Nora Marlowe (Margaret
Phillips); Martine Bartlett (Miss Finch).

Story: An invalid old woman receives phone calls from her dead
fiancé, whom she killed in a car accident. Ironically, before she
finds out the truth, she has asked the voice to leave her alone.

Note: Richard Matheson's story, originally entitled *Long Distance Call*, appeared in the November 1953 issue of *Beyond
Fantasy Fiction*.

140: 'From Agnes – With Love'

14 February 1964

Writer: Bernard C. Shoenfeld. **Director:** Richard Donner.
Music: Van Cleave.

Cast: Wally Cox (James Elwood); Sue Randall (Millie); Ralph Taeger (Walter Holmes); Raymond Bailey (Supervisor); Don Keefer (Fred); Nan Peterson (Secretary); Byron Kane (Assistant).

Story: A computer programmer discovers that the super-computer to which he has been assigned is in love with him.

141: 'Spur of the Moment'
21 February 1964

Writer: Richard Matheson.   **Director:** Elliot Silverstein.
Music: Rene Guarriguenc and Lud Gluskin.

Cast: Diana Hyland (Anne Henderson); Roger Davis (David Mitchell); Robert Hogan (Robert Blake); Marsha Hunt (Mrs Henderson); Philip Ober (Mr Henderson); Jack Raine (Reynolds).

Story: A young woman out riding is chased by an older woman on a similar horse. She eventually discovers it was her older self, trying to warn her not to marry the wrong man – someone of whom her parents disapproved, but whom she married nevertheless.

142: 'An Occurrence at Owl Creek Bridge'
(La Rivière du Hibou)
28 February 1964

Writer: Robert Enrico.   **Story:** Ambrose Bierce.
Director: Robert Enrico.   **Producer:** Marcel Ichac.
Director of Photography: **Music:** Henri Lanoë.
Jean Bofferty.

Cast: Roger Jacquet (Peyton Farquhar); Anne Cornaly (Mrs Farquhar); Anker Larsen, Stéphane Fey, Jean-François Zeller, Pierre Danny, Louis Adelin (Union Soldiers).

Story: During the Civil War, a Confederate spy who is about to be hanged miraculously escapes and manages to return home. But the whole thing was only a dream, and he dies on the gallows.

Note: Ambrose Bierce's story originally appeared in his collection *Tales of Soldiers and Civilians*, published in 1891. In order to save money, producer William Froug purchased the rights of this French short feature, which had won a prize at the 1962 Cannes Film Festival. A new introduction was recorded by Serling and the re-edited version went on to win an Oscar. It is, not, however, part of the regular syndicated *Twilight Zone* package.

143: 'Queen of the Nile'
6 March 1964

Writers: Jerry Sohl and Charles Beaumont.

Director: John Brahm.
Music: Lucien Morawack and Lud Gluskin.

Cast: Ann Blyth (Pamela); Lee Phillips (Jordan); Celia Lovsky (Viola); Frank Ferguson (Krueger); James Tyler (Jackson); Ruth Phillips (Maid).

Story: A journalist discovers that a seemingly ageless movie star is really an ancient Egyptian witch who has been stealing other people's life forces.

Note: While Charles Beaumont was ill, Jerry Sohl helped script this story, but was uncredited.

144: 'What's in the Box?'
13 March 1964

Writer: Martin Goldsmith.

Director: Richard Bare.

Cast: Joan Blondell (Phyllis Britt); William Demarest (Joe

Britt); Sterling Holloway (Repair Man); Sandra Gould (Woman); Herbert Lytton (Dr Saltman); Howard Wright (Judge); John L. Sullivan (Duke); Ted Christy (Panther Man); Ron Stokes (Car Salesman); Douglas Bank (Prosecutor); Tony Miller (Announcer).

Story: After an argument with a television repair man, an unfaithful cab driver's television set starts showing his extramarital activities. He is eventually driven to murder his wife, just as the set had predicted.

145: 'The Masks'
20 March 1964

Writer: Rod Serling.   **Director:** Ida Lupino.
Special make-up: William Tuttle.

Cast: Robert Keith (Jason Foster); Milton Selzer (Wilfred); Alan Sues (Wilfred Jr); Virginia Gregg (Emily); Brooke Hayward (Paula); Willis Bouchey (Doctor); Bill Walker (Butler).

Story: A dying old man forces his greedy heirs to wear mardi gras masks shaped to display their own vices. When they take them off, they discover their faces have come to resemble the masks.

146: 'I am the Night – Color Me Black'
27 March 1964

Writer: Rod Serling.   **Director:** Abner Biberman.

Cast: Michael Constantine (Sheriff Charlie Koch); Paul Fix (Colbey); Terry Becker (Jagger); Ivan Dixon (Reverend Anderson); George Lindsey (Pierce); Eve McVeagh (Ella); Douglas Bank, Ward Wood (Men); Elizabeth Harrower (Woman).

Story: The sun does not rise on a town the day it is going to hang a young man who murdered a bigot. Eventually, the prisoner is hanged, and the darkness created by hate begins to spread.

147: 'Sounds and Silences'

3 April 1964

Writer: Rod Serling.   **Director:** Richard Donner.

Cast: John McGiver (Roswell G. Flemington); Penny Singleton (Mrs Flemington); Michael Fox (Psychiatrist); Francis Defales (Doctor); Renee Aubrey (Secretary); William Benedict (Conklin).

Story: A loud, overbearing man who thrives on noise gets his comeuppance: first, he becomes over sensitive to sounds, then everything ends up sounding too weak.

Note: This episode was the subject of a lawsuit by a writer who alleged that he had previously submitted a similar story to the show. As a result, it is not included in the regular syndicated package.

148: 'Caesar and Me'

10 April 1964

Writer: A. T. Strassfield.   **Director:** Robert Butler.
Music: Richard Shores.

Cast: Jackie Cooper (Jonathan West); Suzanne Cupito (Susan); Sarah Selby (Mrs Cudahy); Olan Soule (Mr Smiles); Stafford Repp (Pawnbroker); Sidney Marion (Watchman); Ken Konopka (Mr Miller); Don Gazzaniga (Detective).

Story: A failed ventriloquist commits a burglary on the advice of his dummy. After he is arrested, the dummy teams up with a vicious little girl.

149: 'The Jeopardy Room'
17 April 1964

Writer: Rod Serling.   **Director:** Richard Donner.

Cast: Martin Landau (Kuchenko); John Van Dreelen (Vassiloff); Robert Kelljan (Boris).

Story: A would-be Russian defector has three hours in which to find a bomb hidden in his hotel room by a KGB assassin. It is in the telephone, set to explode when the receiver is picked up. He escapes, then turns the tables on his opponent.

150: 'Stopover in a Quiet Town'
24 April 1964

Writer: Earl Hamner, Jr.   **Director:** Ron Winston.

Cast: Barry Nelson (Bob Frazier); Nancy Malone (Millie); Denise Lynn (Little Girl); Karen Norris (Mother).

Story: After a night of heavy drinking, a couple wakes up to find themselves in a deserted town, made of props. The only sign of life is the distant laugh of a little girl. They eventually discover they have been kidnapped by a giant alien and have become her daughter's toys.

151: 'The Encounter'
1 May 1964

Writer: Martin Goldsmith.   **Director:** Robert Butler.

Cast: Neville Brand (Fenton); George Takei (Taro).

Story: A WWII veteran and a young Japanese-American gardener become trapped in an attic. Eventually, it is revealed that the veteran murdered an enemy who had surrendered in cold blood, while the gardener's father was a traitor. Egged on by their mutual guilt, the two men end up destroying each other.

Note: Because of its perceived racist connotations, this episode is not included in the regular syndicated package.

152: 'Mr. Garrity and the Graves'
8 May 1964

Writer: Rod Serling. **Story:** Mike Korologos.
Director: Ted Post. **Music:** Tommy Morgan.

Cast: John Dehner (Jared Garrity); J. Pat O'Malley (Gooberman); Stanley Adams (Jensen); Percy Helton (Lapham); Norman Leavitt (Sheriff); John Mitchum (Ace); Kate Murtagh (Zelda); John Cliff (Peterson); Patrick O'Moore (Man).

Story: A western con artist pretends he can raise the dead, then charges money not to. As he leaves, the dead actually come back to life.

153: 'The Brain Center at Whipple's'
15 May 1964

Writer: Rod Serling. **Director:** Richard Donner.

Cast: Richard Deacon (Wallace V. Whipple); Paul Newlan (Hanley); Ted De Corsia (Dickerson); Burt Conroy (Watchman); Jack Crowder (Technician); Shawn Michaels (Bartender); Dion Hansen (Robot).

Story: A factory owner remorselessly fires his employees and replaces them with robots. He is then, in turn, fired and replaced with a robot.

154: 'Come Wander with Me'
22 May 1964

Writer: Anthony Wilson.   **Director:** Richard Donner.

Cast: Gary Crosby (Floyd Burney); John Bolt (Billy Rayford); Bonnie Beecher (Mary Rachel); Hank Patterson (Old Man).
Story: A folk singer who routinely steals his material, hears a girl singing a haunting melody in the woods. He accidentally kills her boyfriend, and discovers that the song foretells his death.

Note: Writer Anthony Wilson created the classic television series *Land of the Giants* and *The Invaders*.

155: 'The Fear'
29 May 1964

Writer: Rod Serling.   **Director:** Ted Post.

Cast: Mark Richman (Robert Franklin); Hazel Court (Charlotte Scott).

Story: A frightened woman and a state trooper encounter what they, at first, believe to be giant aliens, but eventually discover to be tiny ones. The aliens flee in fear of the giant humans, proving that terror is relative.

156: 'The Bewitchin' Pool'
19 June 1964

Writer: Earl Hamner, Jr.   **Director:** Joseph M. Newman.

Cast: Mary Badham (Sport Sharewood); Tim Stafford (Jeb Sharewood); Kim Hector (Whitt); Georgia Simmons (Aunt T.); Tod Andrews (Gil); Dee Hartford (Gloria); Harold Gould (Announcer).

Story: The children of two feuding parents about to get a divorce find peace and happiness on the other side of a magical pool with the loving Aunt T.

Rod Serling's Night Gallery

After the demise of *The Twilight Zone*, and in spite of his public protestations about being tired of the show, Serling tried to sell it to other networks. Since CBS owned 60 per cent of the series, and therefore more than half the name *The Twilight Zone*, Serling tried to package the same concept, under different names. His agent pitched an anthology show to the ABC network, entitled *Rod Serling's Triple W: Witches, Warlocks and Werewolves* after the title of one of Serling's paperback anthologies. Serling later revamped the concept to that of a wax museum, in which each statue would provide the launching point of a story. But no one showed any interest.

Perhaps that fact, as well as the constant harping by CBS about the alleged unprofitability of *The Twilight Zone*, were the determining factors which convinced Serling to actually sell to CBS his 40 per cent interest in the show in March, 1965. When *The Twilight Zone* entered the syndication market soon afterwards, and proved hugely successful, Serling realised that he had made a bad decision, and must have decided to have another go at it.

This time, he wrote a script for a *Twilight Zone* television feature made up of three stories: *Eyes*, *Escape Route* and *Color Scheme*. CBS passed on it. Undaunted, Serling tried to sell the project under the title *Three Nightmares* – CBS being understandably reluctant to let anyone else use a title which they now fully owned – but failed. Finally, Serling took *Eyes*, *Escape Route* and *Color Scheme* and wrote them as novellas, which he incorporated in a book entitled *The Season to be Wary* (Little, Brown, 1967).

He then sent copies of the book, along with a new story, *Cemetery*, to various Hollywood studios, pitching the concept of a horror anthology series, but this time changing the concept from a wax museum to that of a night gallery. Of all the studios, only Universal expressed interest and that was mostly because producer William Sackheim championed the material, and eventually obtained the green light to turn it into a two-hour television special.

In February 1969, Serling signed with Universal to write and host the three *Night Gallery* stories, making it amply clear that he saw the proposed feature as a 'backdoor' pilot. *Rod Serling's Night Gallery* aired on 8 November 1969, on NBC and garnered very impressive ratings, validating Sackheim's faith in the material. In spite of this, neither Universal nor NBC rushed to launch the series Serling craved. Instead, they reluctantly scheduled only six hour-long episodes of *Night Gallery*, to screen alternately with three other shows, *McCloud*, *The Psychiatrist* and *San Francisco International* as *Four-In-One*, starting in late 1970. More frustratingly, Universal had no faith in Serling's ability as a show runner. Since Sackheim did not want to be involved with the production of a weekly show, Universal handed all the reins of power to producer Jack Laird. Laird's credits included writing for *Have Gun – Will Travel*, *Ben Casey*, *The Alfred Hitchcock Hour* and *The Psychiatrist*, which he had also produced.

Despite the fact that Serling was not in control, the first season of *Night Gallery* reflected his unique vision. However, creative conflicts soon developed with Laird, who had a more conventional approach than Serling, and certainly not as much faith in the public's ability to warm to a higher-brow, more literary-inspired brand of fiction. Laird wanted a mass market show, not a cult classic, and consequently ended up heavily rewriting everything Serling wrote.

By the second season, *Rod Serling's Night Gallery* may have been more truthfully entitled *Jack Laird's Night Gallery*. Serling had become just a front man, performing his introductions in a style that was almost a caricature of himself. His creative overtures were either spurned or rejected outright. He understandably grew very bitter and deemed *Night Gallery* the worst creative experience of his life. It is almost certain that the show contributed to driving him away from California. Yet, *Night Gallery*, at best, even without Serling, was not without merit: it contained many good literary adaptations, from H. P. Lovecraft, Conrad Aiken, André Maurois, etc. and could boast often surprisingly high production values. Where *The Twilight Zone* had been a writer's show, *Night Gallery* often was a director's show, and many talented artists worked on it: directors Steven Spielberg, Jeannot Szwarc, John Badham; actors Orson Welles, Agnes Moorehead, Joan Crawford, Edward G. Robinson, William Windom and Mickey Rooney, to name but a few.

However, this was an age of commercial television. Laird wanted to compete with CBS's *Mannix*, against which *Night Gallery* was slotted. In its third, and last, season, he emphasised monsters and cheap frights, but to no avail. *Night Gallery* was cut down to half-an-hour, yet still withered, both creatively and commercially, and was mercifully cancelled. Fate, however, handed Serling his revenge on the proverbial silver platter.

Universal wanted to syndicate *Night Gallery*, but did not have enough episodes to meet the demands of the syndication market. (They needed about a hundred or so.) Consequently, they decided to repackage *The Sixth Sense*, a mediocre, hour-long series about Dr. Rhodes, a parapsychology investigator played by Gary Collins, as part of the *Night Gallery*. But for this, they needed Serling to record new on-camera introductions. For that one day's work, Serling charged Universal the considerable sum of $200,000.

In order to fit the half-hour syndication format, Universal butchered the hour-long *Night Gallery*, sometimes adding totally extraneous material, often cutting up the stories to the extent that longer episodes such as the wonderful *They're Tearing Down Tim Riley's Bar* virtually made no sense. The same fate befell the hour-long episodes of *The Sixth Sense* which, in their half-hour version, are literally incomprehensible. (We provide at the end of our *Night Gallery* episode guide, a list of *The Sixth Sense* episodes, even though they have nothing to do with the former, in order to help viewers to separate these from the original *Night Gallery*.)

Serling tried again to sell *The Twilight Zone* to ABC in 1975, in partnership with his friend, the powerful producer Aaron Spelling, but the network, sensing perhaps that Serling's time was past, did not bite. The torch of *The Twilight Zone* would now pass into other hands.

Pilot

Producer: William Sackheim.
Assistant Producer: John Badham.
Director of Photography: Richard Batcheller,
William Margulies.
Music: William Goldenberg.
Paintings by: Jaroslav Gebr.

1.

8 November 1969

a: 'The Cemetery'

Writer: Rod Serling.   **Director:** Boris Sagal.

Cast: Roddy McDowall (Jeremy); Ossie Davis (Osmond Portifoy); George MacReady (William Hendricks); Barry Atwater (Carson).

Story: A man murders his rich, old uncle, then sees the corpse crawling out of the grave in one of the old man's paintings.

80

Driven mad, he falls to his death. The butler is revealed to have been behind the plot, but now he too starts seeing his victims come back to life in the painting.

b: 'Eyes'

Writer: Rod Serling.   **Director:** Steven Spielberg.

Cast: Joan Crawford (Claudia Menlo); Barry Sullivan (Frank Heatherton); Tom Bosley (Sidney Resnick).

Story: A domineering old woman, blind from birth, blackmails a surgeon into doing an eye transplant. As she recovers her sight, a power blackout causes her to believe the operation has failed. She eventually falls to her death.

c: 'The Escape Route'

Writer: Rod Serling.   **Director:** Barry Shear

Cast: Richard Kiley (Josef Strobe/Helmut Arnt); Sam Jaffe (Bleum); Norma Crane (Gretchen); George Murdock (Agent).

Story: A former nazi is discovered by an Auschwitz survivor, then pursued by Israeli agents. His only refuge is in a painting in a museum, but instead of landing in the 'peaceful fisherman on a lake' scene he had earlier admired, he ends up in a concentration camp crucifixion.

First Season

(As part of *Four-in-One*, rotating with *McCloud*,
The Psychiatrist and *San Francisco International*.)

Producer: Jack Laird.
Director of Photography: Richard C. Glouner,
William Margulies.

Music: Benny Carter, Robert Prince.
Theme Music: Gil Mellé.
Make-up: Bud Westmore, John Chambers.
Paintings by: Tom Wright.
Sculptures by: Logan Elston, Phil Vanderlei.

2.

16 December 1970

a: 'The Dead Man'

Writer: Douglas Heyes.   **Story:** Fritz Leiber.
Director: Douglas Heyes.

Cast: Carl Betz (Dr Max Redford); Louise Sorel (Velia Redford); Jeff Corey (Dr Miles Talmadge); Michael Blodgett (John Fearing); Glenn Dixon (Minister).

Story: A doctor hypnotises a man into believing he is dead, then fails to bring him back to life. A year later, it is revealed that he did it on purpose because the subject was having an affair with his wife. Once the proper signal is given, the corpse comes back to life and kills the doctor.

Note: Fritz Leiber's story originally appeared in the November 1950 issue of *Weird Tales*.

b: 'The Housekeeper'

Writer: Matthew Howard.   **Director:** John Meredyth Lucas.

Cast: Larry Hagman (Cedric Acton); Suzy Parker (Carlotta); Jeanette Nolan (Miss Wattle); Cathleen Cordell (Miss Beamish); Howard Morton (Waiter).

Story: A man uses a spell to transfer the mind of a good-hearted cleaning lady into the body of his beautiful, but allegedly selfish, wife. It turns out that he is the selfish one, has done this before, and will continue to do it – until he 'gets it right'.

Note: Matthew Howard was a pseudonym of Douglas Heyes.

3.
23 December 1970
a: 'Room with a View'

Writer: Hal Dresner.   **Story:** Hal Dresner.
Director: Jerrold Freeman.

Cast: Joseph Wiseman (Mr B); Angel Tompkins (Lila); Diane Keaton (Nurse); Larry Watson (Vic, the Chauffeur); Morgan Farley (Charles).

Story: An invalid man manipulates his nurse into killing his unfaithful wife and her lover, who is also the nurse's fiancé.

Note: Hal Dresner's story originally appeared in the July 1962 issue of *Alfred Hitchcock's Mystery Magazine*.

b: 'The Little Black Bag'

Writer: Rod Serling.   **Story:** Cyril M. Kornbluth.
Director: Jeannot Szwarc.

Cast: Burgess Meredith (Dr Fall); Chill Wills (Heppelwhite); George Furth (Gilling); E. J. Andre (Charlie Peterson); Arthur Malet (Ennis); Eunice Suarez (Mother); Marion Val (Girl); Johnny Silver (Pawnbroker); Robert Terry (Dr Nodella); Lindsay Workman, Matt Pelto (Doctors); Ralph Moody, William Challee (Old Men).

Story: A washed-out doctor finds a medical bag from the future, which he plans to use for good. He is murdered by a greedy hobo, who steals the bag. When scientists from the future find out about the murder, they deactivate the bag, causing the hobo to kill himself while demonstrating the bag's powers.

Note: Cyril M. Korbluth's story first appeared in the July 1950 issue of *Astounding Science-Fiction*.

c: 'The Nature of the Enemy'

Writer: Rod Serling.   **Director:** Allen Reisner.

Cast: Joseph Campanella (Simms); Richard Van Vleet (Steve, The Space Man); James B. Sikking, Jason Wingreen, Albert Popwell (Reporters); Jerry Strickler (Man).

Story: A lunar mission is attacked by a giant mouse.

4.

30 December 1970

a: 'The House'

Writer: Rod Serling.   **Story:** André Maurois.
Director: John Astin.

Cast: Joanna Pettet (Elaine Chambrun); Paul Richards (Peugeot); Steve Franken (Dr Mitchell).

Story: A young woman purchases a country house she has seen repeatedly in her dreams, and which has the reputation of being haunted. She eventually discovers that she herself is the ghost haunting the house.

Note: André Maurois's story was originally published in France in 1935.

b: 'Certain Shadows on the Wall'

Writer: Rod Serling.   **Story:** Mary E. Wilkins-Freeman.
Director: Jeff Corey.

Cast: Louis Hayward (Dr Stephen Brigham); Agnes Moorehead (Emma Brigham); Rachel Roberts (Rebecca Brigham); Grayson Hall (Ann Brigham).

Story: A brother poisons his sister to get her inheritance, but cannot get rid of her shadow on the wall. He, in turn, is accidentally poisoned by another of his sisters, and his shadow goes to join his victim's on the same wall.

Note: Mary E. Wilkins-Freeman's story, originally entitled *The Shadows on the Wall*, was first published in 1903 in her collection *The Wind in the Rosebush and Other Stories of the Supernatural*.

5.

6 January 1971

a: 'Make Me Laugh'

Writer: Rod Serling.   **Director:** Steven Spielberg.

Cast: Godfrey Cambridge (Jackie Slater); Jackie Vernon (Chatterje); Al Lewis (Myron Mishkin); Tom Bosley (Jules Kettleman); Sidney Clute (David Garrick); Gene Kearney, Sonny Klein (Bartenders); John J. Fox (Heckler); Tony Ribbel (Director); Michael Hart (Wilson); Georgia Schmidt (Flower Lady); Sid Rushakoff, Don Melvoin (Laughers).

Story: A magician gives a washed-up comic the miracle he asked for: the ability to make people laugh. But the comic grows bored with his success and wants to make audiences cry. The magician agrees; the comic crosses the street to test his new gift and gets run over by a car, his death at last making people cry.

b: 'Clean Kills and Other Trophies'

Writer: Rod Serling.   **Director:** Walter Doniger.

Cast: Raymond Massey (Colonel Archie Dittman); Tom Troupe (Mr Pierce); Barry Brown (Archie Dittman Jr); Herbert Jefferson Jr (Tom).

Story: A young man who hates hunting is coerced into killing a deer by his brutal, insensitive father. Their African butler prays to his native gods, who take the father's life and mount his head among his other hunting trophies.

Note: Serling restored the original ending of this episode in its novelisation for his anthology *Night Gallery*. In it, there are no African gods, and it is the young man who decapitates his father.

6.

13 January 1971

a: 'Pamela's Voice'

Writer: Rod Serling.   **Director:** Richard Benedict.

Cast: Phyllis Diller (Pamela); John Astin (Jonathan).

Story: A husband who killed his wife because he could no longer stand her shrieking and nagging meets her ghost, who reveals that he has just died and has been condemned to listen to her for all eternity.

b: 'Lone Survivor'

Writer: Rod Serling.   **Director:** Gene Levitt.

Cast: John Colicos (Survivor); Torin Thatcher (*Lusitania* Captain); Hedley Marringly (*Lusitania* Doctor); Charles Davis (*Lusitania* Officer); Brendan Dillon (*Lusitania* Quartermaster); William Beckley (Richards); Terence Pushman (Helmsman); Edward Colmans (*Andrea Doria* Captain); Pierre Jalbert (*Andrea Doria* Officer); Carl Milletaire (*Andrea Doria* Quartermaster).

Story: A coward who escaped from the *Titanic* by disguising himself as a woman, is condemned to go from sinking ship to sinking ship for all eternity: first the *Lusitania* (where no one believes his story about an incoming torpedo attack); then the *Andrea Doria*.

c: 'The Doll'

Writer: Rod Serling.   **Story:** Algernon Blackwood.
Director: Rudi Dorn.

Cast: Shani Wallis (Miss Danton); Henry Silva (Pandit Chola); John Williams (Colonel Masters); Jewel Blanch (Monica); Than Wyenn (Indian); John Barclay (Butler).

Story: An Indian rebel, whose brother was killed by a British Colonel, sends to the latter's niece a magical doll which eventually comes to life and kills the Colonel with its poisoned bite. The Colonel's posthumous revenge is to send a similar doll to the Indian.

Note: Algernon Blackwood's story originally appeared in 1907 in his collection *The Listener and Other Stories*.

7.

20 January 1971

a: 'The Last Laurel'

Writer: Rod Serling.   **Story:** Davis Grubb.
Director: Daryl Duke.

Cast: Jack Cassidy (Marius Davis); Martine Beswick (Susan Davis); Martin E. Brooks (Dr Armstrong).

Story: A former decathlon champion, now paralysed, has learned how to project his astral body and manipulate objects through telekinesis. He plots to murder his wife's lover, but because of a power failure, ends up smashing his own head instead.

Note: Davis Grubb's story, originally entitled *The Horsehair Trunk*, was first published in 1948.

b: 'They're Tearing Down Tim Riley's Bar'

Writer: Rod Serling.   **Director:** Don Taylor.

Cast: William Windom (Randolph Lane); Diane Baker (Lynn Alcott); Bert Convy (Doane); John Randolph (Pritkin); Henry Beckman (McDermott); David Astor (Blodgett); Robert Herrman (Tim Riley); Gene O'Donnell (Bartender); Frederic Downs (Father); John Ragin (Policeman); David Frank (Intern); Susannah Darrow (Kathy Lane); Mary Gail Hobbs (Miss Trevor); Margie Hall (Operator); Don Melvoin, Matt Pelto (Workmen).

Story: A lonely salesman, a widower, unhappy about the pressures of modern life, is grief-stricken when he learns that his favourite bar is about to be torn down. He experiences visions of his past, and gets fired. But his secretary, who is in love with him, gets him rehired and restores his hope in life and in the present.

Second Season

(one-hour episodes)
Producer: Jack Laird.
Director of Photography: Gerald Perry Finnerman, Lionel Lindon, William Margulies, Leonard J. South, E. Charles Straumer, Bud Thackery.
Music: Paul Glass, Hal Mooney, Oliver Nelson, Robert Prince, Eddie Sauter.
Theme Music: Gil Mellé.
Make-up: Bud Westmore, John Chambers.
Paintings by: Tom Wright.
Sculptures by: Logan Elston, Phil Vanderlei.

8.

15 September 1971

a: 'The Boy who Predicted Earthquakes'

Writer: Rod Serling.   **Story:** Margaret St Clair.
Director: John Badham.

Cast: Clint Howard (Herbie Bittman); Michael Constantine (Wellman); Bernie Kopell (Reed); William Hansen (Godwin); Ellen Weston (Dr Peterson); Gene Tyburn (Director); Rance Howard (Cameraman); Rosary Nix (Secretary); John Donald (Grip).

Story: A ten-year-old boy with the gift of prophecy cannot bring himself to reveal that the sun is going to go nova and destroy the Earth.

Note: Margaret St Clair's story originally appeared in 1950 in *Maclean's Magazine*.

b: 'Miss Lovecraft Sent Me'

Writer: Jack Laird.   **Director:** Gene Kearney.

Cast: Joseph Campanella (Father); Sue Lyon (Betsy).

Story: In this story, the first in a series of short-short fillers of five minutes or less, a prospective babysitter runs away from a house of monsters.

c: 'The Hand of Borgus Weems'

Writer: Alvin T. Sapinsley.   **Story:** George Langelaan.
Director: John Meredyth Lucas.

Cast: Ray Milland (Dr Archibald Ravadon); George Maharis (Peter Lacland); Joan Huntington (Susan Douglas); Patricia Donahue (Dr Innokenti); William Mims (Brock Ramsey); Peter

Mamakos (Nico Kazanzakis); Robert Hoy (Everett Winterreich).

Story: A man whose hand has become animated with a murderous will of its own, has it removed by a surgeon. Further investigation reveals that the will behind the hand's actions belongs to an occultist who lived in the same building, was murdered by his niece and her boyfriend, and is now bent on getting revenge. The occultist's ghost then takes over the surgeon's hand.

Note: George Langelaan's story, originally entitled *The Other Hand*, appeared in the October 1961 issue of *The Magazine of Fantasy and Science-Fiction*.

d: 'The Phantom of What Opera?'

Writer: Gene Kearney.   **Director:** Gene Kearney.

Cast: Leslie Nielsen (The Phantom); Mary Ann Beck (The Singer).

Story: In this short-short, the Phantom of the Opera falls in love with a singer who turns out to be as ugly as he is.

9.

22 September 1971

a: 'A Death In The Family'

Writer: Rod Serling.   **Story:** Miriam Allen DeFord.
Director: Jeannot Szwarc.

Cast: E. G. Marshall (Soames); Desi Arnaz, Jr (Doran); Noam Pitlik (Driver); James B. Sikking, John Williams Evans, Bill Elliott (Troopers); Bud Walls (Gravedigger).

Story: An insane, misanthropic mortician has turned the corpses of the recently deceased into a perfect 'family'. A young convict on the run stumbles upon the grisly secret; the two men end up killing each other.

b: 'The Merciful'

Writer: Jack Laird.   **Story:** Charles L. Sweeny, Jr.
Director: Jeannot Szwarc.

Cast: Imogene Coca (Wife); King Donovan (Husband).

Story: In this filler, one is led to believe that a woman is walling up her husband because he is dying from an incurable disease, but in fact, she is walling herself up for the same reason.

c: 'The Class of '99'

Writer: Rod Serling.   **Director:** Jeannot Szwarc.

Cast: Vincent Price (Professor); Brandon De Wilde (Johnson); Randolph Mantooth (Elkins); Frank Hotchkiss (Clinton); Hilly Hicks (Barnes); Suzanne Cohane (Miss Fields); Hunter Von Leer (Templeton); John Davey (McWhirter); Barbara Shannon (Miss Peterson); Richard Doyle (Bruce); Lenore Kasdorf (Miss Wheeton).

Story: On a future Earth where pollution and wars have finally killed off the human population, androids created by man in his image learn the basics of bigotry and intolerance in order to act just like men.

d: 'The Witches' Feast'

Writer: Gene Kearney.   **Director:** Jerrold Freeman.

Cast: Agnes Moorehead, Ruth Buzzi, Fran Ryan, Allison McKay (Witches).

Story: A short filler written in verse. Three witches are cooking up disgusting ingredients when a fourth witch arrives with normal sandwiches.

10.

29 September 1971

a: 'Since Aunt Ada Came To Stay'

Writer: Alvin T. Sapinsley.   **Story:** A. E. Van Vogt.
Director: William Hale.

Cast: James Farentino (Craig Lowell); Jeanette Nolan (Aunt Ada); Michelle Lee (Joanna Lowell); Jonathan Harris (Nicholas Porteus); Eldon Quick (Frank Heller); Charles Seel (Caretaker); Alma Platt (Housekeeper); Arnold Turner (Messenger).

Story: An old witch comes to visit her niece, intending to steal her younger body. But the niece's husband gets wise to her scheme, and eventually defeats her with a green carnation. Or does he?

Note: A. E. Van Vogt's story, originally entitled *The Witch*, appeared in the February 1943 issue of *Unknown Worlds*.

b: 'With Apologies To Mr Hyde'

Writer: Jack Laird.   **Director:** Jeannot Szwarc.

Cast: Adam West (Mr Hyde); Jack Laird (Assistant).

Story: A short filler in which Mr Hyde berates his lab assistant for having put too much vermouth in his cocktail.

c: 'The Flip Side of Satan'

Writers: Malcolm Marmorstein   **Story:** Hal Dresner.
and Gerald Sanford.   **Director:** Jerrold Freeman.
Cast: Arte Johnson (J. J. Wilson).

Story: An amoral disc jockey has been booked by his agent (whose wife he drove to suicide) on a radio station that only plays demonic music. He refuses to repent and is taken to hell while his photo goes to join those of the other DJs.

11.

6 October 1971

a: 'A Fear of Spiders'

Writer: Rod Serling.   **Story:** Elizabeth Walter.
Director: John Astin.

Cast: Patrick O'Neal (Justus); Kim Stanley (Elizabeth); Tom Pedi (Boucher).

Story: A writer who brutally turned down the advances of a neighbour infatuated with him, begins to be plagued by visions of a giant spider. When he turns to the neighbour for help, she eventually locks him up with the spider.

Note: Elizabeth Walter's story, originally entitled *The Spider*, appeared in 1967 in *The Second Fontana Book of Great Horror Stories*.

b: 'Junior'

Writer: Gene Kearney.   **Director:** Theodore J. Flicker.

Cast: Wally Cox (Father); Barbara Flicker (Mother); Bill Svanoe (Junior).

Story: A short filler in which a couple's crying baby is revealed to look like Frankenstein's monster.

c: 'Marmalade Wine'

Writer: Jerrold Freeman.   **Story:** Joan Aiken.
Director: Jerrold Freeman.

Cast: Robert Morse (Roger Blacker); Rudy Vallee (Dr Francis Deeking).

Story: A man with the ability to predict the future is taken prisoner by a mad surgeon who amputates his feet so that his victim can't escape.

Note: Joan Aiken's story originally appeared in 1969 in her collection *The Windscreen Weepers*.

d: 'The Academy'

Writer: Rod Serling.
Story: David Ely.
Director: Jeff Corey.

Cast: Pat Boone (Holston); Leif Erickson (Director); Larry Linville (Sloane); Ed Call (Drill Instructor); Stanley Waxman (Bradley); Robert Gibbons (Gatekeeper); E.A. Sirianni (Chauffeur); John Gruber (Cadet).

Story: After a guided tour, a father decides to send his undisciplined son to a military academy for boys, where he will spend the rest of his life.

Note: David Ely's story originally appeared in *Playboy*, and was later anthologized in 1968 in his collection *Time Out*.

12.

20 October 1971

a: 'The Phantom Farmhouse'

Writer: Halsted Welles.   **Story:** Seabury Quinn.
Director: Jeannot Szwarc.

Cast: David McCallum (Psychiatrist); Linda Marsh (Mildred); David Carradine (Gideon); Ivor Francis (Pierre); Ford Rainey (Sheriff); Trina Parks (Betty); Bill Quinn (Dr Tom); Martin Ashe (Mr Squire); Gail Bonney (Mrs Squire); Ray Ballard (Mr Grouch); Frank Arnold (Shepherd).

Story: A psychiatrist falls in love with a ghostly woman cursed with lycanthropy. At her request, he reads burial prayers over her grave, giving her spirit the peace she has been craving.

Note: Seabury Quinn's story originally appeared in the October 1923 issue of *Weird Tales*.

b: 'Silent Snow, Secret Snow'

Writer: Gene Kearney.   **Story:** Conrad Aiken.
Director: Gene Kearney.   **Narrator:** Orson Welles.

Cast: Radames Pera (Paul); Lisabeth Hush (Mother); Lonny Chapman (Father); Jason Wingreen (Doctor); Francis Spanier (Mrs Buel).

Story: A man becomes so completely obsessed with snow that he totally shuts himself off from reality.

Note: Conrad Aiken's story was first published in 1934.

13.

27 October 1971

a: 'A Question of Fear'

Writer: Theodore Flicker.   **Story:** Bryan Lewis.
Director: Jack Laird.

Cast: Leslie Nielsen (Colonel Dennis Malloy); Fritz Weaver (Dr Mazi); Jack Bannon (Al); Owen Cunningham (Walter); Ivan Bonar (Fred).

Story: The son of a pianist needlessly tortured by a colonel during the war, gains revenge by convincing him that he has fed him a drug that will dissolve his bones and turn him into a slug-like creature. The Colonel shoots himself, but it was all a bluff.

Note: Bryan Lewis's story originally appeared in 1970 in *The*

Eleventh Pan Book of Horror Stories.

b: 'The Devil Is Not Mocked'

Writer: Gene Kearney. **Story:** Manly Wade Wellman.
Director: Gene Kearney.

Cast: Helmut Dantine (General); Francis Lederer (Dracula); Hank Brandt (Kranz); Martin Kosleck (Hugo); Gino Gottarelli (Radio Man); Mark De Vries (Gunner).

Story: Count Dracula tells his grandson how he fought the Nazis during WWII.

Note: Manly Wade Wellman's story originally appeared in the June 1943 issue of *Unknown Worlds*.

14.

3 November 1971

a: 'Midnight Never Ends'

Writer: Rod Serling. **Director:** Jeannot Szwarc.

Cast: Susan Strasberg (Ruth/Writer's Wife); Robert F. Lyons (Vincent Riley/Writer); Joseph Perry (Bateman); Robert Karnes (Sheriff).

Story: A woman and a hitch-hiker go through a series of senseless events until they realise they are fictional characters in the hands of a writer looking for a plot.

b: 'Brenda'

Writer: Matthew Howard. **Story:** Margaret St Clair.
Director: Allen Reisner.

Cast: Laurie Prange (Brenda); Glenn Corbett (Richard Alden);

Barbara Babcock (Flora Alden); Robert Hogan (Jim Emsden); Sue Taylor (Elizabeth); Pamelyn Ferdin (Frances Anne); Fred Carson (Creature).

Story: A lonely, bratty girl falls in love with a mud creature.

Note: Matthew Howard was a pseudonym of Douglas Heyes. Margaret St Clair's story originally appeared in the March 1954 issue of *Weird Tales*.

15.

10 November 1971

a: 'The Diary'

Writer: Rod Serling.   **Director:** William Hale.

Cast: Patty Duke (Holly Schaeffer); Virginia Mayo (Carrie Crane); David Wayne (Dr Mills); Lindsay Wagner (Nurse); Robert Yuro (Jeb Harlan); James McCallion (George); Floy Dean (Receptionist); Diana Chesney (Maid).

Story: A vicious gossip columnist drives an old movie star to commit suicide. But before her death, the actress gives the writer a diary which magically fills itself with predictions of the future. When the diary pages remain blank, the columnist goes insane.

b: 'A Matter of Semantics'

Writer: Gene Kearney.   **Director:** Jack Laird.

Cast: Cesar Romero (Dracula); E. J. Peaker (Nurse); Monie Ellis (Candy Striper).

Story: In this filler, Dracula applies for a loan at a blood bank.

c: 'The Big Surprise'

Writer: Richard Matheson.   **Story:** Richard Matheson.

Director: Jeannot Szwarc.

Cast: John Carradine (Mr Hawkins); Vincent Van Patten (Chris); Marc Vahanian (Jason); Eric Chase (Dan).

Story: A strange old man tells three boys to look for a 'big surprise' under an oak tree. They dig out a box. The old man steps out shouting 'surprise!'

Note: Richard Matheson's story (also known as *What was in the Box?*) originally appeared in the April 1959 issue of *Ellery Queen's Mystery Magazine*.

d: 'Professor Peabody's Last Lecture'

Writer: Jack Laird.   **Director:** Jerrold Freeman.

Cast: Carl Reiner (Professor Peabody); Johnnie Collins III (Lovecraft); Richard Annis (Bloch); Larry Watson (Derleth); Louise Lawson (Miss Heald).

Story: A college professor reads the names of the Old Ones from the *Necronomicon* despite the warnings of students Lovecraft, Derleth and Bloch. He is turned into a monster.

16.
17 November 1971
a: 'House – With Ghost'

Writer: Gene Kearney.   **Story:** August Derleth.
Director: Gene Kearney.

Cast: Bob Crane (Ellis); Jo Anne Worley (Iris); Bernard Fox (Mr Canby); Eric Christmas (Mr Chichester); Trisha Noble (Sherry); Alan Napier (Doctor).

Story: A man, who is trying to get rid of his wife, leases a house haunted by the ghost of a ruthless businessman. The ghost ends up killing the wife, then extorts payment from the husband.

Note: August Derleth's story originally appeared in 1962 in his collection, *Lonesome Places*.

b: 'A Midnight Visit to the Neighborhood Blood Bank'

Writer: Jack Laird.   **Director:** William Hale.

Cast: Victor Buono (Vampire); Journey Laird (Victim).

Story: In this filler, a woman tells a vampire she already gave at the office.

c: 'Dr Stringfellow's Rejuvenator'

Writer: Rod Serling.   **Director:** Jerrold Freeman.

Cast: Forrest Tucker (Dr Stringfellow); Don Pedro Colley (Rolpho); Murray Hamilton (Snyder); Lou Frizzell (Man).

Story: In the old West, a pedlar of phony miracle cures sells his medicine to the father of a dying girl. Later, he sees the girl's ghost and dies of a heart attack.

d: 'Hell's Bells'

Writer: Thedore Flicker.   **Story:** Harry Turner.
Director: Theodore Flicker.

Cast: John Astin (Hippie); Theodore Flicker (Devil); Jody Gilbert (Fat Lady); John J. Fox, Cecil Cabot (Tourists); Jack Laird, Theodore Flicker, Gene Kearney (Demons).

Story: A hippie ends up in hell which, to him, is a room filled with incredibly boring 'normal' people. The Devil remarks that it is also someone else's idea of Heaven.

Note: Harry Turner's story originally appeared in 1970 in *The Eleventh Pan Book of Horror Stories*.

17.

24 November 1971

a: 'The Dark Boy'

Writer: Halsted Welles.　　**Story:** August Derleth.
Director: John Astin.

Cast: Elizabeth Hartman (Mrs Timm); Gale Sondergaard (Abigail Moore); Michael Baseleon (Tom Robb); Hope Summers (Lettie Moore); Steven Lorange (Edward); Ted Foulkes (Fourth Grader); Michael Laird (Joel).

Story: A teacher's school is haunted by the ghost of a boy who died when he fell from a ladder. She and the boy's father eventually lay the boy's soul to rest.

Note: August Derleth's story originally appeared in the February 1957 issue of *The Magazine of Fantasy and Science-Fiction*.

b: 'Keep In Touch – We'll Think of Something'

Writer: Gene Kearney.　　**Director:** Gene Kearney.

Cast: Alex Cord (Erik Sutton); Joanna Pettet (Claire Foster); Richard O'Brien (Sergeant Joe Brice); David Morick (Hruska); Paul Trinka (Policeman); Mike Robelo (Chauffeur).

Story: By making up a story about being assaulted, a man finds the woman he has seen in his dreams. She falls in love with him and tells him that her husband dreams of being murdered by a man with a scar on his hand. Because he has no scar, she cuts his hand, hoping to make the prediction come true.

18.

1 December 1971

a: 'Pickman's Model'

Writer: Alvin T. Sapinsley.   **Story:** H. P. Lovecraft.
Director: Jack Laird.

Cast: Bradford Dillman (Richard Upton Pickman); Louise Sorel (Mavis Goldsmith); Donald Moffat (Uncle George); Jock Livingston (Larry Rand); Joshua Bryant (Eliot Blackman); Joan Tompkins (Mrs De Witt); Robert Prohaska (Creature).

Story: Seventy-five years in the past, a young girl falls in love with a painter whose works depict ghoulish, rodent-like creatures living beneath the city. Eventually, she discovers that the painter himself belongs to the ghouls' race – his hands are like claws. He is taken underground by a ghoul and the tunnels below are sealed. They are reopened in the present.

Note: H. P. Lovecraft's story originally appeared in the October 1927 issue of *Weird Tales*.

b: 'The Dear Departed'

Writer: Rod Serling.   **Story:** Alice-Mary Schnirring.
Director: Jeff Corey.

Cast: Steve Lawrence (Mark); Harvey Lembeck (Joe); Maureen Arthur (Angela); Stanley Waxman (Mr Harcourt); Patricia Donahue (Mrs Harcourt); Rose Hobart (Mrs Hugo); Steve Carlson (Policeman).

Story: A phony medium covets his partner's beautiful wife. After the partner's death in a car accident, he thinks they may be forced to go out of business, but the partner returns as a ghost and tells him that they will stay a team for ever.

Note: Alice-Mary Schnirring's story originally appeared in the May 1944 issue of *Weird Tales*.

c: 'An Act of Chivalry'

Writer: Jack Laird.   **Director:** Jack Laird.

Cast: Rod Stein (Spectre); Deirdre Hudson (Blonde); Jimmy Cross (Passenger).

Story: In this short filler, Death removes its head in the presence of a lady.

19.

8 December 1971

a: 'Cool Air'

Writer: Rod Serling.   **Story:** H. P. Lovecraft.
Director: Jeannot Szwarc.

Cast: Barbara Rush (Agatha Howard); Henry Darrow (Dr Juan Munos); Beatrice Kay (Mrs Gibbons); Larry Blake (Mr Crowley); Karl Lukas (Iceman).

Story: A man has forestalled death for ten years through the sheer power of his will, but has been unable to stop the decay of his body, which is why he must never leave his refrigerated apartment. When the machines break down, he finally rots away.

Note: H. P. Lovecraft's story originally appeared in the March 1928 issue of *Tales of Magic and Mystery*.

b: 'Camera Obscura'

Writer: Rod Serling.   **Story:** Basil Copper.
Director: John Badham.

Cast: Ross Martin (Mr Gingold); Rene Auberjonois (William

Sharsted); Arthur Malet (Abel Joyce); Brendan Dillon (Drucker); Milton Parsons (Lamplighter); John Barclay (Sharsted Sr); Phillip Kenneally (Driver).

Story: A mysterious Mr Gingold uses a camera obscura (a device made up of prisms and a mirror) to banish a greedy and heartless usurer back in time to a place populated by his peers: ghouls, grave robbers and bloodsuckers.

Note: Basil Copper's story originally appeared in 1965 in *The Sixth Pan Book of Horror Stories*.

c: 'Quoth the Raven'

Writer: Jack Laird.   **Director:** Jeff Corey.

Cast: Marty Allen (Poe).

Story: In this short filler, a raven helps Poe write his famous poem.

20.

15 December 1971

a: 'The Messiah on Mott Street'

Writer: Rod Serling.   **Director:** Don Taylor.

Cast: Edward G. Robinson (Abraham Goldman); Ricky Powell (Mikey Goldman); Tony Roberts (Dr Levine); Yaphet Kotto (Buckner); Anne Taylor (Miss Moretti); Joseph Ruskin (Fanatic); John J. Fox (Santa Claus).

Story: An ageing Jewish man desperately wants to stay alive to care for his nine-year-old grandson, and see the return of the Messiah. The boy goes looking for the Messiah, and finds a compassionate black man who, indeed, turns out to be the real Messiah.

b: 'The Painted Mirror'

Writer: Gene Kearney.   **Story:** Donald Wandrei.
Director: Gene Kearney.

Cast: Zsa Zsa Gabor (Mrs Moore); Arthur O'Connell (Frank Standish); Rosemary De Camp (Ellen Chase).

Story: A rapacious woman who owns an antique store and has just swindled her partner out of his share of the business, buys a painted mirror hiding a strange prehistoric landscape. She eventually steps into the landscape and becomes trapped within it. Her partner repaints the mirror.

Note: Donald Wandrei's story originally appeared in *Esquire* in 1937.

21.

29 December 1971

a: 'The Different Ones'

Writer: Rod Serling.   **Director:** John Meredyth Lucas.

Cast: Dana Andrews (Paul Koch); Jon Korkes (Victor Koch); Monica Lewis (Official); Peggy Webber, Mary Gregory (Women); Dennis Rucker (Man).

Story: In the future, a man is eventually forced to send his physically-deformed teenage son to another planet, which welcomes him because all the aliens look like him. In exchange, they send one of their 'freaks', who looks just like a human, to Earth.

b: 'Tell David...'

Writer: Gerald Sanford.   **Story:** Penelope Wallace.
Director: Jeff Corey.

Cast: Sandra Dee (Ann Bolt); Jared Martin (Tony Bolt/David

Blessington); Jenny Sullivan (Pat Blessington); Jan Shutan (Jane Blessington); Françoise Ruggieri (Yvonne); Anne Randall (Julie); Chris Patrick (David Bolt).

Story: A young woman meets her own grown-up son from 20 years in the future. He is trying to prevent her from killing her husband in a fit of jealousy, then committing suicide. But she cannot escape her intended fate.

c: 'Logoda's Heads'

Writer: Robert Bloch.   **Story:** August Derleth.
Director: Jeannot Szwarc.

Cast: Patrick Macnee (Major Crosby); Denise Nicholas (Kyro); Brock Peters (Logoda); Tim Matheson (Henley); Zara Culley (Emba); Albert Popwell (Sergeant Imo); Roger E. Mosley (Askari).

Story: In Africa, a witch doctor uses his magic to make shrunken heads speak. A girl who hates him uses her magic to make the heads kill the witch doctor.

Note: August Derleth's story originally appeared in the April 1939 issue of *Strange Stories*. Robert Bloch is also the author of *Psycho* and numerous horror and suspense novels.

22.

5 January 1972

a: 'Green Fingers'

Writer: Rod Serling.   **Story:** R. C. Cook.
Director: John Badham.

Cast: Cameron Mitchell (Michael J. Saunders); Elsa Lanchester (Lydia Bowen); Michael Bell (Ernest); George Keymas (Crowley); Harry Hickox (Sheriff); Bill Quinn (Doctor); Larry

Watson, Jeff Burton (Deputies).

Story: An old woman won't sell her property to a developer, so he has her roughed up by a thug, who accidentally kills her. But she uses her 'green fingers' to return from the grave and drive the man insane.

b: 'The Funeral'

Writer: Richard Matheson.   **Story:** Richard Matheson.
Director: John Meredyth Lucas.

Cast: Werner Klemperer (Ludwig Asper); Joe Flynn (Morton Silkline); Charles Macaulay (The Count); Harvey Jason (Morrow); Jack Laird (Ygor); Laara Lacey (Jenny the Witch); Leonidas D. Ossetynkski, Diana Hale (Vampires); Jerry Summers (Bruce).

Story: A vampire arranges his own funeral, because he feels he never had a proper one. It is attended by other vampires, a werewolf, a witch, etc. Later, he recommends the funeral director to other monsters.

Note: Richard Matheson's story originally appeared in the April 1955 issue of *The Magazine of Fantasy and Science-Fiction*.

c: 'The Tune in Dan's Cafe'

Writer: Gerald Sanford   **Story:** Shamus Frazier.
and Garrie Bateson.   **Director:** David Rawlins.

Cast: Pernell Roberts (Joe Bellman); Susan Oliver (Kelly Bellman); James Davidson (Roy Gleason); Brooke Mills (Red); James Nusser (Dan).

Story: A couple discuss their marital problems in a café where the jukebox plays only one record: the favourite song of a gangster who was betrayed by his girlfriend and shot in the café by the police. The tale helps the couple to reconcile. The gangster's girlfriend returns, to be trapped by her lover's ghost.

23.

12 January 1972

a: 'Lindemann's Catch'

Writer: Rod Serling.   **Director:** Jeff Corey.

Cast: Stuart Whitman (Lindemann); Anabel Garth (Mermaid); Jack Aranson (Dr Nichols); Harry Townes (Suggs); John Alderson (Granger); Jim Boles (Bennett); Ed Bakey (Ollie); Matt Pelto (Phineas); Michael Stanwood (Charlie).

Story: A lonely fisherman falls in love with a mermaid. To turn her into a human, he gives her a magic potion, but instead, it gives her a woman's legs and the head of a fish.

b: 'A Feast of Blood'

Writer: Stanford Whitmore.   **Story:** Dulcie Gray.
Director: Jeannot Szwarc.

Cast: Sondra Locke (Sheila Gray); Norman Lloyd (Henry Mallory); Hermione Baddeley (Mrs Gray); Patrick O'Hara (Frankie); Barry Bernard (Gippo); Cara Burgess (Girl); Gerald S. Peters (Chauffeur).

Story: An ugly, boorish man gives a small fur brooch to the woman who turned down his marriage proposal. It transforms into a blood-sucking monster which kills her. He then gives another brooch to the next woman to whom he intends to propose.

Note: Dulcie Gray's story, originally entitled *The Fur Brooch*, appeared in 1966 in *The Seventh Pan Book of Horror Stories*.

c: 'The Late Mr Peddington'

Writer: Jack Laird.   **Story:** Frank Sisk.

Director: Jeff Corey.

Cast: Kim Hunter (Carla Peddington); Harry Morgan (Thaddeus Conway); Randy Quaid (John).

Story: A woman shops around for the cheapest funeral possible to see if she can afford to kill her stingy husband.

24.

19 January 1972

a: 'The Miracle at Camafeo'

Writer: Rod Serling.   **Story:** C. B. Gilford.
Director: Ralph Senensky.

Cast: Harry Guardino (Rogan); Julie Adams (Gay Melcor); Ray Danton (Joe Melcor); Richard Yñiguez (Priest); Rodolfo Hoyos (Bartender); Margarita Garcia (Woman); Thomas Trujillo (Blind Boy).

Story: A con artist defrauds an insurance company of half-a-million dollars by faking an injury. He plans to 'miraculously' recover by visiting a holy site in Mexico. But when the miracle happens, he 'inherits' a little boy's blindness.

b: 'The Ghost of Sorworth Place'

Writer: Alvin T. Sapinsley.   **Story:** Russell Kirk.
Director: Ralph Senensky.

Cast: Richard Kiley (Ralph Burke); Jill Ireland (Ann Loring); John D. Schofield (Alistair Loring); Mavis Neal (Mrs Ducker); Patrick O'Moore (MacLeod).

Story: In Scotland, an American traveller meets a beautiful, but loveless, woman who implores him to protect her from the ghost of her husband, whom she killed. He falls to his death during his encounter with the ghost, who is banished. He then returns as a ghost himself, only to discover that the woman tricked him, because she can only love someone who is not alive.

Note: Russell Kirk's story, originally entitled *Old Place of Sorworth*, appeared in the February/March 1952 issue of *London Mystery Magazine*.

25.
26 January 1972
a: 'The Waiting Room'

Writer: Rod Serling.   **Director:** Jeannot Szwarc.

Cast: Stephen Forrest (Sam Dichter); Gilbert Roland (Bartender); Buddy Ebsen (Doc Soames); Albert Salmi (Joe Bristol); Lex Barker (Charlie McKinley); Jim Davis (Abe Bennett); Larry Watson (Kid Max).

Story: After riding past a hanging figure, a western gunfighter enters a saloon where he meets a group of dead gunslingers who know everything about his life. The men leave at periodic intervals. In reality, he is dead (he was the hanging figure) and this is the waiting room of hell, where people who lived by the gun are condemned to relive their deaths for all eternity.

b: 'Last Rites for a Dead Druid'

Writer: Alvin T. Sapinsley.   **Director:** Jeannot Szwarc.

Cast: Bill Bixby (Bruce Farraday); Carol Lynley (Jenny Farraday); Donna Douglas (Mildred McVane); Ned Glass (Bernstein); Janya Brannt (Marta).

Story: A young woman buys a statue of an ancient, evil druid, which bears an uncanny resemblance to her husband. The druid's spirit eventually switches places with the husband, who is turned into a statue.

26.

9 February 1972.
a: 'Deliveries in the Rear'

Writer: Rod Serling.   **Director:** Jeff Corey.

Cast: Cornel Wilde (Dr John Fletcher); Rosemary Forsyth (Barbara Bennett); Walter Burke (Jameson); Kent Smith (Bennett); Peter Whitney, John Madison (Grave Robbers); Larry D. Mann (Detective Hannify); Peter Brocco (Dr Shockman); Marjorie E. Bennett (Mrs Woods); Ian Wolfe (Dillingham); Gerald McRaney (Tuttle).

Story: A turn-of-the-century surgeon uses murderous grave robbers to provide him with bodies for his lectures. When warned, he refuses to stop his practice, and eventually discovers, to his horror, that they have brought him the body of his fiancée.

b: 'Stop Killing Me'

Writer: Jack Laird.   **Story:** Hal Dresner.
Director: Jeannot Szwarc.

Cast: Geraldine Page (Frances Turchin); James Gregory (Sergeant Stanley Beverlow).

Story: A woman tells a policeman that her husband is planning to kill her because she refuses to divorce him. After her seemingly accidental death, the sergeant, who is married to the same type of woman, calls the husband to ask how he did it.

c: 'Dead Weight'

Writer: Jack Laird.   **Story:** Jeffry Scott.
Director: Timothy Galfas.

Cast: Bobby Darin (Landau); Jack Albertson (Bullivant); James Metropole (Delivery Boy).

Story: In this short filler, a killer attempting to flee to South America is turned into dog food.

27.

16 February 1972

a: 'I'll Never Leave You – Ever'

Writer: Jack Laird.   **Story:** Rene Morris.
Director: Daniel Haller.

Cast: Royal Dano (Owen); Lois Nettleton (Moira); John Saxon (Ianto); Peggy Webber (Crone).

Story: A woman who has taken a younger lover tries to kill her older, long-ailing husband by burning a magic doll in his likeness. But the doll does not burn completely through, and she is left with an even more crippled husband.

Note: Rene Morris's story originally appeared in 1966 in *The Seventh Pan Book of Horror Stories*.

b: 'There Aren't Any More MacBanes'

Writer: Alvin T. Sapinsley.   **Story:** Stephen Hall.
Director: John Newland.

Cast: Joel Grey (Andrew MacBane); Howard Duff (Arthur Porter); Darrell Larson (Elie Green); Barry Higgins (Mickey Standish); Mark Hamill (Francis, the Messenger Boy); Vincent Van Lynn (Manservant); Ellen Blake (Creature).

Story: A young man uses witchcraft to summon an evil creature to kill his rich uncle, who threatens to disinherit him. But the monster goes on to kill his friends, until he stops it by sacrificing himself.

28.

23 February 1972

a: 'You Can't Get Help Like That Anymore'

Writer: Rod Serling.   **Director:** Jeff Corey.

Cast: Broderick Crawford (Joseph Fulton); Cloris Leachman (Mrs Fulton); Henry Jones (Malcolm Hample); Lana Wood (Maid); Severn Darden (Dr Kessler); Christopher Law (Mr Foster); Pamela Shoop (Mrs Foster); A'leshia Lee (Receptionist); Roberta Carol Brahm (Damaged Maid).

Story: A sadistic couple like to torture their android maids, until the Agency gives them a maid programmed to defend herself. Eventually, the androids become self-aware and replace the humans.

b: 'The Sins of the Fathers'

Writer: Halsted Welles.   **Story:** Christianna Brand.
Director: Jeannot Szwarc.

Cast: Geraldine Page (Mrs Evans); Richard Thomas (Ian Evans); Barbara Steele (Widow Craigill); Michael Dunn (Servant); Cyril Delevanti (Old Man); Alan Napier, Terence Pushman, John Barclay (Mourners).

Story: In nineteeth-century Wales, a young, starving sin-eater is instructed by his mother to only pretend to eat the food from a depraved man's body. He brings the food home, but his mother forces him to eat it from his father's body.

Note: Christianna Brand's story originally appeared in 1964 in *The Fifth Pan Book of Horror Stories*.

29.

1 March 1972
a: 'The Caterpillar'

Writer: Rod Serling.   **Story:** Oscar Cook.
Director: Jeannot Szwarc.

Cast: Laurence Harvey (Steven Macy); Joanna Pettet (Rhona Warwick); Tom Helmore (John Warwick); Don Knight (Tommy Robinson); John Williams (Doctor).

Story: In Borneo, a man plots to murder the husband of a beautiful woman by using an 'earwig', an insect which burrows through the brain of its host. The plan backfires, and instead, he becomes the victim. The earwig somehow comes out without harming him, but then he learns that it was a female, which left her eggs behind.

Note: Oscar Cook's story was originally entitled *Boomerang*.

b: 'Little Girl Lost'

Writer: Stanford Whitmore.   **Story:** E. C. Tubb.
Director: Timothy Galfas.

Cast: William Windom (Professor Puttman); Ed Nelson (Tom Burke); Ivor Francis (Dr Cottrell); John Lasell (Colonel Hawes).

Story: To retain his sanity, a brilliant physicist pretends that his daughter, killed in an accident, is still alive. When he realises his delusion, in order to be with her, he creates a formula which destroys the world.

Note: E. C. Tubb's story first appeared in the October 1955 issue of *New Worlds*.

Third Season

(half-hour episodes)
Producer: Jack Laird.
Director of Photography: Lloyd Ahern,
Gerald Perry Finnerman, Emil Oster, Leonard J. South.
Music: Eddie Sauter.
Theme Music: Gil Mellé.
Make-up: Bud Westmore, John Chambers.
Paintings by: Tom Wright.
Sculptures by: Logan Elston, Phil Vanderlei.

30: 'The Return of the Sorcerer'
24 September 1972

Writer: Halsted Welles.　　　**Story:** Clark Ashton Smith.
Director: Jeannot Szwarc.

Cast: Vincent Price (Carnby); Bill Bixby (Noel Evans); Patricia Sterling (Fern).

Story: A sorcerer hires a young interpreter to decipher an ancient occult manuscript. He is seeking to protect himself from his brother, also a sorcerer, whom he dismembered but who has returned to life. Both sorcerers have been used by their young female assistant, who falls in love with the interpreter.

Note: Clark Ashton Smith's story originally appeared in the September 1931 issue of *Strange Tales*.

31: 'The Girl with the Hungry Eyes'
1 October 1972

Writer: Robert Malcolm Young.　　**Story:** Fritz Leiber.
Director: John Badham.

Cast: James Farentino (David Faulkner); Joanna Pettet (The Girl); John Astin (Munsch); Kip Noven (Harry); Bruce Powers (Man).

Story: A photographer discovers that his new, stunningly beautiful model is a vampiric creature who feeds on men's souls. He destroys her by burning all the negatives of her pictures.

Note: Fritz Leiber's story originally appeared in an anthology of the same name, edited by Donald A. Wollheim (Avon, 1949).

32: 'Fright Night'
15 October 1972

Writer: Robert Malcolm Young.   **Story:** Kurt Van Elting.
Director: Jeff Corey.

Cast: Stuart Whitman (Tom Ogilvy); Barbara Anderson (Leona Ogilvy); Ellen Corby (Miss Patience); Alan Napier (Zachariah Ogilvy); Larry Watson (Longhair); Michael Laird, Glenna Sargent (Goblins).

Story: A young couple inherits a country house from a dead warlock. It contains a trunk whose evil influence almost tears them apart. On Halloween, the warlock's corpse returns to claim the trunk. But then, they find yet another trunk. Unable to wait until next Halloween, they leave and put the house up for sale.

33: 'Rare Objects'
22 October 1972

Writer: Rod Serling.   **Director:** Jeannot Szwarc.

Cast: Raymond Massey (Dr Glendon); Mickey Rooney (August Kolodney); Fay Spain (Molly Mitchell); Davis Fresco (Blockman); Regis J. Cordic (Doctor); Victor Sen Young (Joseph the Butler); Ralph Adano (Tony).

Story: A mobster on the run, afraid that he will be killed, wants out of his criminal lifestyle. He eventually falls into the hands of a doctor who collects rare people. The doctor injects him with a drug that will keep him young, and locks him in a cell alongside Amelia Earhart, Adolph Hitler, etc.

34: 'Spectre in Tap-Shoes'
29 October 1972

Writer: Gene Kearney.   **Story:** Jack Laird.
Director: Jeannot Szwarc.

Cast: Sandra Dee (Millicent/Marion Hardy); Dane Clark (Mr Jason); Christopher Connelly (Sam Davis); Russell Thorson (Dr Coolidge); Michael Laird (Michael); Michael Richardson (Andy the Mailman); Stuart Nisbet (Policeman).

Story: A girl returns to her New England home only to discover that her twin sister has hanged herself. In reality, she has been murdered by her lover, whom she was blackmailing. The man now tries to drive the surviving twin insane. He is about to kill her when the spirit of the dead sister takes over and shoots him.

35: 'The Ring with the Red Velvet Ropes'
5 November 1972

Writer: Robert Malcolm Young.   **Story:** Edward D. Hoch.
Director: Jeannot Szwarc.

Cast: Chuck Connors (Roderick Blanco); Gary Lockwood (James Figg); Joan Van Ark (Sandra Blanco); Ralph Manza (Max); Charles Davis (Hayes); Ji-Tu Cumbuka (Big Dan Anger); James Bacon (Reporter); Frankie Van (Referee).

Story: The newly-crowned heavyweight boxing champion is magically abducted and forced to fight the champion, who has held the title since 1861. When he is defeated, the former champion ages and dies. The new champion is now forced to defend his title for all eternity.

36: 'You Can Come Up Now, Mrs Millikan'
12 November 1972

Writer: Rod Serling.   **Story:** J. Wesley Rosenquist.
Director: John Badham.

Cast: Harriet Nelson (Helena Millikan); Ozzie Nelson (Henry Millikan); Roger Davis (George Beaumont); Michael Lerner (Dr Burgess); Don Keefer (Dr Coolidge); Margaret Muse (Dr Steinhem); Lew Brown (Officer Stacy); Stuart Nisbet (Officer Kimbrough).

Story: An eccentric inventor poisons his absent-minded wife with the intention of bringing her back from the dead with his latest serum. She returns, late as usual; in fact too late to prevent her husband from committing suicide after he thinks he has really killed her.

Note: J. Wesley Rosenquist's story, originally entitled *Return to Death*, appeared in the January 1936 issue of *Weird Tales*.

37: 'The Other Way Out'
19 November 1972

Writer: Gene Kearney.   **Story:** Kurt Van Elting.
Director: Gene Kearney.

Cast: Ross Martin (Bradley Meredith); Burl Ives (Old Man Doubleday); Peggy Feury (Estelle Meredith); Jack Collins (Potter); Elizabeth Thompson (Miss Flannagan); Paul Micale (Paul, the Waiter); Adam Weed (Sonny Doubleday).

Story: The murderer of a dancing girl is lured by the grandfather of his victim into a deadly trap from which there can be no escape, other than suicide.

38: 'Finnegan's Flight'
3 December 1972

Writer: Rod Serling.   **Director:** Gene Kearney.

Cast: Burgess Meredith (Charlie Finnegan); Barry Sullivan (Dr Simsich); Cameron Mitchell (Pete Tuttle); Kenneth Tobey (Warden); Dort Clark, Roger Mobley, Raymond Mayo (Prisoners); John Gilgreen, Michael Masters (Guards).

Story: A convict experiments with hypnosis on a highly suggestible fellow prisoner who cannot stand being locked up. He convinces him that he is flying a jet during a hypnotic trance, but the prisoner 'crashes', causing a real explosion.

39: 'She'll Be Company for You'
24 December 1972

Writer: David Rayfiel.   **Story:** Andrea Newman.
Director: Gerald Perry Finnerman.

Cast: Leonard Nimoy (Henry Auden); Lorraine Gray (Barbara Morgan); Kathryn Hays (June); Bern Hoffman (Reverend).

Story: A cold-hearted widower, too happy to be rid of his crippled wife, is given a cat by one of his late wife's friends. The cat turns into a tiger which eventually kills him.

40: 'Something in the Woodwork'
14 January 1973

Writer: Rod Serling.   **Story:** R. Chetwynd-Hayes.
Director: Edward M. Abroms.

Cast: Geraldine Page (Molly Wheatland); Leif Erickson (Charlie Wheatland); John McMurtry (Jamie Dillman); Barbara Rhodes (Julie); Paul Henkins (Joe Wilson).

Story: A vengeful divorcée plots to use the ghost of a murderer which haunts her attic to kill her weak-hearted ex-husband. Instead, the ghost takes over the husband's body and leaves his spirit behind in the attic.

Note: R. Chetwynd-Hayes's story was originally entitled *Housebound*.

41: 'Death on a Barge'
4 March 1973

Writer: Halsted Welles.   **Story:** Everil Worrell.
Director: Leonard Nimoy.

Cast: Lesley Ann Warren (Hyacinth); Robert Pratt (Ron); Brooke Bundy (Phyllis); Lou Antonio (Jake); Jim Boles (Father); Artie Spain (Coastguard); Dorothy Konrad, De De Young (Customers).

Story: A young man falls in love with a beautiful vampire girl. After she murders a friend of his, he tries to kill her, but fails. Her father finally drives a stake through her heart.

Note: Everil Worrell's story, originally entitled *The Canal*, appeared in the December 1927 issue of *Weird Tales*. This episode was actor Leonard Nimoy's first directing credit. Nimoy went on to direct several *Star Trek* films.

42: 'Whisper'
13 May 1973

Writer: David Rayfiel.   **Story:** Martin Waddell.
Director: Jeannot Szwarc.

Cast: Sally Field (Irene); Dean Stockwell (Charlie); Kent Smith (Dr Kennaway).

Story: An eccentric girl, who has fooled her husband into believing that she has the power to channel the spirits of the dead, ends up doing so, but can no longer return to her own body.

43: 'The Doll of Death'
20 May 1973

Writer: Jack Guss.   **Story:** Vivian Meik.
Director: John Badham.

Cast: Susan Strasberg (Sheila Trent); Alejandro Rey (Raphael); Barry Atwater (Alex Brandon); Murray Matheson (Dr Strang); Henry Brandon (Vereker); Jean Durand (Andrew).

Story: A man uses a voodoo doll to get revenge on his rival, who stole his fiancée at the altar. But the girl turns the tables on him, hiding one of the jilted man's rings on the doll. When he destroys the doll, he kills himself.

Note: Vivian Meik's story originally appeared in 1933 in her collection *Devil's Drums*.

44.
27 May 1973
a: 'Hatred Unto Death'

Writer: Halsted Welles.   **Story:** Milton Geiger.
Director: Gerald Perry Finnerman.

Cast: Stephen Forrest (Grant Wilson); Dina Merrill (Ruth

Left: **Rod Serling introduces *The Twilight Zone*.**

Below: **Pat Carter (Patricia Breslin) tries to save her husband, Don (William Shatner), from an evil fortune-telling machine in 'Nick of Time' (TZ43).**

ASK ME A YES OR NO QUESTION

Right: **Brother Jerome (John Carradine) tries to warn David Ellington (H. M. Wynant) away from 'The Howling Man'** (TZ41).

Below: **A stranded astronaut (Roddy McDowall, with Susan Oliver) discovers that 'People Are Alike All Over'** (TZ25).

Left: **Agnes Moorehead faces 'The Invaders' (TZ51).**

Below: **William Tuttle's superb make-up for 'Eye of the Beholder' (TZ42).**

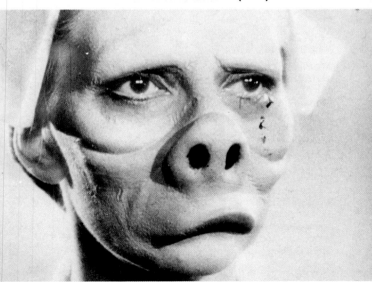

Above: **Mr Dingle (Burgess Meredith) and two Venusians (Donald Losaby, Greg Irvin) from 'Mr Dingle the Strong'** (TZ55).

Right: **Jeannot Szwarc directed many of the most famous episodes of** *Night Gallery*.

Above: **Rod Serling** in the *Night Gallery*.

Left: **Adam West, 'With Apologies to Mr Hyde' (NG10b).**

Above: **A ghoulish encounter from the** *Night Gallery* **(NG2a).**

Right: **Vincent Price prepares himself for 'The Return of the Sorcerer' (NG30).**

Above: Director Joe Dante lines up a low-angle shot for dramatic effect **n** his segment of *Twilight Zone - The Movie*. The motion picture was **roduced** by Steven Spielberg and John Landis based on Rod **erling's** legendary television series. Frank Marshall served as **xecutive** producer of the Warner Bros release.

elow: One of SPFX wizard Rob Bottin's horrific creations for director **oe** Dante's segment of *Twilight Zone - The Movie*.

Above: **Father Costigan (Fritz Weaver) and Dr Chandler (Donald Moffat) seek the secret of 'The Star'.**

Right: **Charity Payne (Kerry Noonan) defies the evil Squire Hacker (Gerald Hiken) in 'A Message from Charity'.**

Wilson); Fernando Lamas (Dr Ramirez); George Barrows (N'Gi); Caro Kenyatta, Ed Rue, David Tyrone (Watusi Warriors).

Story: In Africa, a husband-and-wife writing team come across a strange gorilla which displays a sudden, and inexplicable, hatred for the husband. Back in America, they theorise that it is because the husband and the gorilla were deadly foes in a previous life. Eventually, the gorilla escapes and kills the husband.

b: 'How to Cure the Common Vampire'

Writer: Jack Laird.   **Director:** Jack Laird.

Cast: Richard Deacon (Man with Mallet); Johnny Brown (Man with Stake).

Story: A short filler about killing vampires.

Syndication

Four short fillers, left over from the series' regular network run but subsequently added to the syndication package.

45: 'Die Now, Pay Later'

Writer: Jack Laird.   **Story:** Mary Linn Roby.
Director: Timothy Galfas.

Cast: Slim Pickens (Sheriff Ned); Will Greer (Walt Peckinpah).

Story: A mortician's 'clearance sale' causes a community's death rate to increase because the man is secretly a warlock. After pleading with the mortician to stop the sale, the local sheriff eventually decides to take advantage of it to get rid of his nagging wife.

46: 'Room for One Less'

Writer: Jack Laird.   **Director:** Jack Laird.

Cast: Lee Jay Lambert; James Metropole.

Story: A demon gets rid of an extra passenger in a crowded elevator.

47: 'Satisfaction Guaranteed'

Writer: Jack Laird.   **Director:** Jeannot Szwarc.

Cast: Victor Buono (Vampire); Cathleen Cordell (Mrs Mount).

Story: A vampire interviews job applicants – for lunch.

48: 'Smile, Please'

Writer: Jack Laird.   **Director:** Jack Laird.

Cast: Cesare Danova (Vampire); Lindsay Wagner (Woman).

Story: A vampire lures a woman photographer into his crypt.

The Sixth Sense

Regular Cast: Gary Collins (Dr Michael Rhodes); Catherine Ferrar (Nancy Murphy).

Episodes:
1. *I Do Not Belong to the Human World*
2. *The Heart that Wouldn't Stay Buried*
3. *Lady, Lady, Take My Life*
4. *The House that Cried Murder*
5. *The Man Who Died at Three and Nine*
6. *Death at the Top of the Stairs*
7. *With This Ring, I Thee Kill*

8.   *Witch, Witch, Burning Bright*
9.   *Eye of the Hunted*
10. *Echo of a Distant Scream*
11. *Whisper of Evil*
12. *Shadow in the Well*
13. *Face of Ice*
14. *Two Hour Streets*
15. *Coffin, Coffin, in the Sky*
16. *Dear Joan, We Are Going to Scare You to Death*
17. *Witness Within*
18. *With Affection, Jack the Ripper*
19. *Once Upon a Chilling*
20. *Through a Flame, Darkly*
21. *I Did Not Mean to Slay Thee*
22. *And Scream by the Light of the Moon, the Moon*
23. *If I Should Die Before I Wake*
24. *Five Women Weeping*
25. *Gallows in the Wind*
26. *The Eyes That Would Not Die*

The Twilight Zone: The Movie

The Twilight Zone gave birth to many imitators, some of them very good in their own style: *The Outer Limits*, *Thriller*, *One Step Beyond*, etc., but it was never successfully remade, not even by Rod Serling, hard as he tried, as the semi-failure of *Night Gallery* indicates. Yet, the show, if anything, gained in popularity over the years, and achieved widespread cult status. Rod Serling himself still appears daily on millions of television sets throughout the United States. In his own inimitable tones, he continues to take his fans on a tour through the realm of the imagination.

It was therefore unavoidable that Warner Bros, who had obtained the film rights to *The Twilight Zone* from Carol Serling, would attempt to produce a remake. However, it took Steven Spielberg's indomitable energy to get such a project off the ground.

The director of *E. T.* and *Close Encounters of the Third Kind*, who had been one of *Night Gallery*'s pilot directors, gathered around him other such gifted genre directors as John Landis, Joe Dante and Australian-born George Miller. Veteran *Twilight Zone* writer Richard Matheson was signed up to do the screenplay, and Jerry Goldsmith, who had scored many original *Twilight Zone* episodes, to do the music. The four segments ultimately chosen were an original story by John Landis, and three remakes: *It's A Good Life* (episode 73); *Kick the Can* (episode 86) and *Nightmare at 20,000 Feet* (episode 123).

The Twilight Zone: The Movie, however, was almost cancelled when, on 23 July 1982, at 2.30 a.m., actor Vic Morrow and two Vietnamese children, Renée Shinn Chen, aged six, and

Myca Dinh Le, aged seven, died in a helicopter crash while filming the John Landis segment. The fatal accident occurred on the last day of shooting. Morrow was to run away from a burning Vietnamese village, carrying the two small children with him. At the same time, special effects explosions were timed to go off. The scene was being shot from a camera helicopter which went out of control 20 feet from the ground and crashed, killing the three actors and injuring six crew members, including helicopter pilot Dorcey Wingo, production manager Dan Allingham and two cameramen.

In an interview granted to the *Los Angeles Times*, Steven Spielberg made his feelings known. 'The accident cast a pall on all 150 people who worked on the production. We are still just sick to the centre of our souls. I don't know anybody who hasn't been affected. A movie is a fantasy – it's light and shadow flickering on a screen. No movie is worth dying for.'

This tragic accident would soon involve Warner Bros, Spielberg, executive producer Frank Marshall, Landis, associate producer George Folsey, Jr, the National Transportation Safety Board (NTSB), the Federal Aviation Administration (FAA), the California branch of the Occupational Safety and Health Administration (OSHA), the Los Angeles County Fire Department, the Screen Actors' Guild Safety Committee and a veritable army of lawyers.

A subsequent investigation by the NTSB showed that the tail section of the helicopter had been engulfed in fireballs caused by the explosions, and that the back rotor had been hit by a piece of metal identified as the lid of an explosive can. Furthermore, an OSHA investigation revealed that the two children had been hired by the producers in violation of California's labour laws, unbeknownst to the Warner Bros executives. As a result, fines totalling over $62,000 were levied by OSHA against Warner Bros, Landis, Folsey and Allingham, but were surprisingly withdrawn in 1987.

In the month following the accident, Vic Morrow's estate,

as well as the children's families, also filed various lawsuits against Warner Bros, Spielberg, Landis et al. These suits were eventually settled out of court in 1987 for several millions of dollars.

Despite this host of troubles piled upon the film and its principals, *The Twilight Zone: The Movie* continued, although the Landis segment was heavily re-edited and the release date was postponed from Christmas 1982 to the summer of 1983. The film did poorly at the box office, with George Miller's segment generally considered the most successful. Critic Leonard Maltin summed it up best when he stated that none of the four segments 'provided the all-important moment of revelation that made the [original television] show so memorable, and more tellingly, none improved on the originals.'

In the meantime, a grand jury convened in May 1983 indicted Landis, Folsey, Allingham, Wingo and special effects coordinator Paul Stewart for manslaughter. The case came to trial in September 1986. In May1987, after nine days' deliberation, a jury found all the defendants not guilty. Many theorised that the prosecution had overreached itself by deciding to prosecute for the much harder-to-prove manslaughter charges instead of sticking with the violation of child labour laws and reckless endangerment.

The Twilight Zone: The Movie

Warner Bros, 1983.

Producers: Steven Spielberg, John Landis.

Executive Producer: Frank Marshall.

Music: Jerry Goldsmith.

Narrator: Burgess Meredith.

Project Consultant: Carol Serling.

Prologue/Epilogue

Writer: John Landis.

Director: John Landis.

Assistant Producer: George Folsey, Jr.

Director of Photograhy: Stevan Larner.

Cast: Dan Aykroyd (Passenger); Albert Brooks (Driver; prologue only).

Story: A driver picks up a hitch-hiker who turns out to be a monster. The same character shows up again in the ambulance taking Valentine to the hospital at the end of the film.

1: 'Time Out'

Writer: John Landis.　　　　**Director:** John Landis.
Assistant Producer:　　　　**Director of Photography:**
George Folsey, Jr.　　　　　　Stevan Larner.

Cast: Vic Morrow (Bill); Doug McGrath (Larry); Charles Hallahan (Ray); Remus Peets, Kai Wulff (Germans); Sue Dugan, Debby Porter (Waitresses); Steven Williams (Bar Patron); Annette Claudier (French Mother); Joseph Hieu, Albert Leong (Vietnamese); Stephen Bishop, Thomas Byrd, Vincent J. Isaac, William B. Taylor, Domingo Ambriz (GIs); Eddie Donno, Michael Migram, John Larroquette (KKK); Norbert Weisser (Soldier).

Story: A bigot finds himself transported through time to various periods of oppression and ends up in a train to Auschwitz.

2: 'Kick the Can'

Writers: George Clayton　　**Story:** George Clayton
Johnson, Richard Matheson,　Johnson.
John Rogan.　　　　　　　　**Director:** Steven Spielberg.
Assistant Producer:　　　　**Director of Photography:**
Kathleen Kennedy.　　　　　　Allen Daviau.

Cast: Scatman Crothers (Bloom); Bill Quinn (Mr Conroy); Martin Garner (Mr Weinstein); Selma Diamond (Mrs Weinstein); Helen Shaw (Mrs Dempsey); Murray Matheson (Mr Agee); Peter Brocco (Mr Mute); Priscilla Pointer (Miss Cox); Scott Nemes (Young Mr Weinstein); Tanya Fenmore (Young Mrs Weinstein);

Evan Richards (Young Mr Agee); Laura Mooney (Young Mrs
Dempsey); Christopher Eisenmann (Young Mr Mute); Richard
Swingler (Grey Panther); Alan Haufrect (Conroy's Son); Cheryl
Socher (Conroy's Daughter-in-Law); Elsa Raven (Nurse).

Story: The mysterious Mr Bloom tells the residents of Sunnyvale
Rest Home how to recapture their youth. However, in this version, they eventually choose to return to their real ages.

Note: 'John Rogan' is a pseudonym of Melissa Mathison.

3: 'It's A Good Life'

Writer: Richard Matheson.　　**Story:** Jerome Bixby.
Director: Joe Dante.　　**Assistant Producer:** Michael
Director of Photography:　　Finnell.
John Hora.　　**SPFX:** Rob Bottin.

Cast: Kathleen Quinlan (Helen Foley); Jeremy Licht (Anthony
Fremont); Kevin McCarthy (Walt); Patricia Barry (Mother);
William Schallert (Father); Nancy Cartwright (Ethel); Dick Miller
(Walter Paisley); Cherie Currie (Sara); Bill Mumy (Tim); Jeffrey
Bannister (Charlie).

Story: In this version, schoolteacher Helen Foley comes to a
town terrorised by the all-powerful Anthony Fremont, but eventually teaches him a sense of responsibility.

Note: The name of Helen Foley is taken from *Nightmare as a
Child* (*Twilight Zone* episode 29). This segment is remarkable
for the monstrous cartoon characters brought to life by Anthony
Fremont, designed and built by Rob Bottin.

4: 'Nightmare at 20,000 Feet'

Writer: Richard Matheson.　　**Story:** Richard Matheson.

Director: George Miller.
Director of Photography: Allen Daviau.

Assistant Producer: Jon Davison.
SPFX: Craig Reardon, Michael McCracken.

Cast: John Lithgow (Valentine); Abbe Lane, Donna Dixon (Stewardesses); John Dennis Johnston (Co-Pilot); Larry Cedar (Creature); Charles Knapp (Sky Marshal); Christina Nigra (Little Girl); Lonna Schwab (Mother); Margaret Wheeler (Old Woman); Eduard Franz (Old Man); Margaret Fitzgerald (Young Girl); Jeffrey Weissman (Young Man); Jeffrey Lambert, Frank Toth (Mechanics).

Story: See *Twilight Zone* episode 123 (no significant variations).

The New Twilight Zone

The Twilight Zone: The Movie was not a huge, commercial success, but it was not an abysmal failure either. The concept of reviving old television series had caught the fancy of the television network executives, who believed that, by capitalising on the viewers' familiarity with a well-known and beloved name, they could gain a foothold on their competition. After the 'returns' of *Gilligan's Island*, *Leave it to Beaver* and *The Man from U.N.C.L.E.*, it was only a matter of time before CBS thought of resurrecting Rod Serling's show.

The New Twilight Zone – the official name of the show was *The Twilight Zone*, but we shall call it 'New' to distinguish it from the original – began on CBS in the fall season of 1985. Since network executives travel in packs, that same year also saw the return of the equally famous *Alfred Hitchcock Presents*, as well as the launching of Steven Spielberg's own *Amazing Stories*.

CBS entrusted *The New Twilight Zone* to Philip DeGuere, writer/producer of the hit detective series *Simon and Simon*, *Whiz Kids*, a television adaptation of the Marvel Comics character *Doctor Strange* and an aborted mini-series adaptation of Arthur C. Clarke's SF classic, *Childhood's End*. *The New Twilight Zone* was a one-hour-long show, a format which had previously defeated Serling, and would prove an equal handicap to his would-be successor. It featured two or three stories, often written or adapted by famous science fiction writers such as Harlan Ellison, David Gerrold, Arthur C. Clarke, Ray Bradbury, Stephen King, etc. Like the original *Twilight Zone*, the new show was able to attract a number of first-class directors such as William Friedkin, John Milius, Wes Craven, etc. The show also enlisted the help of noted SF writer Harlan Ellison, billed as 'Creative Consultant'. However, Ellison resigned his position over a dispute with the network's standards and practices department during the first year.

Early on, the decision was made not to replace Serling (whose face appears briefly in the opening credits) as walk-on host, but to substitute instead an off-screen narrator's voice. Charles Aidman, who had appeared in two of the original *Twilight Zones* (episodes 11 and 91) was hired for the job. The new show also featured an updated version of the famous Marius Constant theme music by The Grateful Dead.

The first season of *The New Twilight Zone* delivered a great number of excellent episodes, including some clever remakes of stories from the original *Twilight Zone*. Even though its style was markedly different from the original – as it should have been – its 'batting average' was arguably as good as Serling's, who had been quoted as saying that only one-third of his episodes met his exacting standards of quality. Yet, in spite of everything, *The New Twilight Zone* did not deliver the high ratings the network expected.

Some blamed this on the programme being scheduled in the notoriously difficult Friday night slot, facing tough competition from the other channels. Others felt that the series lacked Serling's voice and unique creative vision, which was, after all, what the original *Twilight Zone* was all about.

The New Twilight Zone was nevertheless renewed for a second season, but primarily because of its attractive 'demographics', meaning that its audience was made up of yuppies with money to spend. Even defenders of the show will accept that the second season did not contain as many memorable episodes as the first. Worse yet, CBS yanked the programme out of its unattractive but regular Friday evening slot to juggle it continuously from place to place, before finally putting it into an hiatus, thereby effectively ensuring its demise. *The New Twilight Zone* then briefly returned as a pathetic half-hour version programmed in what could only be termed a kamikaze move against the mighty *Cosby Show*.

'The show had a very loyal cult following,' Bud Grant, then CBS Entertainment President, said to writer Lee Goldberg, 'but it wasn't enough to sustain a network TV time period.'

That would have been the end of *The New Twilight Zone*, except for the existence of the lucrative syndication market where television series – even mediocre ones – can run for ever and generate an endless stream of cash for their producers. CBS had invested a lot of money in *The New Twilight Zone*, but did not have enough episodes to repackage it as a syndicated series. It had only the equivalent of 60 half-hours, and needed 30 more to meet syndication's requirements. The conclusion was, therefore, obvious: more episodes had to be produced, and for as little money as possible.

'We were looking at the prospect of not getting a return out of our investment,' Donald D. Wear, Senior Vice President and General Manager of CBS Broadcast International, explained candidly to Goldberg. 'The new reality of the business is, if you make a substantial investment, you have to make every effort to make it earn money for you. That means taking an asset and making sure you don't prematurely abandon it before you make it work in every medium.'

A third season of *The New Twilight Zone* was therefore put into production, done on limited budgets in Canada with local actors and directors. Some of the stories seemed derivative and predictable, and the narration by Robin Ward lacked the punch of his predecessors. When there were enough episodes to syndicate, the series was simply shut down.

First Season (CBS)

Executive Producer: Phil DeGuere.
Supervising Producer: James Crocker.
Producer: Harvey Frand.
Executive Story Consultant: Alan Brennert.
Story Editor: Rockne S. O'Bannon.
Creative Consultants: Harlan Ellison (episodes 1–18);
James Crocker (episodes 19–24).
Director of Photography: Bradford May (except where
otherwise indicated); Frank P. Beascoechea
(episodes 12b, 13b, 15, 16a, b, 17, 18b, c, 19); Chuck Arnold
(episodes 20, 21, 22b, 23a); Robert Seaman
(episodes 22a, c, 23b, 24).
Narrator: Charles Aidman.
Music: The Grateful Dead, Merl Saunders (except where
otherwise indicated).

1.

27 September 1985

a: 'Shatterday'

Writer: Alan Brennert.
Director: Wes Craven.

Story: Harlan Ellison.
Music: Bob Weir, Mickey
Hart.

Cast: Bruce Willis (Peter Jay Novins); Dan Gilvezan (Bartender); Murukh (Woman); Johny Carlyle (Clerk); Seth Isler (Alter Ego); Anthony Grumbach (Bellboy).

Story: The better self of an egotistical, unprincipled PR executive gains independent existence and eventually ends up replacing his old self.

Note: Harlan Ellison's story first appeared in *Science-Fiction Monthly* in 1975 and was reprinted in the collection of the same title in 1980.

b: 'A Little Peace and Quiet'

Writer: James Crocker.   **Director:** Wes Craven.

Cast: Melinda Dillon (Penny); Greg Mullavey (Russell); Virginia Kechne (Susan); Brittany Wilson (Janet); Joshua Harris (Russell Jr); Judith Barsi (Bertie); Claire Nono (Newscaster); Elma Veronda Jackson, Pamela Gordon, Laura Waterbury (Shoppers); Todd Allen (Man); Isabelle Walker (Woman).

Story: A harried housewife finds a medallion which gives her the power to freeze time and get some much needed peace and quiet. She eventually ends up using it to stop nuclear missiles that are approaching the United States. But now she can never unfreeze time again.

2.

4 October 1985

a: 'Wordplay'

Writer: Rockne S. O'Bannon. **Director:** Wes Craven.

Cast: Robert Klein (Bill Lowry); Annie Potts (Kathy); Adam Raber (Donnie); Robert J. Downey (Miller); Brian Bradley (Hotshot); Bernard Behrens (Salesman); Anne Betancourt, Alexandra Morgan, Lee Arnone (Nurses); Mimi Neyer Craven (Receptionist); Russ Marin (Doctor); Brynja Willis (Secretary); Raye Birk (Bearded Man); Joseph Whipp (Doug); Dwier Brown (Robbie); Willard Peugh (Man); Helene Udy (Woman)

Story: A salesman wakes up one morning to discover that words have changed meanings ('dinosaur' now means 'lunch'). He eventually adapts and begins learning this new language.

b: 'Dreams For Sale'

Writer: Joe Gannon.   **Director:** Tommy Lee Wallace.

Cast: Meg Foster (Jenny); David Hayward (Mark); Vincent Guastaferro, Lee Anthony (Technicians); Kristi Purdy, Deanna Purdy (Twins).

Story: A woman at a picnic discovers that, in reality, she is a factory worker plugged into a 'Dreamatron' in a grim future. A malfunction kills her, but she remains alive in her dream.

c: 'Chameleon'

Writer: James Crocker.   **Director:** Wes Craven.

Cast: Terrance O'Quinn (Curt Lockridge); Ben Piazza (Vaughn Heilman); John Ashton (Bradley Simmons); Steve Howell Bassett (Gerald Tyson); Iona Morris (Annie); Alma Martinez (Teresa Rojas); Chad Hayes (Peter Iverson); Lin Shaye (Woman).

Story: An alien with shape-changing powers comes to Earth out of curiosity. Two scientists decide to leave with him while a third one chooses to stay.

3.

11 October 1985

a: 'Healer'

Writer: Michael Bryant.   **Director:** Sigmund Neufeld.
Music: Barry De Vorzon.

Cast: Eric Bogosian (Jackie Thompson); Vincent Gardenia (Harry Faulk); Robert Constanzo (Joey Rubello); Joaquin

Martinez (Duende); Adam Ferris (Deaf Boy); Joy Pankin (Mother); Ed Levey (Neighbour); Vivian Bonnell (Black Woman); Anthony Johnson (Guard); Lauren Levian (Amanda's Mom).

Story: A burglar finds an Indian gem with healing powers. His greedy partner turns him into a successful televangelist, but they eventually find that the stone will only work when used unselfishly. Having learned compassion, the burglar returns the stone to the Indians.

Note: 'Michael Bryant' is a pseudonym for Alan Brennert. This episode was later rewritten as a short story by Alan Brennert and appeared in *The Magazine of Fantasy and Science-Fiction* in 1988.

b: 'Children's Zoo'

Writers: Chris Hubbell and Gerrit Graham.

Director: Robert Downey.
Music: Robert Drasnin.

Cast: Lorna Luft (Sheila Cunningham); Steven Keats (Marty Cunningham); Jaclyn Bernstein (Debbie); Sydney Walsh (Melody); Wes Craven, Don Paul, Jack Taloe, Al Alu (Caged Men); Kerry Slattery, Sandy Brown Wyeth, Pamela Brown, Virginia Morris (Caged Women).

Story: Two awful parents are tricked by their daughter into taking her to a children's zoo, where she exchanges them for a set of better parents.

c: 'Kentucky Rye'

Writers: Richard Krzemien and Chip Duncan.

Director: John Hancock.

Cast: Jeffrey DeMunn (Bob Spindler); Michael Greene (Irving

Schlesser); Arliss Howard (Stranger); Clarence Felder (Randy); Philip Bruns (Old Man); Scott Jaeck (Pete); John DeMita (George); Brad Burlingame (Larry); Rosemarie Thomas (Nancy); Gloria Rusch (Laura); Lisa Long (Debbie); John Davey, Tim Russ (Officers).

Story: After an accident, a drunk driver staggers into the Kentucky Rye, a rowdy roadside tavern. After he decides to buy it, he discovers that he is really dead, killed in the accident and that he has bought his own, private hell.

4.
18 October 1985
a: 'Little Boy Lost'

Writer: Lynn Barker.   **Director:** Tommy Lee Wallace.
Music: Robert Drasnin.

Cast: Season Hubley (Carol Shelton); Nicholas Surovy (Greg); Scott Grimes (Kenny); Nancy Kyes (Housewife).

Story: A female photographer meets her own son from a possible future, but in spite of this, chooses a first-rate assignment over marriage to her boyfriend. As a result of her choice, the boy vanishes.

b: 'Wish Bank'

Writer: Michael Cassutt.   **Director:** Rick Friedberg.

Cast: Dee Wallace Stone (Janice Hammill); Julie Carmen (Mary Ellen Bradshaw); Peter Land (Brent); Harvey Vernon (Willoughby); Julie Payne (Clerk).

Story: After finding a magic lamp, a housewife trying to get her three wishes from a genie is confronted with mind-boggling bureaucracy, forcing her to wish that she had never found the lamp in the first place. Her wish is granted.

c: 'Nightcrawlers'

Writer: Philip DeGuere.   **Story:** Robert McCammon.
Director: William Friedkin.

Cast: Scott Paulin (Price); James Whitmore, Jr (Dennis Wells); Robert Swan (Bob); Exene Cervenka (Waitress); Sandy Martin (Lindy); Bobby Bass (Ray); Matt Levin (Ricky).

Story: A Vietnam veteran who fled and abandoned his unit is endowed with the power of mind over matter. While he sleeps, ghostlike soldiers materialise, destroy the diner where he is staying and eventually kill him, before vanishing again. We learn that there are four other vets with similar powers.

Note: Robert McCammon's story first appeared in the anthology *Masques* edited by J. N. Williamson in 1984.

5.

25 October 1985

a: 'If She Dies'

Writer: David Bennett Carren. **Director:** John Hancock.
Music: Jerrold Immel.

Cast: Tony LoBianco (Paul Marano); Jenny Lewis (Sarah); Nan Martin (Sister Agnes); Andrea Barber (Cathy Marano); John Gowans (Dr Brice); Donna-Jean Lansing (Nun); Adele Miller (Nurse).

Story: A widower's daughter goes into a deep coma following a car accident. However, the ghost of another little girl eventually restores her to life.

b: 'Ye Gods'

Writer: Anne Collins.   **Director:** Peter Medak.

Cast: David Dukes (Todd Ettinger); Robert Morse (Cupid); Carolyn Seymour (Magaera); John Myhers (Bacchus); Andrew Masset (Peter); Patti Karr (April); Ingrid Boulting (Woman).

Story: A yuppie must first straighten out the relationship between Cupid and Magaera before finding love himself.

6.

1 November 1985

a: 'Examination Day'

Writer: Philip DeGuere.   **Story:** Henry Slesar.
Director: Paul Lynch.

Cast: Christopher Allport (Richard Jordan); David Mendenhall (Dickie Jordan); Elizabeth Normant (Ruth Jordan); Ed Krieger, Myrna White, Jeffrey Alan Chandler (Clerks).

Story: In a dystopian future, a twelve-year old child is put to death because his IQ exceeds Government standards.

Note: Henry Slesar's story first appeared in *Playboy* in 1957.

b: 'A Message from Charity'

Writer: Alan Brennert.   **Story:** William M. Lee.
Director: Paul Lynch.   **Music:** Basil Poledouris.

Cast: Kerry Noonan (Charity Payne); Duncan McNeil (Peter Wood); Gerald Hiken (Squire Jonas Hacker); James Cromwell (Obediah Payne); Vanessa Brown (Aunt Beulah); Michael Fox (Tom Carter); Jennifer Parsons (Ursula Miller); Jack Wells (Dr Maxwell); Philip Proctor (Mr Wood); Barbara Lindsay (Mrs Wood).

Story: Charity, an eighteenth-century girl, and Peter, a twentieth-century boy, become mentally linked after experiencing the same illness. Betrayed by a local girl, Charity is accused of being a witch by the corrupt Squire. Peter uses information available in the future about the Squire to help Charity secure her release. The two friends agree to sever their link, but much later, Peter finds a message from Charity carved into a rock.

Note: William M. Lee's story first appeared in *The Magazine of Fantasy and Science Fiction* in 1967.

7.

8 November 1985

a: 'Teacher's Aide'

Writer: Steven Barnes.   **Director:** B. W. L. Norton.
Music: Craig Safan.

Cast: Adrienne Barbeau (Miss Peters); Adam Postil (Wizard); Miguel Nunez (Fury); Josh Richman (Trojan); Fred Morsell (Hugh Costin); Brian Robbins (Twelfth Grader); Sarah Partridge (Student Teacher); Richard Brainard (Younger Brother); Suzanne Sasson (Jennifer); Al Christy (Guard); Noelle Harling (Amanda).
Story: An English teacher becomes possessed by an evil gargoyle and starts behaving extremely aggressively with her rebellious students. Seeing what she has become, she backs off. A thunderbolt smashes the gargoyle.

b: 'Paladin of the Lost Hour'

Writer: Harlan Ellison.   **Story:** Harlan Ellison.
Director: Alan Smithee.   **Music:** Robert Drasnin.

Cast: Danny Kaye (Gaspar); Glynn Turman (Billy Kineta); John Bryant, Corky Ford (Punks); Mike Reynolds (Driver).

Story: Gaspar, an old man, is the custodian of a magic watch seemingly stuck at eleven o'clock. If he dies without passing it on, the last hour will start to tick and mankind will be doomed. Gaspar eventually bequeaths it to Billy, a Vietnam veteran and, before dying, uses up one minute to help Billy resolve his guilt over the death of a man who saved his life during the war.

Note: Harlan Ellison's story was written simultaneously with the teleplay and appeared in the anthology *Universe*, edited by Terry Carr, in 1985. 'Alan Smithee' is a generic Directors' Guild pseudonym, used in this instance by Gilbert Cates.

8.

15 November 1985

a: 'Act Break'

Writer: Haskell Barkin.   **Director:** Ted Flicker.
Music: Lance Rubin.

Cast: James Coco (Maury Winkler); Bob Dishy (Harry/Shakespeare); Avery Schreiber (Landlord).

Story: A dying playwright gives a magic amulet to his partner, Harry. But instead of using it to save his partner's life, Harry wishes to become Shakespeare's partner. When the amulet eventually falls into Shakespeare's hands, Harry ends up being forced to write Shakespeare's plays.

b: 'The Burning Man'

Writer: J. D. Feigelson.   **Story:** Ray Bradbury.
Director: J. D. Feigelson.   **Music:** Lance Rubin.

Cast: Piper Laurie (Aunt Neva); Andre Gower (Doug); Roberts Blossom (The Man); Danny Cooksey (The Boy).

Story: A woman and her nephew, out for a swim on a blazing hot summer's day pick up a strange hitch-hiker, a ranting old man. They throw him out of the car, but on their way home, they pick up a boy, who turns out to be the same creature.

Note: Ray Bradbury's story appeared in his collection *Long After Midnight* in 1976.

c: 'Dealer's Choice'

Writer: Donald Todd.   **Director:** Wes Craven.

Cast: Dan Hedaya (Nick); M. Emmet Walsh (Peter); Garrett Morris (Jake); Barney Martin (Tony); Morgan Freeman (Marty).

Story: The Devil turns up at a poker game, and deals for one of the players' souls. He seems to win, but is revealed to have been cheating. He departs in a generous mood. The players decide to mend their ways.

9.

22 November 1985
a: 'Dead Woman's Shoes'

Writer: Lynn Barker.   **Story:** Charles Beaumont.
Director: Peter Medak.   **Music:** Craig Safan.

Cast: Helen Mirren (Maddy Duncan); Jeffrey Tambor (Kyle Montgomery); Theresa Saldana (Iñez); Sasha Von Scherler (Eileen); Robert Pastorelli (Man); Hardy Rawls (Hyatt); Tyra Ferrell (Maid); Julie Dolan, Leslie Bega (Girls); Nana Visitor (Lori); Lance Nichols (Cabbie); Pia Gronning (Sara Montgomery).

Story: A mousy saleslady puts on the shoes of a murdered woman and is almost forced to kill the husband who killed her.

She escapes, but the husband is finally done in by a maid who finds the shoes.

Note: This is a remake, with a gender variant, of episode 47 of *The Twilight Zone* and was based on Charles Beaumont's teleplay.

b: 'Wong's Lost and Found Emporium'

Writer: Alan Brennert.   **Story:** William F. Wu.
Director: Paul Lynch.   **Music:** Craig Safan.

Cast: Brian Tochi (David Wong); Anna Maria Poon (Melinda); Carol Bruce (Mrs Whitford); Stacy Keach, Sr (Old Man); Jack Jozefson (Cashier); Marty Levy (Customer).

Story: Wong, a young Chinese-American, discovers a magic place where anything lost can be found. He finds his lost compassion and, along with a young woman who had lost her sense of humour, decides to run the place.

Note: William F. Wu's story originally appeared in *Amazing Stories* in 1983.

10.
29 November 1985
a: 'The Shadow Man'

Writer: Rockne S. O'Bannon.   **Director:** Joe Dante.

Cast: Jonathan Ward (Danny Hayes); Michael Rich (Peter Wilcox); Heather Haase (Liannna); Jason Presson (Eric); Jeff Calhoun (Shadow Man); Kathleen Coyne (Mother); Melissa Moultrie (Janie); Amy O'Neill, Tricia Bartholome, Julia Hendler (Girls); Christopher Gosch, Marc Bently, David Goldsmith (Boys).

Story: A boy who is teased by his schoolmates uses a mysterious 'shadow man' who lives under his bed to get his revenge. The shadow man has promised never to hurt the person under whose bed he lives, but after the boy becomes popular but obnoxious, he is done in by a shadow man living under someone else's bed.

b: 'The Uncle Devil Show'

Writer: Donald Todd.   **Director:** David Steinberg.
Music: Craig Safan.

Cast: Murphy Dunne (Uncle Devil); Joel Polis (Father); Wendy Phillips (Mother); Gregory Mier (Joey).

Story: A strange videotape teaches a neglected child a variety of incredible magic tricks.

c: 'Opening Day'

Writers: Chris Hubbell   **Director:** John Milius.
and Gerrit Graham.   **Music:** Craig Safan.

Cast: Martin Kove (Joe Farrell); Jeff Jones (Carl Wilkerson); Elan Oberon (Sally); Molly Morgan (Kerri); Shawn Donahue (Joe Jr); Andrea Hall Lovell (Beverly); Michael Nissman (Ned); Frank McRae (Sheriff); Shelby Billington (Girl); Gary Hollis (Man).

Story: A woman and her lover plot to murder her obnoxious husband during the opening day of the duck-hunting season. The deed done by the lover, he returns to find the tables have been turned: he has become the husband and the husband is now the lover whom he knows is about to murder him.

11.

6 December 1985

a: 'The Beacon'

Writers: Martin Pasko and Rebecca Parr.

Director: Gerd Oswald.
Music: Morton Stevens.

Cast: Charles Martin Smith (Dr Barrows); Martin Landau (William Cooper James); Vonni Ribisi (Teddy); Cheryl Anderson, Scott Lincoln, Hayley Taylor Block (Townspeople).

Story: A doctor discovers a small coastal town where the citizens live in terror of a beacon whose light kills those upon whom it shines. He tries to incite them to revolt, but is instead killed himself.

b: 'One Life, Furnished in Early Poverty'

Writer: Alan Brennert.
Director: Don Carlos Dunaway.

Story: Harlan Ellison.
Music: Harry Betts.

Cast: Peter Riegert (Gus 'Harry' Rosenthal); Jack Kehoe (Lou Rosenthal); Chris Hebert (Gus Rosenthal); Barbara Tarbuck (Girlfriend); Susan Wheeler Duff (Mrs Rosenthal); Biff Yeager (Jack Wheeldon, Cabbie); Gary Karp (Wheeldon kid).

Story: An angry writer returns to his home town and travels back in time to meet himself as a child. He makes peace with his father, finds solace and becomes a better person.

Note: Harlan Ellison's story originally appeared in the anthology *Orbit*, edited by Damon Knight in 1970.

12.

13 December 1985

a: 'Her Pilgrim Soul'

Writer: Alan Brennert.   **Director:** Wes Craven.
Music: William Goldstein.

Cast: Kristoffer Tabori (Kevin Drayton); Betsy Jane Licon (Nola Granville, aged four); Danica McKellar (Nola, aged ten); Anne Twomey (Nola, adult); Gary Cole (Daniel Gaddis); Wendy Girard (Carol Drayton); Katherine Wallach (Susan); Richard McGonagle (Lester); Nelson Welch (Ruskin).

Story: A female fœtus mysteriously appears inside a holographic simulation and begins growing with amazing speed. A young scientist becomes emotionally involved with the rapidly-ageing woman. She is eventually revealed to be his mother, who died during childbirth.

Note: This episode was made into an off-Broadway musical entitled *Weird Romance* in 1992: music by Alan Menken, lyrics by David Spencer, book by Alan Brennert, directed by Barry Harman. Danica McKellar later starred in *The Wonder Years*.

b: 'I of Newton'

Writer: Alan Brennert.   **Story:** Joe Haldeman.
Director: Kenneth Gilbert.

Cast: Sherman Hemsley (Sam); Ron Glass (The Devil).

Story: A scientist unwittingly offers to sell his soul to the Devil to solve some equations, but eventually tricks the demon by ordering him to 'get lost'.

Note: Joe Haldeman's story originally appeared in *Fantastic Stories* in 1970. Alan Brennert's teleplay was later adapted for the stage at the University of Rochester in 1992.

13.

20 December 1985

a: 'Night of the Meek'

Writer: Rockne S. O'Bannon. **Story:** Rod Serling.
Director: Martha Coolidge. **Music:** Morton Stevens.

Cast: Richard Mulligan (Henry Corwin); William Atherton (Dundee); Bill Henderson, Jeff Kober (Policemen); Teddy Wilson (Henderson); Shelby Leverington (Mother); Joanne Barron (Mrs Beacham); Thomas F. Duffy (Businessman); Hugo Stanger (Dobson); Elizabeth Ward (Girl); Charles Swiegart (Bartender); Wayne Morton (Manager); Monty Ash (Old Man); Patricia Wilson (Caroler); Wilson Camp (Man); Benjie Gregory, Paul Stout (Boys); Georgia Schmidt (Wife); Muriel Minot (Mother); Enid Rodgers (Spinster); Brian Muehl (Father); Toria Crosby (Little Girl); Larenz Tate (Older Brother); Harry Governick (Man on roof); Phyllis Erlich (Woman on phone).

Story: See *The Twilight Zone* episode 47 (no significant variations).

b: 'But Can She Type?'

Writers: Martin Pasko **Director:** Shelley Levinson.
and Rebecca Parr.

Cast: Pam Dawber (Gloria Billings); Charles Levin (Burt); Jeannie Elias (Marcy); Jonathan Frakes (Single Guy); Deborah Harmon (Hostess); Michael Prince (Edward Rehnquist); Amzie Strickland (Cleaning Woman); Jolina Collins (Model); Douglas Bair (Limo Driver); Ken Sagoes (Workman).

Story: A broken photocopier inadvertently transports a harried secretary saddled with an incompetent, dictatorial boss to a world where secretaries are on the top of the social pyramid.

c: 'The Star'

Writer: Alan Brennert.   **Story:** Arthur C. Clarke.
Director: Gerd Oswald.   **Music:** Morton Stevens.

Cast: Fritz Weaver (Matthew Costigan); Donald Moffat (Dr Chandler); Elizabeth Huddle (Captain).

Story: In the future, a priest discovers that a star which went nova, destroying an advanced civilisation, was the star that shone over Bethlehem.

Note: Arthur C. Clarke's story originally appeared in *Infinity Science-Fiction* in 1955.

14.

3 January 1986

a: 'Still Life'

Writers: Gerrit Graham   **Director:** Peter Medak.
and Chris Hubbell.   **Music:** Ken Wannberg,

Cast: Robert Carradine (Dan Arnold); John Carradine (Professor Alexander Stottel); Marilyn Jones (Rebecca Arnold).

Story: A young couple find an old camera which belonged to an anthropologist who took pictures of Indians in the Amazon. The Indians magically leave the photographs and attack the couple, but are retrapped inside a modern camera.

b: 'The Little People of Killany Woods'

Writer: J. D. Feigelson.   **Director:** J. D. Feigelson.
Music: Morton Stevens.

Cast: Hamilton Camp (Liam O'Shaughnessy); Michael Alldredge (Mike Mulvaney); James Scally (Kelly); Tim

Donoghue (Eddie Donovan); Anthony Palmer (McGinty); Hal Landon (O'Dell); Pat Crawford Brown (Mrs Finnegan).

Story: An Irish teller of tall tales is not believed when he claims to have seen the 'little people' – until he starts paying for his beer with triangular gold coins. The 'little people' are revealed to be aliens who have stopped to repair their ship. The Irishman leaves with them.

c: 'The Misfortune Cookie'

Writer: Steven Rae.   **Story:** Charles E. Fritch.
Director: Allan Arkush.

Cast: Elliot Gould (Harry Folger); Bennett Ohta (Mr Lee); Caroline Lagerfelt (April Hamilton); Frederick Coffin (Max); Claire Carter (Gourmette); John G. Scanlon (O'Malley); Elven Havard (Guard); Albert Leong (Chinese Proprietor).

Story: A nasty restaurant critic who unfairly trashed a Chinese restaurant gets his comeuppance through fortune cookies which really do predict the future. But in his case his future is death followed by his endless hell – of Chinese food.

Note: Charles E. Fritch's story originally appeared in *The Magazine of Fantasy and Science-Fiction* in 1971. 'Steven Rae' is a pseudonym for Rockne S. O'Bannon.

15.

24 January 1986

a: 'Monsters!'

Writer: Robert Crais.   **Director:** B.W. L. Norton.
Music: Basil Poledouris.

Cast: Ralph Bellamy (Emile Francis Bendictson); Oliver Robins (Tobey Michaels); Kathleen Lloyd (Mrs Michaels); Bruce Solomon (Mr Michaels); Lewis Dauber (Lou); Mary Margaret Lewis (Liz); Roger Hampton (Mover); Eve Brenner, Teryn Jenkins (Neighbours).

Story: A boy who is crazy about monsters befriends an old vampire. The vampire reveals that the real monsters are humans who turn into creatures of the night genetically programmed to destroy beings like him.

b: 'A Small Talent for War'

Writers: Carter Scholz and Alan Brennert.

Director: Claudia Weill.
Music: Christopher Young.

Cast: John Glover (Alien Ambassador); Peter Michael Goetz (American Ambassador Fraser); Stefan Gierasch (Russian diplomat); Fran Bennett (UN Chairman); Jose Santana (Aide); Gillian Eaton (British Delegate); Richard Brestoff (British Aide).

Story: Mankind unites after an alien ambassador comes to Earth and tells the UN that they are unhappy about our progress. But what the aliens really wanted were warriors, not peace-lovers.

c: 'A Matter of Minutes'

Writer: Rockne S. O'Bannon.   **Story:** Theodore Sturgeon.
Director: Sheldon Larry.   **Music:** Christopher Young.

Cast: Karen Austin (June Wright); Adam Arkin (Michael Wright); Adolph Caesar (Supervisor); Marianne Muellerleile (Woman); Alan David Gelman (Man).

Story: A couple wake up to discover faceless, blue construction workers literally taking apart their house and neighbourhood. In reality, they have slipped backstage and ahead in time where everything in every minute is being built from scratch.

Note: Theodore Sturgeon's story, originally entitled *Yesterday Was Monday*, appeared in *Unknown Worlds* in 1941.

16.

31 January 1986

a: 'The Elevator'

Writer: Ray Bradbury.   **Director:** R. L. Thomas.
Music: Arthur Kempel.

Cast: Stephen Geoffreys (Will); Robert Prescott (Roger); Douglas Emerson (Young Roger); Brandon Bluhm (Young Will).

Story: The two sons of a mad scientist become the victims of their father's experiments to create a new source of food that induces gigantism in animals.

b: 'To See the Invisible Man'

Writer: Steven Barnes.   **Story:** Robert Silverberg.
Director: Noel Black.   **Music:** Craig Safan.

Cast: Cotter Smith (Mitchell Chaplin); Karlene Crockett (Invisible Woman); Mary Robin Redd (Margaret); Peter Hobbs (Blind Man); Bonnie-Campbell Britton (Woman); Jack Gallagher (Comic); Kenneth Danziger (Maître d'); Richard Jamison (Guard); Chris McCarty (Businessman); Karla Richards (Waitress); Rebecca Robertson (Nurse); Dean Fortunato (Tough); Steve Peterson (Server); Terri Lynn Wood (Crying Girl); Whitby Hertford (Boy).

Story: An antisocial man is condemned to be socially 'invisible' for a year. Afterwards, he chooses further 'invisibility' rather than refuse to show compassion for an 'invisible' woman.

Note: Robert Silverberg's story originally appeared in the April 1963 issue of *Worlds of Tomorrow*.

c: 'Tooth and Consequences'

Writer: Haskell Barkin.   **Director:** Robert Downey.
Music: Craig Safan.

Cast: David Birney (Dr Myron Mandel); Kenneth Mars (Tooth Fairy); Teresa Ganzel (Lydia Bixby); Oliver Clark (Dr Walter Rinkham); Peggy Pope (Mrs Schulman); Mina Kolb (Mrs Taylor); Jane Ralston (Receptionist); Ermal Williamson (Mr Frank); Martin Azarow (Man); Mitzi McCall (Woman); William Utay, Nat Bernstein, Jack Lindine, Ron Ross (Hobos).

Story: The tooth fairy rescues a suicidal dentist and magically grants him the love he is seeking, but too much love drives him to become a hobo – a road taken by many other dentists before him.

17.

7 February 1986

a: 'Welcome to Winfield'

Writer: Les Enloe.   **Director:** Bruce Bilson.

Cast: Jonathan Caliri (Matt); Joann Willette (Amy); Gerrit Graham (Griffin St George); Henry Gibson (Mayor); Alan Fudge (Sheriff); Elisha Cook (Weldon); Dennis Fimple (Ray Bob); Chip Heller (Elton); Sally Klein (Marnie); Claudia Bryar, David Morick (Townspeople).

Story: To lay claim to a dying young man, an Agent of Death comes to an old Western town which was bypassed by the previous Grim Reaper. The inhabitants appeal to his compassion, and he eventually leaves without collecting anyone.

b: 'Quarantine'

Writer: Alan Brennert.   **Story:** Philip DeGuere and

Director: Martha Coolidge.   Stephen Bochco.
Music: Dennis McCarthy.

Cast: Scott Wilson (Matthew Foreman); Tess Harper (Sarah); Larry Riley (Joshua); Jeanne Mori (Irene); D. W. Brown (John).

Story: After 324 years in hibernation, a man awakens to a Utopian future where technology has been replaced by psychic powers and biogenetics. Its inhabitants trick him into using old weapons to destroy a spaceship from the past carrying nuclear weapons.

18.

14 February 1986
a: 'Gramma'

Writer: Harlan Ellison.   **Story:** Stephen King.
Director: Bradford May.   **Music:** Mickey Hart.

Cast: Barret Oliver (George); Darlanne Fluegel (Mother); Frederick Long (Gramma).

Story: A boy discovers his monstrous, dying grandmother is a witch. She eventually takes over his body.

Note: Stephen King's story originally appeared in *Weird Book* magazine in 1984 and was later collected in *Skeleton Crew* (1986). Barret Oliver starred in *The Never-Ending Story*.

b: 'Personal Demons'

Writer: Rockne S. O'Bannon. **Director:** Peter Medak.
Music: Arthur Kempel.

Cast: Martin Balsam (Rockne S. O'Bannon); Clive Revill (Paul Connell); Joshua Shelley (Herman Gold); Marlena Giovi (Widow); Penny Baker (Pam); Stephen Flanigan (Gary); Tommy

Madden, Billy Curtis, Gary Friedkin, Kevin Thompson, Dan Frishman, Lou Carry, Jerry Maren (Creatures).

Story: A burned-out writer starts seeing gnome-like creatures bent on destroying his possessions. To get rid of them, he must write about them.

c: 'Cold Reading'

Writers: Martin Pasko and Rebecca Parr.

Director: Gus Trikonis.
Music: Artie Butler.

Cast: Dick Shawn (Nelson Westbrook); Joel Brooks (Jack Holland); Lawrence Poindexter (Milo Trent); Annette McCarthy (Carla); Janet Carroll (Marilyn Cavendish); Ralph Manza (Sol); Kevin Scannell (Announcer); Mike Pniewski (Page); Paul Keith (Paul Loomis); Thomas Bellin (Ed Winter); Jon Melichar (Engineer).

Story: A megalomaniacal radio producer doing a show about Africa wishes for authentic sound effects. His wishes are magically granted by a voodoo artifact, creating chaos in the studio. Next week's show: *Invaders from Mars!*

19.

21 February 1986

a: 'The Leprechaun-Artist'

Writer: Tommy Lee Wallace. **Story:** James Crocker.
Director: Tommy Lee Wallace. **Music:** Arthur Kempel.

Cast: Cork Hubbert (Shawn McGool); Bradley Gregg (Richie); Joey Green (J. P.); Danny Nucci (Buddy); James Hess (Sergeant Brewer); Marguerite DeLain (J. P.'s Mother); Burr Middleton (Richie's Dad); Chuck Stransky (Buddy's Dad); Melinda Peterson (Buddy's Mother).

Story: Three boys capture a vacationing leprechaun who grants them three wishes (x-ray vision, power over their parents and a car). Each wish turns out to be more than they can handle.

b: 'Dead Run'

Writer: Alan Brennert. **Story:** Greg Bear.
Director: Paul Tucker.

Cast: Steve Railsback (John Davis); John DeLancie (The Dispatcher); Barry Corbin (Pete); James Lashly (Merle); Ebbe Roe Smith (Gary Frick); Paul Jenkins, John Barlow (Truckers); John Le May (Gay Man); Ritch Brinkley (Middle-aged Man); Brent Spiner (Draft Dodger); Nancy Lenehan (Addict); Howard Munco, Brian Libby (Employees); Gertrude Flynn (Elderly Woman); David Wells (Bald Man); Pat Ast (Fat Woman); Brad Fisher (Ferret); Jimmie F. Skaggs (Mean Man); Andy Landis (Young Woman); Virginia Lantry (Young Girl); Donna Lyn Leavy, Lisa Cloud (Women); Gregory Wagrowski (Man).

Story: A washed-out trucker with a bad driving record finds that the only work left for him is ferrying people to Hell. But he discovers that some of the people sent there do not deserve it, because Hell is being run by Man, and he starts releasing them.

Note: Greg Bear's story originally appeared in *Omni* in 1985.

20.

7 March 1986

a: 'Profile in Silver'

Writer: J. Neil Schulman. **Director:** John Hancock.
Music: Basil Poledouris.

Cast: Andrew Robinson (President Kennedy); Lane Smith (Professor Joseph Fitzgerald); Louis Giambalvo (Livingston); Barbara

Baxley (Dr Kate Wange); Jerry Hardin (Lyndon B. Johnson); Mark Taylor (Inspector); Charles Lanyer (Anchorman); David Sage (Professor); Ken Hill (Aide); Huck Liggett (Texan); Gerard Bocaccio (Student).

Story: Professor Fitzgerald, a descendent of President Kennedy, who has travelled back in time, prevents his famous ancestor from being assassinated, but discovers that his actions have doomed the world. To put things right, Fitzgerald sacrifices himself to die in Dallas instead of Kennedy, who is transported to the future.

b: 'Button, Button'

Writer: Logan Swanson.   **Story:** Richard Matheson.
Director: Peter Medak.   **Music:** Robert Folk.

Cast: Mare Winningham (Norma Lewis); Brad Davis (Arthur Lewis); Basil Hoffman (Steward).

Story: A poor couple is given a box with a button. If they press it, someone they do not know will die and they will receive $200,000. The husband refuses to use it, but his wife eventually does. She gets the money, but is told that the box will now pass into the hands of someone who does not know her.

Note: 'Logan Swanson' is a pseudonym for Richard Matheson. Matheson's story was first written for the original *Twilight Zone*, but never produced. It then appeared in *Playboy* in 1970. In the story's original ending, the husband dies, because he is someone his wife didn't really know.

21.

21 March 1986

a: 'Need to Know'

Writer: Mary Sheldon.   **Story:** Sidney Sheldon.

Director: Paul Lynch.   **Music:** Ron Ramin.

Cast: William L. Petersen (Edward Sayers); Robin Gammell (Jeffrey Potts); Frances McDormand (Amanda Strickland); Harold Ayer (Mr Strickland); Eldon Quick (Dr Benitz); Ellen Albertini Dow (Mrs Hotchkiss); Shay Garner (Dr Fall); Ray Ballard (Jack Henries); Clarence Brown (Wiley Whitlow).

Story: A man who has discovered the secret of the meaning of life drives an entire town insane.

b: 'Red Snow'

Writer: Michael Cassutt.   **Director:** Jeannot Szwarc.
Music: Elliot Kaplan.

Cast: George Dzundza (Colonel Ulyanov); Barry Miller (Povin); Vladimir Skomarovsky (Mayor Titov); Victoria Tennant (Valentina Orlova); Rod Colbin (Minister); Andrew Divoff (Vladimir); Lilliam Adams (Babushka); Jack Ross Obney (Grishenko); Kimberly Ann Morris (Galya); Mike Kulcsar (Golodkin); Tom Maier (Villager).

Story: A disillusioned KGB Colonel discovers that dissidents sent to an Arctic village in the Gulag have become vampires. He eventually chooses to become a vampire himself to fight the system from within.

22.
28 March 1986
a: 'Take My Life... Please!'

Writer: Gordon Mitchell.   **Director:** Gus Trikonis.

Cast: Tim Thomerson (Billy Diamond); Ray Buktenika (Max); Jim MacKrell (Marty Gibbons); Xander Berkeley (Dave).

Story: A dead comedian who led a self-centred, rotten life discovers that hell is being forced to perform that life as a stand-up act for eternity.

b: 'Devil's Alphabet'

Writer: Robert Hunter.   **Story:** Arthur Gray.
Director: Ben Bolt.

Cast: Ben Cross (Frederick); Hywell Bennett (Grant); Robert Schenkkan (Cornelius); Wayne Alexander (Deva); Osmond Bullock (Andrew); Ethan Phillips (Bolivius); Jim Piddock (Eli); Stuart Dowling (Creditor); Christopher Carroll (Chimney Sweep); Christopher Grove (Assistant).

Story: The six members of a university club swear to continue meeting after their deaths, which they do. The last surviving member and the five ghosts eventually agree to dissolve the club.

Note: Arthur Gray's story, originally entitled *The Everlasting Club*, appeared in *Tedious Brief Tales of Granta and Gramarye* in 1919.

c: 'The Library'

Writer: Anne Collins.   **Director:** John Hancock.
Music: Dennis McCarthy.

Cast: Uta Hagen (Gloria); Frances Conroy (Ellie Pendleton); Lori Petty (Lori Pendleton); Joe Santos (Doug Kelleher); Candy Azzara (Carla Mollencami); Alan Blumenfeld (Edwin Dewett); Jay Gerber (Man); Mimi Monaco (Woman).

Story: A woman hired to work in a library where the books are a record of everyone's life, starts rewriting her neighbours' lives. Ultimately, her tampering results in her sister's death.

23.

4 April 1986

a: 'Shadow Play'

Writer: James Crocker.   **Story:** Charles Beaumont.
Director: Paul Lynch.

Cast: Peter Coyote (Adam Grant); Guy Boyd (Mark Ritchie); Janet Eilber (Erin Jacobs); Deborah May (Carol Ritchie); William Schallert (Father Grant); Raymond Bieri (Flash); William Smith (Guard); Earl Billings (Jimmy); George Petrie (Judge); Ella Raino Edwards (Foreman); Hank Garrett (Warden); Gilbert De La Pena (Muñoz).

Story: See *The Twilight Zone* episode 62 (no significant variations).

b: 'Grace Note'

Writer: Patrice Messina.   **Director:** Peter Medak.
Music: Robert Drasnin.

Cast: Julia Migenes Johnson (Rosemarie Miletti); Sydney Penny (Mary Miletti); Rhoda Gemignani (Angelina); Kay E. Kuter (Maestro Barbieri); Catherine Paolone (Dorothy, aged 35); Gina Marie Vinaccia (Dorothy, aged 9); Ross Evans (Sam); Ruth Zakarian (Teresa); Elliott Scott (Joey); Toni Sawyer (Old Woman); Tom Finnegan (Cabbie); Craig Schaefer (Guard); Sandy Lipton (Woman).

Story: A dying girl's last wish provides her would-be opera singer sister, who is plagued with doubt, with a vision of a future where she has become a diva.

24.

11 April 1986

a: 'A Day in Beaumont'

Writer: David Gerrold.   **Director:** Philip DeGuere.
Music: Fred Steiner.

Cast: Victor Garber (Dr Kevin Carlson); Stacey Nelkin (Faith);
Jeff Morrow (H. G. Orson); John Agar (Pops); Kenneth Tobey
(Sheriff Haskins); Warren Stevens (Major Whitmore); Richard
Partlow (Sergeant); Myles O'Brien (Young Man).

Story: In the 1950s, a young couple witness the landing of a
flying saucer. No one in the neighbouring town of Beaumont
appears to believe them until it turns out the entire town has
been invaded. It is eventually revealed that they are themselves
aliens training for the real invasion of Earth.

b: 'The Last Defender of Camelot'

Writer: George R. R. Martin.   **Story:** Roger Zelazny.
Director: Jeannot Szwarc.   **Music:** Elliot Kaplan.

Cast: Richard Kiley (Lancelot); Jenny Agutter (Morgan Le
Fay); Norman Lloyd (Merlin); John Cameron Mitchell (Tom);
Anthony LaPaglia, Don Stark (Punks).

Story: Lancelot and Morgan Le Fay team up to prevent a re-
vived Merlin from using his powers to force his outmoded ideas
upon the modern world. Lance and his young squire Tom then
choose to remain in the faerie world.

Note: Roger Zelazny's story originally appeared in *Isaac
Asimov's Science-Fiction Magazine* in 1979.

Second Season (CBS)

Executive Producer: Phil DeGuere.
Supervising Producers: Anthony and Nancy Lawrence.
Producer: Harvey Frand.
Executive Story Consultant: Alan Brennert.
Story Consultant: Rockne S. O'Bannon.
Story Editors: George R. R. Martin, Martin Pasko
and Rebecca Parr.
Director of Photography: Bradford May (except where
otherwise indicated); Chuck Arnold (episodes 29, 32b, 35);
Robert Collins (episodes 33a,b, 34b).
Narrator: Charles Aidman.
Music: Merl Saunders (except where otherwise indicated).

25.

27 September 1986

a: 'The Once and Future King'

Writer: George R. R. Martin.   **Story:** Bryce Maritano.
Director: Jim McBride.   **Music:** Richard Stone.

Cast: Jeff Yagher (Gary Pitkin/Elvis Presley); Lisa Jane Persky (Sandra Mitchison); Red West (Boss Harris); Banks Harper (Marion Keisker); Paul Eiding (Sam Phillips); Brian Hatton (Bill); Mitch Carter (Scotty); Cynthia Sanders (Waitress); Nancy Throckmorton (Barmaid).

Story: Gary, an Elvis impersonator, travels back in time and meets the real 'King' before he became a star. But this Elvis is nothing like the one Gary remembers. After a fight during which Elvis dies, Gary ends up impersonating him.

b: 'A Saucer of Loneliness'

Writer: David Gerrold.   **Story:** Theodore Sturgeon.

Director: John Hancock.   **Music:** Robert Folk.

Cast: Shelley Duvall (Margaret); Nan Martin (Mother); Richard Libertini (Lonely Man); Edith Diaz (Religious Woman); Mari Gorman (Friend); Andrew Masset (Dream Date); Myrna White (Psychiatrist); Michael Zand (Clerk); Brick Karnes (Boyfriend); James Edward Thomas (Hank Charles); Bruno Aclin (Officer); Laura Harlan (Waitress); Geoff Witcher (Anchorman); Mary Ingersoll, David Hayward, Shannon Lee Avnsoe, J. Omar Hansen (Reporters).

Story: A lonely girl receives a message from a flying saucer, but refuses to divulge it. As she is about to commit suicide, she is rescued by an equally lonely man and reveals that the saucer's message was about loneliness and hope.

Note: Theodore Sturgeon's story originally appeared in *Galaxy* in 1953. Shelley Duvall played Olive Oyl in *Popeye* (1980).

26.

4 October 1986

a: 'What Are Friends For?'

Writer: J. Michael Straczynski.   **Director:** Gus Trikonis. **Music:** J. A. G. Redford.

Cast: Tom Skerritt (Alex Mattingly); Fred Savage (Jeff Mattingly); Lukas Haas (Mike); Joy Claussen (Allyson Conrad); Michael Ennis (Ross Conrad); Mark-Paul Gosselaar (Tim); Johnny Green (Larry); Jennifer Roach (Cindy); David Selberg (Doctor).
Story: The son of a divorced father starts playing with an imaginary friend, who unwittingly lures him into danger. The father realises it is the same entity that he used to play with as a kid. The father eventually convinces the entity to release its hold on his son in the name of friendship.

b: 'Aqua Vita'

Writers: Jeremy Bertrand Finch and Paul Chitlik.

Director: Paul Tucker.
Music: Gary Malkin-Remal.

Cast: Mimi Kennedy (Christie Copperfield); Joseph Hacker (Marc); Christopher McDonald (Delivery Man); Barbra Horan (Shauna Allen); Martin Doyle (News Editor); Bob Delegall (Sales Manager); John Le May (Ted); Harry Stephens (Young Man); Cynthia Kania (Young Woman).

Story: An anchorwoman worried about ageing starts taking youth-restoring 'Aqua Vita', but it proves horribly addictive and expensive. Worse, stopping it causes her to age in an accelerated fashion. Her boyfriend's love eventually helps her to realise what is really important and he too drinks some Aqua Vita to look as old as she does.

27.

11 October 1986

a: 'The Storyteller'

Writer: Rockne S. O'Bannon. **Director:** Paul Lynch.
Music: Ron Ramin.

Cast: Glynnis O'Connor (Dorothy Livingston); David Faustino (Micah Frost); Parley Baer (Grandfather Frost); Nike Doukas (Heather); Ellen Albertini Dow (Old Woman); Robert Britton (Bus Driver); Patricia Allison (Mrs Dockweiller); Morgan Saint John (William); Tony Anton (Daniel); Billy Anton (Nathaniel); Melissa Clayton (Girl); Billie Joe Wright (Farmboy); Bill Sak (Doctor); Frank Moon (Man).

Story: Like his father before him, a mountain boy somehow keeps his great-grandfather alive by reading him stories. A schoolteacher stumbles upon his secret and eventually uses it to keep her own mother alive.

b: 'Nightsong'

Writer: Michael Reaves.   **Director:** Bradford May.
Music: John Debney, Michael
Wetherwax, Stephen Stills.

Cast: Lisa Eilbacher (Andrea Fields); Antony Hamilton (Simon
Locke); Kenneth David Gilman (Ace).

Story: A DJ plays an album by a former boyfriend who disappeared five years earlier. He returns, makes peace with her and
helps her let go – as she eventually discovers he died in an
unreported accident.

28.

18 October 1986

a: 'The After Hours'

Writer: Rockne S. O'Bannon.   **Story:** Rod Serling.
Director: Bruce Malmuth.   **Music:** Robert Folk.

Cast: Terry Farrell (Marsha Cole); Ned Bellamy (Mysterious
Man); Ann Wedgeworth (Toy Store Saleslady); Chip Heller
(Workman); Lori Michaels (Mother); Edan Gross (Boy); Evan
Malmuth, Alan David (Security); Alvie Selznick, Deborah
Bennett (Mannequins); Caprice Spenser-Roth (Bin Mannequin);
Michael Dobo (Owner).

Story: See *The Twilight Zone* episode 34 (no significant variations).

b: 'Lost and Found'

Writer: George R. R. Martin.   **Story:** Phyllis Eisenstein.
Director: Gus Trikonis.

Cast: Akosua Busia (Jennifer Templeton); Cindy Harrell (Kathy); Leslie Ackerman, Raye Birk (Time Travellers).

Story: A young student keeps losing small, personal things. She eventually discovers they have been taken by collectors from the future because she'll become Earth's first black, female president.

Note: Phyllis Eisenstein's story originally appeared in *Analog* in 1978.

c: 'The World Next Door'

Writer: Lan O'Kun.   **Director:** Paul Lynch.

Cast: George Wendt (Barney Schlessinger); Bernadette Birkett (Katie Schlessinger); Tom Finnegan (Steve); Jeffrey Tambor (Milton Baumsey); Victoria Bass (Lucille); Dinah Lenney (Francine); Jon Menick (Henry the Butler).

Story: A misunderstood inventor finds a passage into another world where he is a rich and respected man. He has, in fact, switched places with his other self, who is tired of his responsibilities.

29.

4 December 1986

'The Toys Of Caliban' (half-hour episode)

Writer: George R. R. Martin.   **Story:** Terry Matz.
Director: Thomas J. Wright.

Cast: Richard Mulligan (Ernest Ross); Anne Haney (Mary Ross); David Greenlee (Toby Ross); Alexandra Borrie (Mandy Kemp); Earl Bullock (Minister); Richard Biggs (Resident).

Story: A retarded boy who has the power to make things materialise from pictures goes out of control, killing his mother. After a social worker stumbles upon his secret, his father has no choice but to arrange their deaths.

Note: Director Thomas J. Wright did several of the paintings shown in the opening of *Night Gallery*.

30.

11 December 1986

'The Convict's Piano' (half-hour episode)

Writer: Patrice Messina.   **Story:** James Crocker.
Director: Thomas J. Wright.   **Music:** Artie Kane.

Cast: Joe Penny (Rick Frost); Norman Fell (Eddie O'Hara); Tom O'Brien (Mickey Shaughnessy); John Hancock (Dr Puckett); Sam Scarber (Max); Cristen Kauffman (Ellen); Tony De Longis (Thompson); Burton Collins (Shorty); Raymond O'Keefe (Guard); Ezekiel Moss (Peters); James MacIntire (Prisoner); Chad Krentzman (Soldier).

Story: A convict, unjustly imprisoned for murder, uses an old piano to travel into the past and switches place with a prohibition gangster.

31.

18 December 1986

The Road Less Travelled (half-hour episode)

Writer: George R. R. Martin.   **Director:** Wes Craven.
Music: Dennis McCarthy.

Cast: Cliff DeYoung (Jeff McDowell); Margaret Klenck (Denise McDowell); Jaclyn-Rose Lester (Megan); Clare Nono (Susan); John Zarchen (Jack); Christopher Brown (Grunt).

Story: A draft dodger who fled to Canada rather than serve in Vietnam experiences visions of the war, then meets his other self who did go to Vietnam, and ends up sharing memories with him.

32.

21 February 1987

a: 'The Card'

Writer: Michael Cassutt.   **Director:** Bradford May.
Music: William Goldstein.

Cast: Susan Blakely (Linda Wolfe); Virginia Kiser (Katherine Foley); William Atherton (Brian Wolfe); Ken Lerner (Salesman); Beverly Eilbacher (Receptionist); Coleby Lombardo (Evan Wolfe); Zachary Bostrom (Matthew Wolfe); Frank Mangano (Tow Truck Driver).

Story: A compulsive spender acquires 'The Card' with unlimited spending power. But the price is the repossession of her entire family if she can't pay.

b: 'The Junction'

Writer: Virginia Aldridge.   **Director:** Bill Duke.

Cast: William Allen Young (John Parker); Chris Mulkey (Ray Dobson); John Dennis Johnston (Charley); William Frankfather (Reverend Bailey); Michael Alldredge (Schmidt); Tanya Boyd (Melissa Parker); James Lashly (Bobby); John Walcutt (Les); Ann Doran (Mrs Clark); Karen Landry (Sarah Dobson); Joe Unger, Christopher Kriesa (Rescuers); Dianna Patton (Woman); Bobby Hosea (Stretcher Bearer).

Story: After a cave-in, a mine engineer finds a man who was trapped down there in 1912. When the earlier miner is rescued, he sends a letter from the past to the engineer's wife, which leads to his rescue.

33.

21 May 1987

a: 'Joy Ride'

Writer: Cal Willingham.   **Director:** Gil Bettman

Cast: Rob Knepper (Alonzo); Brooke McCarter (Gregory); Heidi Kozak, Tamara Mark (Girlfriends); Burr Middleton, Danny Spear (Policemen); Randy Hall (Fireman).

Story: Two teenage couples steal a dead gangster's 1950 Oldsmobile for a joyride. The car appears to take them back in time. In fact, they haven't left the garage: they are trapped inside the car, reliving its owner's crime spree.

b: 'Shelter Skelter'

Writers: Ron Cobb   **Story:** Ron Cobb.
and Robin Love.   **Director:** Martha Coolidge.

Cast: Joe Mantegna (Harry Dobbs); Joan Allen (Sally Dobbs); Jonathan Gries (Nick Gatlin); Adam Raber (Jason Dobbs); Danica McKellar (Deidre Dobbs); Lauren Levian (Wendy); Diana Lewis (Reporter); Tamara Taylor (Newscaster); Geoff Witcher (Announcer).

Story: A survivalist believes he has lived through a nuclear war in his shelter. In reality, it was an accident which destroyed his town and contributed to bringing peace to Earth, and he has been entombed for ever.

Note: Ron Cobb is a renowned conceptual artist whose credits include *Alien* (1979) and *The Abyss* (1989).

c: 'Private Channel'

Writer: Edward Redlich.   **Director:** Peter Medak.

Music: Robert Folk.

Cast: Scott Coffey (Keith); Andrew Robinson (Williams); Claudia Cron (Gloria); Louise Fitch (Old Woman); Joan Foley (Girl); Rebeccah Bush (Clerk); Alex Daniels (Host); Jackson Hughes (Paul); Juliette Sorci (Little Girl).

Story: After a bolt of lightning strikes his aeroplane, an obnoxious teenager can hear thoughts through his radio. These include those of the man sitting next to him who plans to blow up the plane because his family was killed in a plane crash. He stops him by making him listen to the other passengers' thoughts.

34.

10 July 1987

a: 'Time and Teresa Golowitz'

Writer: Alan Brennert.   **Story:** Parke Godwin.
Director: Shelley Levinson.   **Music:** William Goldstein.

Cast: Gene Barry (Prince of Darkness); Kristi Lynes (Teresa Golowitz); Grant Heslov ('Binki' Blaustein); Paul Sand (Bluestone); Gina Gershon (Laura); Beau Dremann (Bob); Heather Haase (Mary Ellen Cosgrove); Wally Ward (Nelson); J. D. Roth (Boy); Laurel Green (Girl).

Story: A dead pianist asks the Prince of Darkness for the chance to make it with his teenage crush. He ends up turning around the life of a frumpy girl who becomes a superb diva.

Note: Parke Godwin's story, originally entitled *Influencing the Hell out of Time and Teresa Golowitz*, appeared in *The Twilight Zone Magazine* in 1982.

b: 'Voices in the Earth'

Writer: Alan Brennert.   **Director:** Curtis Harrington.

Music: Robert Folk.

Cast: Martin Balsam (Donald Knowles); Jenny Agutter (Jacinda); Tim Russ (Archer); Dennis Haskins (Bledsoe); Ted Lehman (Old Man); Eve Brenner (Old Woman); Sandra Ganzer (Girl); Cesca Lawrence (Young Woman); Christopher Lofton (Man).

Story: A historian from the future returns to a devastated Earth scheduled for strip mining. He starts seeing ghosts of the people left behind when his ancestors abandoned the planet, who plot to take over his body and escape. Instead, he talks them into sacrificing their energy to recreate life.

35.
17 July 1987
a: 'Song of the Younger World'

Writers: Anthony and Nancy Lawrence.	**Director:** Noel Black.
	Music: Robert Folk.

Cast: Peter Kowanko (Tanner Smith); Jennifer Rubin (Amy Hawkline); Roberts Blossom (Hawkline); Paul Benedict (Okie).

Story: The director of a reformatory farm threatens to kill the boy his daughter loves. The two reincarnate their souls into wolves to escape his wrath.

b: 'The Girl I Married'

Writer: J. M. DeMatteis.   **Director:** Philip DeGuere.

Cast: James Whitmore, Jr (Ira Richman); Linda Kelsey (Valerie Richman); Dennis Patrick (Marvin).

Story: A successful lawyer yearning for his youth encounters his wife as she was 20 years before, but eventually comes to realise he has matured. Meanwhile, his wife has been undergoing the same experience with his younger self.

Third Season (Syndicated)

Executive Producers: Mark Shelmerdine, Michael MacMillan.
Producer: Seaton McLean.
Story Editors: Paul Chitlik, Jeremy Bertrand Finch, J. Michael Straczynski.
Production Designer/Associate Producer: David Moe.
Narrator: Robin Ward.
(*Because these episodes were shown directly in syndication, i.e. at various dates and times around the United States, there are no official first dates of broadcasting. However, they were generally screened during the 1988 season.*)

1: 'The Curious Case of Edgar Witherspoon'

Writer: Haskell Barkin.
Director: René Bonnière
Director of Photography: Ludek Bogner.

Story: Haskell Barkin, J. Michael Straczynski.
Music: John Tucker.

Cast: Harry Morgan (Edgar Witherspoon); Cedric Smith (Dr Jeremy Sinclair); Barbara Chilcott (Mrs Milligan); Eve Crawford (Cynthia); Pixie Bigelow (Miss Walker).

Story: A psychiatrist sent to investigate an old man discovers that he has built a complicated contraption which prevents the world from falling apart. The psychiatrist ends up inheriting his burden.

2: 'Extra Innings'

Writer: Tom Palmer.

Director: Doug Jackson.

Director of Photography: **Music:** Louis Natale.
Ron Orieux.

Cast: Marc Singer (Ed Hamler/Monty Hanks); Amber Lea Weston (Paula); Tracey Cunningham (Cindy Hamler); J. Winston Carroll (McIntyre); James O'Regan (Umpire); Lynn Vogt (Receptionist); Don Chevrier (Announcer).

Story: An injured baseball player is magically transported back to 1909 by a baseball card showing a player who looks just like him. He ends up staying in the past and becoming a champion.

3: 'The Crossing'

Writer: Ralph Phillips.   **Director:** Paul Lynch.
Director of Photography: **Music:** John Welsman.
Ron Orieux.

Cast: Ted Shackelford (Father Mark Cassidy); Gerard Parkes (Monsignore); Serge Leblanc (Billy); Shelagh Harcourt (Kelly); Bunty Webb (Maggie Dugan).

Story: A stressed-out priest experiences visions of car crashes, caused by the guilt he feels over the death of a friend who died in a car accident from which he escaped. He eventually trades his life for hers.

4: 'The Hunters'

Writers: Paul Chitlik and   **Director:** Paul Lynch.
Jeremy Bertrand Finch.   **Director of Photography:**
Music: Louis Natale.   Ludek Bogner.

Cast: Louise Fletcher (Dr Cline); Michael Hogan (Sheriff Roy); Steven Andrade (Steve [Bob]); Bob Warner (Farmer Jacob); Les Carlson (Jim Hilsen [Holsen]); Jonathon Potts (John [Teaching Assistant]).

Story: After a prehistoric archaeological site is discovered, local animals are found slaughtered. The cave paintings on the walls come to life and murder an archaeologist, but the local sheriff erases them.

Note: Some characters' names are incorrectly identified in the end credits. We have listed both versions, with the end credits between square brackets.

5: 'Dream Me A Life'

Writer: J. Michael Straczynski.   **Director:** Allan King.
Director of Photography: **Music:** Christopher Dedrick.
Ludek Bogner.

Cast: Eddie Albert (Roger Simpson Leads); Frances Hyland (Laura Kincaid); Barry Morse (Frank); Joseph Shaw (Kincaid); Michelyn Emille (Nurse); Jack Mather, Warren Van Evera (Boarders).

Story: A grief-stricken widower meets an equally grief-stricken widow in his dreams. Helped by her husband's shade, he pulls her out of her autism and together, they rediscover the joys of life.

6: 'Memories'

Writer: Bob Underwood.   **Director:** Richard Bugajski.
Director of Photography: **Music:** Louis Natale.
Andreas Poulsson.

Cast: Barbara Stock (Mary McNeal); Nigel Bennett (Jim Sinclair); James Kidnie (Vigilante); Judy Sinclair (Mrs Gustin); Deidre Flanagan (Mrs Vivencore); Alan Rosenthal (Man); Lucy Filippone (Woman).

Story: A regression therapist finds herself transported to a universe where everybody remembers their past lives, and ends up teaching people how to forget them.

7: 'The Hellgramite Method'

Writer: William Selby.   **Director:** Gilbert Shilton.
Director of Photography: **Music:** Carlos Lopes,
Andreas Poulsson.   Aidan Mason.

Cast: Timothy Bottoms (Miley Judson); Leslie Yeo (Dr Eugene Murrich); Julie Khaner (Annie Judson); Alec Willows (Jamie); Illya Woloshyn (Chad); Gerry Salsberg (Stranger).

Story: An alcoholic discovers that the pill he has taken to quit drinking has released a worm into his body that will kill him unless he stops drinking. Eventually, he overcomes his addiction.

8: 'Our Sylena is Dying'

Writer: J. Michael Straczynski.   **Story:** Rod Serling.
Director: Bruce Pittman.   **Director of Photography:**
Music: Louis Natale.   Robin Miller.

Cast: Terri Garber (Debra Brockman); Jennifer Dale (Sylena Brockman); Charmion King (Diane (Martha) Brockman); R. H. Thompson (Dr Burrell); Aileen Taylor Smith (Martha (Diane) Brockman); Paul Bettis (Orville); Patricia Idette (Susan); Jackie McLeod, Ann Turnbull (Nurses); Rob McClure (Doctor); Tim Koetting (Specialist); Ron Payne (Officer).

Story: A dying old woman steals the life-force of her niece, but the local doctor discovers the plot. The old woman dies in a fire and the niece recovers her youth. But the old woman's sister, who stole her own daughter's life, escapes.

Note: This story was based on an unproduced *Twilight Zone* outline by Rod Serling.

9: 'The Call'

Writer: J. Michael Straczynski.   **Director:** Gilbert Shilton.
Director of Photography: **Music:** John Welsman.
Andreas Poulsson.

Cast: William Sanderson (Norman Blane); Dan Redican (Co-Worker); Julie Khaner (Voice of Mary-Ann Lindeby); Jill Frappier (Museum Patron); Ian Nothnagel (Museum Attendant); Djanet Sears (Information Lady).

Story: A lonely man finds himself talking on the telephone with the ghost of a sculptress who committed suicide. He eventually turns into a statue.

10: 'The Trance'

Writers: Jeff Stuart and   **Director:** Randy Bradshaw.
J. Michael Straczynski.   **Director of Photography:**
Music: John Welsman.   Andreas Poulsson.

Cast: Peter Scolari (Leonard Randall); Neil Munro (Don); Jeanne Beker (Daphne Blake); Ted Simonett (Gerry); Hrant Alianak (Dr Greenburg); Mona Matteo (Julia); Glynis Davies (Believer).

Story: A con artist who pretends to channel Delos, an ancient Atlantean, becomes possessed by a real spirit who destroys his career by telling the truth.

11: 'Acts of Terror'

Writer: J. Michael Straczynski.   **Director:** Brad Turner.
Director of Photography: **Music:** Louis Natale.
Andreas Poulsson.

Cast: Melanie Mayron (Louise Simonson); Kenneth Welsh

(Jack Simonson); Kate Lynch (Sister); Lee J. Campbell (Phil); James Barron (Postman); Trevor Bain (Policeman).

Story: A housewife abused by her husband is avenged by a porcelain dog which becomes real.

12: '20/20 Vision'

Writer: Robert Walden.
Director of Photography: Robin Miller.
Director: Jim Purdy.
Music: Glenn Morley, Lawrence Shragge.

Cast: Michael Moriarty (Warren Cribbens); David Hemblen (Cutler); Cynthia Belliveau (Sandy); Grant Roll (Vern Slater); Diane Douglass (Teller); Evelyn Kaye (Mrs Slater); Calum McGeachie (Slater Boy).

Story: A kind-hearted banker's new glasses enable him to see into the future, help a farmer on the verge of foreclosure and thwart his greedy boss.

13: 'There Was an Old Woman'

Writer: Tom J. Astle.
Director of Photography: Andreas Poulsson.
Director: Otta Hanus.
Music: Micky Erbe, Maribeth Solomon.

Cast: Colleen Dewhurst (Alley Parker); Maria Ricossa (Nancy Harris); Alf Humphreys (Mr Harris); Zachary Bennett (Brian Harris); David Hughes (Librarian); Marilyn Smith (Real Estate Agent); Karl Pruner (Martin Glazer); Ferne Downey (Page Glazer).

Story: An ageing, discouraged writer of children's books is given new hope by the ghost of a boy to whom she gave one of her autographed books.

14: 'The Trunk'

Writers: Paul Chitlik and Jeremy Bertrand Finch.
Music: Carlos Lopes, Aidan Mason.

Director: Steve DiMarco.
Director of Photography: Ron Orieux.

Cast: Bud Cort (Willy Gardner); Lisa Schrage (Candy); Milan Cheylov (Danny); Rummy Bishop (Old Man); Elena Kudara (Mrs Kudaba); Kelly Denomme (Young Woman); Gerry Quigley (Cap); Mark Danton (Rocco).

Story: The kind-hearted manager of a fleabag hotel finds a trunk that creates whatever one wishes. After he appears to have become rich, the trunk saves him from thugs who want to rob him, then helps him find love.

15: 'Appointment on Route 17'

Writer: Haskell Barkin.
Director of Photography: Peter Benison.

Director: René Bonnière.
Music: John Welsman.

Cast: Paul Le Mat (Tom Bennett); Marianna Pascal (Mary-Jo); Rosemary Dunsmore, Chris Bondy (Co-Workers); Lori Hallier (Waitress); Tannis Burnett, Lucinda Neilsen (Secretaries).

Story: A man who had a heart-transplant experiences a change in personality and falls in love with the girlfriend of the man whose heart he now has.

16: 'The Cold Equations'

Writer: Alan Brennert.
Director: Martin Lavut.
Music: Micky Erbe, Maribeth Solomon.

Story: Tom Godwin.
Director of Photography: Robin Miller.

Cast: Terence Knox (Thomas Bartin); Christianne Hirt (Marilyn Lee Cross); Barclay Hope (Gerry Cross); Michael J. Reynolds (Commander Delhart); Nicky Guadagni (Clerk).

Story: Because he doesn't have enough fuel to complete his vital mission, the pilot of an emergency dispatch spaceship is forced to jettison a teenage girl stowaway.

Note: Tom Godwin's story originally appeared in *Astounding Science-Fiction* (later *Analog*) in 1954.

17: 'Strangers in Possum Meadows'

Writers: Paul Chitlik and Jeremy Bertrand Finch.
Music: Louis Natale.

Director: Sturla Gunnarsson.
Director of Photography: Peter Benison.

Cast: Steve Kanaly (Danny Wilkins); Laura Press (Mrs Wilkins); Benjamin Barrett (The Scout).

Story: A single mother and a boy meet an alien scout who shows compassion by not taking them back as samples.

18: 'Street of Shadows'

Writer: Michael Reaves.
Director of Photography: Peter Benison.

Director: Richard Bugajski.
Music: John Tucker.

Cast: Charles Haid (Steve Cranston); Angela Gei (Elaine Cranston); Reiner Schwarz (Attorney); Shawn Lawrence (Frederick Perry); James Mainprize (Butler); Marla Lukofsky (Counsellor); Lisa Jakub (Lisa); Philip Williams (Repair Man).

Story: A desperate unemployed man is shot during a burglary. He trades places with the heartless businessman who shot him, just long enough to save his homeless shelter.

19: 'Something in the Walls'

Writer: J. Michael Straczynski.   **Director:** Allan Kroeker.
Director of Photography: **Music:** Jon Goldsmith.
Robert Fresco.

Cast: Deborah Raffin (Sharon Miles); Damir Andrei (Dr Mallory Craig); Lally Cadeau (Rebecca Robb); Kate Parr (Maid); Douglas Carrigan, Janice Green, Aaron Ross Fraser, Martha Cronyn (Wall People).

Story: In a sanatorium, a psychiatrist meets a woman who is terrified by creatures who live in the patterns on the walls and carpets. They end up taking over her body and turning her into a pattern.

Note: This story was reportedly based on the short story *Wood* by Michael Langford, published in 1986 in the anthology *Afterlives*, edited by Pamela Sargent and Ian Watson.

20: 'A Game of Pool'

Writer: George Clayton   **Director:** Randy Bradshaw.
Johnson.   **Director of Photography:**
Music: Louis Natale.   Brian R. R. Hebb.

Cast: Maury Chaykin (Fats Brown); Esai Morales (Jesse Cardiff); Paul Jolicoeur (Customer); Guy Sanvido (Owner); Elliot McIver (Player).

Story: Pool player Jesse Cardiff bets his life to challenge Fats Brown, the greatest player who ever lived. He loses and, instead of immortality, is condemned to a life of being second-best.

Note: This is a remake of *The Twilight Zone* episode 70, but with George Clayton Johnson's original ending.

21: 'The Wall'

Writer: J. Michael Straczynski. **Director:** Atom Egoyan.
Director of Photography: **Music:** Jon Goldsmith.
Brian R. R. Hebb.

Cast: John Beck (Major Alexander McAndrews); Patricia
Collins (Village Leader); George R. Robertson (General Greg
Slater); Eugene Clark (Captain Henry Kincaid); Robert Collins
(2nd Lieutenant Emilio Perez); Sharon Corder (Technician);
Jack Blum, Steve Atkinson (Advisors).

Story: A test pilot is sent through a gate into another dimension and discovers a Utopian society. Unlike the previous vol-
unteers, he chooses to do his duty and return to Earth, but when
he finds that the military are planning to destroy the Utopia, he
destroys the gate and returns there.

22: 'Room 2426'

Writers: Jeremy Bertrand **Director:** Richard Bugajski.
Finch and Paul Chitlik. **Director of Photography:**
Music: John Tucker. Robert Fresco.

Cast: Dean Stockwell (Martin Decker); Brent Carver (Josef);
Peter Boretski (Dr Ostroff); Walter Massey (Professor); Nicholas
Pasco, Al Therrien (Orderlies).

Story: A scientist being tortured by a totalitarian state is tricked
into believing he can escape through teleportation; he then really escapes through the power of his mind.

23: 'The Mind of Simon Foster'

Writer: J. Michael Straczynski. **Director:** Doug Jackson.
Director of Photography: **Music:** Louis Natale.
Robert Fresco.

Cast: Bruce Weitz (Simon Foster); Geza Kovacs (Quint); Ilse Von Glatz (Counsellor); Rafe MacPherson (Manager); Reg Dreger (Principal); Jennifer Griffin (Carolyn); Alyson Court (Beverly).

Story: An unemployed man desperate for money is forced to sell his memories, until he realises the extent of his loss, and forces the broker to cram his head full of other people's memories.

24: 'Cat and Mouse'

Writer: Christy Marx.　　**Director:** Eric Till.
Director of Photography:　**Music:** John Welsman.
Andreas Poulsson.
Cast: Pamela Bellwood (Andrea Moffitt); Page Fletcher (Guillaume De Marchaux); Gwynyth Walsh (Elaine); John Blackwood (Carl); Peg Christopherson (Assistant Vet).

Story: A mousey pharmacist's new cat turns into the Prince Charming she has been waiting for, but he turns out to be an unfaithful cad so she has him fixed.

25: 'Many, Many Monkeys'

Writer: William Froug.　　**Director:** Richard Bugajski.
Director of Photography:　**Music:** Mark Korven.
Andreas Poulsson.

Cast: Karen Valentine (Nurse Claire Hendricks); Jackie Burroughs (Jean Reed); Ken Pogue (Dr Eddie Peterson); Jan Filips (Dr Friedman); Norah Grant (Nurse Susan); Warren Van Evera (Mr Wells); John Gardiner (Mr Reed).

Story: A cold-hearted hospital nurse believes that lack of compassion is what really triggered an epidemic of blindness, and becomes psychosomatically blind herself.

Note: This story was based on an unproduced *Twilight Zone* script written by producer William Froug.

26: 'Rendezvous in a Dark Place'

Writer: J. Michael Straczynski. **Director:** René Bonnière.
Director of Photography: **Music:** Louis Natale.
Andreas Poulsson.

Cast: Janet Leigh (Barbara LeMay); Stephen McHattie (Death); Malcom Stewart (Jason LeMay); Todd Duckworth (Trent); Lorne Gossette (Minister); Michael Miller (Detective); Eric House (Dying Man).

Story: An old woman obsessed by death meets the Grim Reaper and eventually becomes his assistant.

27: 'Special Service'

Writer: J. Michael Straczynski. **Director:** Randy Bradshaw.
Director of Photography: **Music:** John Welsman.
Andreas Poulsson.

Cast: David Naughton (John Sellick); Keith Knight (Archie the Repair Man); Susan Roman (Leslie Sellick); Elias Zarou (Network Manager); Marlon McGann (Receptionist); Barbara Von Radicki (Fan).

Story: A man discovers that his life is the subject of all the programmes on a television channel.

28: 'Love is Blind'

Writer: Cal Willingham. **Director:** Gilbert Shilton.
Director of Photography: **Music:** Carlos Lopes,
Andreas Poulsson. Aidan Mason.

Cast: Ben Murphy (Jack Haines); Sneezy Waters (Blind Singer);

Eric Keenleyside (Bartender); Steve Adams (Taylor); Cindy Girling (Elaine Haines); John Novak (Man).

Story: A jealous trucker who has planned to kill his wife and her suspected lover (who turns out to be just a friend) meets a blind singer who knows his plans and literally shows him the error of his ways.

29: 'Crazy as a Soup Sandwich'

Writer: Harlan Ellison.
Director of Photography: Robert Fresco.

Director: Paul Lynch.
Music: Louis Natale.

Cast: Anthony Franciosa (Arky Lockner); Wayne Robson (Nino Lancaster); Susan Wright (Miss Thorne); Laurie Paton (Cassandra Fishbine); George Buza (Gus); B. J. McQueen (Bork); Garry Robbins (Volkerps); Thick Wilson (Voice of Volkerps).

Story: A petty thief who has sold his soul to a crafty demon confesses to a crime lord. The gangster gets rid of the demon, but is revealed to be a master of demons himself.

30: 'Father and Son Game'

Writers: Paul Chitlik and Jeremy Bertrand Finch.
Music: John Welsman.

Director: Randy Bradshaw.
Director of Photography: Brian R. R. Hebb.

Cast: Ed Marinaro (Darius Stevens); Patricia Phillips (Anita Stevens); Eugene Robert Glazer (Michael Stevens); Richard Monette (Dr Wilson); George Touliatos (Dave); Mark Melymick (Larry).

Story: An ageing industrialist has his memories transplanted into an artificial body, but his son challenges his right to say he is alive. The pressure kills the android, but the personality goes on to fight as a disembodied computer intelligence.

The Twilight Zone:
Rod Serling's Lost Classics

The latest incarnation of *The Twilight Zone* was a two-hour television special aired by CBS in May 1994, during a period known as the 'rating sweeps', when networks attempt to boost their percentages of the viewing audience in order to increase their future advertising revenues.

Lost Classics began with an unproduced Serling screenplay, *Where the Dead Are*, and various treatments discovered by Carol Serling, Rod's widow and literary executor, while sorting out material for the Serling Archives for Ithaca College where Serling taught. Mrs Serling handed these to her lawyer, Rene Golden, who passed them on to his clients, producers Michael O'Hara and Lawrence Horowitz, whose credits include the mini-series *Switched at Birth* and a tele-film, *Moments of Truth*.

Where the Dead Are was a welcome change of pace from the usual TV-movie fare,' declared O'Hara in an interview with the *Los Angeles Times*. 'It's no fault of the writers writing the material because fact-based stories are the market, but those are narrow. This is pure imagination, a period piece, literate – some might say wordy. If Rod Serling's name weren't on it, it wouldn't have a chance of getting made.'

Since the networks wanted a two-hour special for the May sweeps period, the producers called in Richard Matheson to script *The Theatre*, a 30-minute story based on one of Serling's treatments.

According to Carol Serling, there are five or six more unproduced treatments and one other screenplay still in existence. 'A lot of people out there want to do a remake [of *The Twilight Zone*], but I'm not rushing to do that,' said Mrs Serling. 'If something was done right the first time, why do it again?'

Executive Producers: Michael O'Hara, Lawrence Horowitz.
Producer: S. Bryan Hickox.
Supervising Producer: Carol Serling.
Associate Producers: Bob Phillips, Joseph Plager.
Director of Photography: Jacek Laskus.
Music: Patrick Williams.
Narrator: James Earl Jones.

1: 'The Theatre' (half-hour episode)

26 May 1994

Writer: Richard Matheson.   **Story:** Rod Serling.
Director: Robert Markowitz.

Cast: Amy Irving (Melissa Sanders); Gary Cole (Dr Jim McCain); Heidi Swedberg, Priscilla Pointer, Scott Burkholder, Don Bloomfield, Michael Burgess, Grey Silbley, Alex Van, Deborah Winstead (Extras).

Story: A sculptress who refuses to marry her doctor boyfriend goes to see a Cary Grant movie (*His Girl Friday*). What she actually sees is a movie about her own future. She eventually dies just as the movie had predicted.

Note: In the original Serling treatment, Melissa was a secretary in love with a co-worker.

2: 'Where the Dead Are'
(one-and-a-half-hour episode)

Writer: Rod Serling.   **Director:** Robert Markowitz.

Cast: Jack Palance (Jeremy Wheaton); Patrick Bergen (Dr

Benjamin Ramsey); Jenna Stern (Susan Wheaton); Julia Campbell (Maureen Flannagan); Peter McRobbie, Bill Bolender, Malachy McCourt, J. Michael Hunter, Stan Kelly, Tony Pender, Hank Troscianiec, Mark Joy, Richard K. Olsen, Chris O'Neill (Extras).

Story: In 1868, a surgeon obsessed with fighting death travels to an isolated island where a chemist has discovered a drug which brings the dead back to life. He has injected the drug into the island's population and has become their prisoner. When he realises that he, himself, is about to die, he replaces the drug with water. The islanders begin to revert to a corpse-like state. The doctor escapes with the chemist's young niece, but she turns out to have been a reanimated corpse as well. However, he is now reconciled to the ineluctability of death.

Note: Jack Palance won an Emmy when he starred in Serling's television classic *Requiem for a Heavyweight*.

The Twilight Zone: Showtime Version

In spite of the low ratings garnered by Rod Serling's *Lost Classics*, *The Twilight Zone* will once again resurface on American television, this time as two two-hour 'specials', each comprised of four half-hour episodes, scheduled to be broadcast during 1995 on the US cable network Showtime.

This *Twilight Zone* 'revisited' is a co-production between CBS (which owns the rights to the show) and the Canadian company Atlantis, which has already been involved in the production of the syndicated version of *The New Twilight Zone*. The shows will be made in Canada.

The eight new half-hour episodes are written by J. D. Feigelson, whose credits include writing and directing *The Burning Man* (episode 8b) and *The Little People of Killany Woods* (episode 14b) on *The New Twilight Zone*. According to Feigelson, these are original stories, but follow the Rod Serling 'format' (including a yet-to-be-cast host).

The titles of the episodes are: 1. *Night Sighting*; 2. *The Wormhole Crossing*; 3. *The Skirmishers*; 4. *Snow*; 5. *The First Ding*; 6. *Croaked*; 7. *Perfect Strategy* and 8. *Wishful Thinking*.

SPOTLIGHTS

Spotlight: Rod Serling

Rodman Edward Serling was born on Christmas Day, 1924, in Syracuse, New York, the second son of Sam and Esther Serling. Soon after his birth, his parents moved to the small town of Binghamton, where they opened a grocery store. As a child, Serling was precocious, frenetic and gifted with a sharp intelligence and an obvious love for language. But he was also insecure and needed to be the focus of attention; these were all qualities that would shape the rest of his life. Helen Foley, Rod's seventh grade teacher, whom he later immortalised in *The Twilight Zone* episode *Nightmare as a Child*, encouraged him to develop his public-speaking and writing abilities. Soon, young Serling began writing articles for the West Falls school paper, which he ended up editing during high school.

Throughout his formative years, Serling also became a fervent devotee of radio dramas, such as those produced by Norman Corwin, Orson Welles – Serling was 14 when Welles broadcast his famous *War of the Worlds* Mercury Theatre adaptation – and Arch Oboler. The latter's *Lights Out* programme was a clear forerunner of *The Twilight Zone*, with Oboler introducing ghastly stories in a spooky voice: 'This is the witching hour. It is the hour when dogs howl and evil is let loose on the sleeping world. Want to hear about it? Then turn off your lights!'

On 15 January 1943, three weeks after his eighteenth birthday, Serling graduated from high school and, the next morning, enlisted in the army, ending up as a paratrooper. He fought bravely in the Pacific, was badly injured in the Philippines and was awarded a Purple Heart. During his time in the army, Serling also learned to box, eventually taking part in sixteen fights. On

6 August 1945, the same day that Japan surrendered, Rod's father passed away.

Upon his return to the US, Serling decided to enrol at Antioch University in Ohio. There, he began once more to write, publishing Hemingway-influenced short stories about war and boxing in the local literary magazine. He would later reuse some of that material in his plays. His first experience as a scriptwriter came in the autumn of 1946, when he began selling scripts to a local radio station, WNYC. In November 1948, Serling was appointed manager of the university radio station, a job which enabled him to write, direct and often act in his own dramatic anthology show, getting a taste of creative freedom which he rarely, if ever, experienced in the future. It was while he was at Antioch that he met his wife, then Carolyn Kramer.

In 1949, *To Live A Dream*, one of Serling's scripts written for the university radio station, won third prize in a competition sponsored by *The Dr Christian Show*. This award brought Serling a prize of $500, much local fame and, more importantly, confirmed his career choice. However, Serling was smart enough to sense that his future was not in radio, but in the rapidly growing new medium of television. He soon found a job at WLW in Cincinnati doing minor scripting chores. The following year, he made his first freelance sale: a radio script entitled *A Little Guy Named Johnny O'Neil* to CBS's *Grand Central Station* and, soon afterwards a television script entitled *Grady Everett for the People* to *Stars over Hollywood*. More freelance sales soon followed, even though some of the plays would not appear until the following year. Serling had, at last, broken into television.

Serling remained at WLW for a year and a half before moving on to greener pastures. During that time, he contributed a dozen scripts to *The Storm*, a brand-new live anthology show produced by another local television station, WKRC. These undoubtedly helped him hone his talent for the new medium. At the end of 1951, Serling felt comfortable and secure enough to go freelance full-time. The following year turned out to prove him right. The increasing penetration of television into American homes was a blessing for Serling's budding writing career. That year, he sold ten scripts to a variety of prestigious shows such as *The Armstrong Circle Theater*, *The Lux Video Theater*, *Hallmark Hall of Fame*, etc. In 1953 and 1954, Serling sold an average of fifteen scripts per year, becoming a staple of the television industry and a local celebrity. The Serling family, which had grown to include two daughters, Jody and Nan, finally moved to New York in 1954.

Serling's first big, critical break came in 1955 with *Patterns*, an intense tale of corporate intrigue, which won him the first of his six Emmys, and which was immediately remade into a feature film the following year. In 1956, Serling wrote the equally critically acclaimed *The Rack*, and *Requiem for a Heavyweight*, the tragic story of a fighter on the decline, for which he won another Emmy. Both were also made into films. Then came *The Comedian* in 1957, an adaptation of an Ernest Lehman story, which won Serling a third Emmy. By the end of 1957, Serling could legitimately lay claim to being the most successful writer in television. Hollywood beckoned, and the Serlings moved west to California.

Even though Serling was now one of the major writers in the industry, he had also discovered that the business carried with it many frustrations. Producers wanted to change his scripts. Sponsors were always wary of controversial ideas, or asked for changes for absurd commercial considerations: a gas company sponsoring a show reportedly asked that no mention be made of gas chambers in a World War II story, and a man could not commit suicide because one of the sponsors was a life assurance company. Serling met violent opposition on *Noon on Doomsday* and *A Town Has Turned to Dust*, both intended to be strong attacks on racism. In *The Velvet Alley*, written in 1958 for the prestigious *Playhouse 90*, Serling wrote a semi-autobiographical story highlighting what he saw as the corrupting effect of Hollywood: 'They give you a thousand dollars a week and they keep giving it to you until you can't live without it. Then they start to talk about taking it away and there isn't anything you won't do to keep that thousand dollars a week.'

Serling could no longer afford to quit an industry that paid him so well. Yet, he needed to find a refuge from its constant aggravations. One solution appeared to be the genre of fantasy. Because it was perceived as unconnected to reality, it was left relatively untouched by the networks' and the sponsors' meddling hands. Serling had had more than a passing acquaintance with the genre, having previously written an unadapted screenplay based on John Christopher's *No Blade of Grass*, and an SF adaptation for *Playhouse 90*, *Forbidden Area*.

As a consequence, Serling began pitching the concept of a fantasy anthology show, *The Twilight Zone*. In 1958, he wrote an ingenious time-paradox story, *The Time Element*, as a pilot, which he later sold to *The Westinghouse-Desilu Playhouse*. Its success clinched the sale of the show to CBS, and *The Twilight Zone* was born. (For a brief history of the show, see the relevant chapter elsewhere in this book.)

The Twilight Zone won Serling two more Emmys. It also made him rich and, more importantly, it made him a true star, recognised by millions. During *The Twilight Zone*, Serling reached the pinnacle of his creative years, and won the fame that he would later be able to convert into various commercial jobs. For Serling, *The Twilight Zone* proved to be the 'Velvet Alley' of his earlier play.

After *The Twilight Zone* was cancelled, Serling tried to take the next, logical career step, writing screenplays for motion pictures. His experiences in the field were not unqualified successes. Among his most famous screenplays of the period are John Frankenheimer's *Seven Days in May*, perhaps the most frightening story ever made about the dangers of a military coup in the United States, and the film adaptation (with Michael Wilson) of Pierre Boulle's classic SF novel, *Planet of the Apes*.

The twist ending where the sight of a half-buried Statue of Liberty reveals to Charlton Heston that he has not really left Earth must, in particular, be attributed to Serling. Yet, in spite of everything, Serling never became a fully-fledged movie writer. Television had taught him to write short, and to write fast. Features required, if not different skills, at least a different mindset.

In television, Serling found himself increasingly at odds with the system. In 1965, he created *The Loner*, trying to do with Westerns what he had done with fantasy in *The Twilight Zone*. The show, an ambitious, philosophical odyssey of one man (played by Lloyd Bridges) looking for personal fulfilment after the Civil War, did not prove hugely popular. Worse, Serling publicly feuded with CBS, causing its executives public embarrassment. This was certainly a major factor in the cancellation of the show after 26 episodes.

In 1966, Serling, borrowing a real-life anecdote from his brother Bob, wrote a television film entitled *The Doomsday Flight* for NBC. This story of a terrorist who plants a pressure-sensitive bomb on an aeroplane sparked many copycat hoaxes, and forced Serling to apologise publicly. It was at about that time that Serling began capitalising on his public persona by appearing on inane game shows, commercials and mediocre pseudo-documentaries. His only respectable venture in this otherwise blighted field was acting as the narrator to the outstanding *Undersea World of Jacques Cousteau* series.

In 1969, one of Serling's attempts at relaunching *The Twilight Zone* eventually resulted in the production of *Rod Serling's Night Gallery*. (For a brief history of the show, see the relevant chapter elsewhere in this book.) However, that series quickly turned into a horribly frustrating creative experience for Serling, undoubtedly the last nail in the coffin. It drove him away from Hollywood for good. From 1972 onwards, he would spend at least half of the year lecturing and teaching at Ithaca College on the East Coast.

Serling's work in the early seventies included *A Storm in*

Summer, written in 1970 for *The Hallmark Hall of Fame*, which he thematically cannibalised for the *Night Gallery* episode *The Messiah on Mott Street*, and which later became a pilot for a series that never sold, as well as a stage play; a story for Irwin Allen's *Time Travelers*, a *Time Tunnel* television spin-off and, finally, a screenplay adaptation of *The Man*, from a book by Irving Wallace about the first black president of the US.

On 28 June 1975, Serling died during open-heart surgery. He was the only television writer to have won six Emmys. After his death, he was hailed by *The Hollywood Reporter* as one of 'the most important figures of the Golden Age of Television'.

The Works of Rod Serling

Because of the enormous amount of work produced by Rod Serling during his life, in various media, there is no exhaustive bibliography and filmography of this remarkable writer. We are, however, indebted to Gordon F. Sander of the Museum of Broadcasting and to the Wisconsin Center for Film and Theater Research, where Serling's scripts are kept, for much of the information provided here. Details concerning the scripts written for *The Twilight Zone* and *Rod Serling's Night Gallery* are, of course, listed separately under these show's respective entries in the Programme Guide section of this book.

Because this filmography is not exhaustive, and because the vast majority of the shows listed below are neither readily accessible to today's viewing public, nor germane to the focus of this book, the information contained therein has not been included in the indices.

Feature Films:

1. 'Patterns' (United Artists, 1956)

Producers: Michael Myerberg, Jed Harris.
Director: Fielder Cook.
Writer: Rod Serling.
Cast: Van Heflin, Everett Sloane, Ed Begley, Beatrice Straight, Elizabeth Wilson.
Story: A merciless struggle in the world of corporate politics pits young executive Fred Staples against his boss, Ramsey.

2. The Rack (MGM, 1956)

Producer: Arthur M. Loew, Jr.
Director: Arnold Laven.
Writer: Stewart Stern.
Story: Rod Serling.
Cast: Paul Newman, Wendell Corey, Walter Pidgeon, Anne Francis, Lee Marvin, Cloris Leachman, Robert Blake, Dean Jones, Rod Taylor.
Story: A brainwashed Korean War veteran is put on trial for treason.

3. Saddle the Wind
(MGM, 1957)
Producer: Armand Deutsch.
Director: Robert Parrish.
Writer: Rod Serling.
Story: Thomas Thompson.
Cast: John Cassavetes, Robert Taylor, Julie London, Donald Crisp, Royal Dano, Charles McGraw.
Story: In the old West, two brothers are on a collision course.

4. Incident in an Alley
(United Artists, 1962)
Producer: Robert E. Kent.
Director: Edward L. Cahn.
Writers: Harold Medford, Owen Harris.
Story: Rod Serling.
Cast: Chris Warfield, Erin O'Donnell, Harp McGuire.

5. Requiem for a Heavyweight
(Columbia, 1962)
Producer: David Susskind.
Director: Ralph Nelson.
Writer: Rod Serling.
Cast: Anthony Quinn, Jackie Gleason, Mickey Rooney, Julie Harris, Nancy Cushman, Madame Spivy, Muhammad Ali.
Story: A fighter whose boxing career is over is forced into a life of corruption.

6. The Yellow Canary
(20th Century Fox, 1963)
Producer: Maury Dexter.
Director: Buzz Kulik.
Writer: Rod Serling.
Based on the novel *Evil Come, Evil Go* by Whit Masterson.
Cast: Pat Boone, Barbara Eden, Steve Forrest, Jack Klugman, Jesse White, Milton Selzer, Harold Gould, John Banner, Jeff Corey.
Story: A spoilt pop singer must rescue his kidnapped son.

7. Seven Days in May
(Paramount, 1964)
Producer: Edward Lewis.
Director: John Frankenheimer.
Writer: Rod Serling.
Based on the novel by Fletcher Knebel and Charles W. Bailey II.
Cast: Kirk Douglas, Burt Lancaster, Fredric March, Ava Gardner, Edmond O'Brien, Marin Balsam, John Houseman.
Story: A US general plots to overthrow the President.

8. Assault on a Queen
(Paramount, 1966)
Producer: William Goetz.
Director: Jack Donohue.
Writer: Rod Serling.
Based on the novel by Jack Finney.
Cast: Frank Sinatra, Virna Lisi, Tony Franciosa, Richard Conte, Reginald Denny.
Story: Gangsters break into the HMS *Queen Elizabeth*'s vault.

9. Planet of the Apes
(20th Century Fox, 1968)
Producer: Arthur P. Jacobs.

Director: Franklin J. Schaffner.
Writers: Michael Wilson, Rod Serling.
Based on the novel by Pierre Boulle.
Cast: Charlton Heston, Kim Hunter, Roddy McDowall, Maurice Evans, James Whitmore, James Daly, Linda Harrison.
Story: An astronaut crash lands on a planet where apes rule and humans are enslaved.

10. The Man
(Paramount, 1972)
Producer: Lee Rich.
Director: Joseph Sargent.
Writer: Rod Serling.
Based on the novel by Irving Wallace.
Cast: James Earl Jones, Martin Balsam, Burgess Meredith, Lew Ayres, William Windom, Barbara Rush, Janet MacLachlan, Jack Benny.
Story: A black senator becomes US president.

11. The Enemy Within
(HBO, 1994)
Producers: Peter Douglas, Robert Papazian.
Director: Jonathan Darby.
Writers: Darryl Ponicsan and Ron Bass. Based on the screenplay by Rod Serling and the novel by Fletcher Knebel and Charles W. Bailey II.
Cast: Forest Whitaker, Sam Waterston, Dana Delany, Jason Robards, Josef Sommer, George Dzunda, Isabel Glasser, Dakin Matthews, William O'Leary, Lisa Summerour, Willie Norwood Jr, Rory Aylward, Greg Brickman, David Combs.
Story: A remake of *Seven Days in May* (No. 7 above).

Made-For-Television Feature Films:

1. 13 December 1966
The Doomsday Flight
(Universal, World Premiere Theater, NBC)
Producer: Frank Price.
Director: William A. Graham.
Writer: Jackson Gillis.
Story: Rod Serling, Irwin Allen.
Cast: Jack Lord, Edmond O'Brien, Van Johnson, Katherine Crawford, John Saxon, Michael Sarrazin, Edward Asner, Greg Morris, Richard Carlson, Don Stewart.
Story: A lunatic blackmails an airline with an altitude-sensitive bomb.

2. 8 November 1969
Night Gallery (pilot)
(Universal, World Premiere Theater, NBC)
(see Programme Guide)

3. 1976
The Time Travellers
(20th Century Fox, ABC)
Producer: Irwin Allen.

Director: Alexander Singer.
Writer: Jackson Gillis.
Story: Rod Serling and Irwin Allen.
Cast: Sam Groom, Tom Hallick, Richard Basehart, Trish Stewart, Francine York, Booth Coleman.
Story: Two scientists looking for a cure for an epidemic find themselves in Chicago, 1871.
Note: This was a pilot for a never-launched series.

Television Series:

(The shows are listed in alphabetical order; however, each script has been numbered in chronological order.)

Appointment with Adventure (CBS)

45. 17 April 1955
The Fateful Pilgrimage
Producer: David Susskind.
Director: Robert Stevens.
Writer: Rod Serling.
Cast: William Prince, Viveca Lindfors, George Macready, Martin Kosleck, Theodore Bikel.

Armstrong Circle Theater (NBC)

3. 29 April 1952
The Sergeant
Producer: David Susskind.
Writer: Rod Serling.
Cast: Don Hanmer.

38. 4 January 1955
Save Me from Treason
Producer: David Susskind.
Director: William Corrigan.
Writer: Rod Serling.
Cast: Ed Begley, Mildred Dunnock.

Bob Hope Presents The Chrysler Theater (NBC)

148. 4 October 1963
A Killing at Sundial
Producer: Dick Berg.
Director: Alex Segal.
Writer: Rod Serling.
Cast: Melvyn Douglas, Stuart Whitman, Angie Dickinson, Joseph Callera, Robert Emhardt.

156. 20 December 1963
It's Mental Work
Producer: Dick Berg.
Writer: Rod Serling.
Story: John O'Hara.
Cast: Harry Guardino, Lee J. Cobb, Gena Rowlands, Archie Moore.

160. 27 March 1964
Slow Fade To Black
Producer: Dick Berg.
Director: Ron Winston.
Writer: Rod Serling.
Cast: Rod Steiger, Robert Culp, Janes Dunn, Sally Kellerman.

165. 22 May 1964
The Command
Producer: Dick Berg.
Director: Fielder Cook.
Writer: Rod Serling.

Cast: Robert Stack, Andrew Duggan, Robert Walker, Milton Selzer, Edward Binns.

168. 22 January 1965
Exit From a Plane in Flight
Producer: Dick Berg.
Writer: Rod Serling.
Cast: Hugh O'Brian, Lloyd Bridges, Constance Townes, Sorrell Brooke.

Campbell Television Soundstage (NBC)

27. 25 December 1953
The Happy Headline
Producer: Martin Harrell.
Directors: Gary Simpson, Don Appell.
Writer: Rod Serling.
Cast: James Costigan, Richard Bishop.

Catholic Hour (NBC)

55. 15 April 1956
Beloved Outcasts
Writer: Rod Serling.

Center Stage (ABC)

33. 24 August 1954
The Worthy Opponent
Writer: Rod Serling.
Cast: Charles Coburn, Thomas Gomez, Parker Fennelly.

Chrysler Medallion Theater (CBS)

20. 22 August 1953
The Quiet Village
Producer: William Spier.
Director: Seymour Robbie.
Writer: Rod Serling.
Cast: Robert Preston, Rod Steiger.

25. 19 December 1953
Twenty-Four Men in a Plane
Producer: Mort Abrahams.
Director: Don Medford.
Writer: Rod Serling.
Cast: Leslie Nielsen, Jackie Cooper.

28. 26 December 1953
They Call Them Meek
Producer: William Spier.
Director: Ralph Nelson.
Writer: Rod Serling.
Cast: Thomas Gomez, Gene Raymond.

Climax (CBS)

43. 31 March 1955
The Champion
Producer: Martin Manulis.
Director: Allen Reisner.
Writer: Rod Serling.
Story: Ring Lardner.
Cast: Rory Calhoun, Wallace Ford, Ray Collins, Geraldine Brooks.

48. 23 June 1955
To Wake at Midnight
Producer: Martin Manulis.

Director: John Frankenheimer.
Writer: Rod Serling.
Cast: George Voskovec, Wendell
Corey, Maria Riva, Akim Tamiroff.

51. 24 November 1955
Portrait in Celluloid
Producer: Martin Manulis.
Director: John Frankenheimer.
Writer: Rod Serling.
Cast: Kim Hunter, Jack Carson,
Don Taylor, Audrey Totter.

Danger (CBS)

35. 14 September 1954
One for the Angels
Producer: Stanley Niss.
Director: Byron Paul.
Writer: Rod Serling.

37. 7 December 1954
Knife in the Dark
Producer: Stanley Niss.
Writer: Rod Serling.
Cast: Paul Newman, James
Gregory.

The Doctor (NBC)

8. 5 October 1952
No Gods to Serve
Producer: Marion Parsonnet.
Director: Don Siegel.
Writer: Rod Serling.
Cast: Robert North, Dabbs Greer,
Harlan Wade.

9. 19 October 1952
Those Who Wait
Producer: Marion Parsonnet.

Director: Don Siegel.
Writer: Rod Serling.
Cast: Bernadine Hayes.

Fireside Theater (NBC)

49. 13 September 1955
The Director
Producer: Frank Wisbar.
Director: Herschell Daugherty.
Writer: Rod Serling.
Cast: Jack Carson, James Barton,
Nancy Gates.

Ford Television Theater (NBC)

36. 18 November 1954
The Summer Memory
Producer/Director: Jules Bricken.
Writer: Rod Serling.
Cast: Richard Kiley, Claire Trevor,
James Barton.

42. 24 March 1955
Garrity's Sons
Producer/Director: Jules Bricken.
Writer: Rod Serling.
Cast: Rory Calhoun, May Wynn,
Vince Edwards.

General Electric Theater (CBS)

46. 15 May 1955
A Man with a Vengeance
Writer: Rod Serling.
Cast: Luther Adler, Barry Sullivan,
Neva Patterson.

Hallmark Hall of Fame
(NBC)

5. 3 August 1952
The Carlson Legend
Producer/Director: Albert McCleery.
Writer: Rod Serling.
Cast: Tod Andrews.

6. 17 August 1952
I Lift up my Lamp
Producer/Director: William Corrigan.
Writer: Rod Serling.
Cast: Maria Riva.

14. 8 March 1953
Horace Mann's Miracle
Producer/Director: William Corrigan.
Writer: Rod Serling.

17. 21 June 1953
Man Against Pain
Producer/Director: William Corrigan.
Writer: Rod Serling.

186. 6 February 1970
A Storm in Summer
Producer: Alan Landsburg.
Director: Buzz Kulik.
Writer: Rod Serling.
Cast: Peter Ustinov, N'Gai Dixon, Peter Bonerz, Marlyn Mason, Penny Stanton, Frances Robinson.
Note: This story was reshot in 1971 as a pilot for an unsold series entitled *Shaddick*, produced by Alan Landsburg, directed by Carl Reiner,

starring Herschel Bernardi. That year, it was also partly cannibalised by Serling for his *Night Gallery* episode, *The Messiah on Mott Street*. In 1972, it was adapted as a stage play directed by James Burrows, starring Sam Jaffe and Rodney Bingley.

Insight

183. 29 April 1966
The Hate Syndrome
(Syndicated)
Executive Producer/Host: Ellwood E. Keiser.
Writer: Rod Serling.

Kaiser Aluminium Hour
(NBC)

57. 25 September 1956
Mr Finchley versus the Bomb
Producer/Director: Fielder Cook.
Writer: Rod Serling.
Cast: Henry Hull, Roland Winters.

Kraft Television Theater
(NBC)

15. 8 April 1953
Next of Kin
Producers: Maury Holland, Richard Dunlap, Harry Herrmann.
Writer: Rod Serling.
Cast: Frederick Tozere, James Daly, Pat Ferris, Jack Arthur.

16. 27 May 1953
The Twilight Rounds
Producers: Maury Holland,
Richard Dunlap, Harry Herrmann.
Writer: Rod Serling.
Cast: Barbara Baxley, J. Pat
O'Malley, Tony Canzoneri.

18. 5 August 1953
Old MacDonald had a Curve
Producers: Maury Holland,
Richard Dunlap, Harry Herrmann.
Writer: Rod Serling.
Cast: Cameron Prud'homme, Olin
Howlin.

21. 26 August 1953
The Blues for Joey Menotti
Producers: Maury Holland,
Richard Dunlap, Harry Herrmann.
Writer: Rod Serling.
Cast: Dan Morgan, Constance
Ford.

23. 11 November 1953
A Long Time Till Dawn
Producers: Maury Holland,
Richard Dunlap, Harry Herrmann.
Writer: Rod Serling.
Cast: James Dean, Naomi Riordan,
Ted Osborn.

39. 12 January 1955
Patterns
Producer/Director: Fielder Cook.
Writer: Rod Serling.
Cast: Richard Kiley, Ed Begley,
Everett Sloane, Joanna Roos,
Elizabeth Wilson.

169–82. The Loner (CBS)

Executive Producer: William
Dozier. Producer: Andy White.
Created by: Rod Serling.
Regular Cast: Lloyd Bridges
(William Colton).

1. 18 September 1965
An Echo Of Bugles
Director: Alex March.
Writer: Rod Serling.
Cast: Tony Bill, Whit Bissell, John
Hoyt.

2. 25 September 1965
The Vespers
Director: Leon Benson.
Writer: Rod Serling.
Cast: Jack Lord, Joan Freeman,
Ron Soble.

3. 2 October 1965
The Lonely Calico Queen
Director: Allen Miner.
Writer: Rod Serling.
Cast: Jeanne Cooper, Edward
Faulkner, Tracy Morgan.

4. 9 October 1965
The Kingdom of McComb
Director: Leon Benson.
Writer: Rod Serling.
Cast: Leslie Nielsen, Tom Lowell,
Ken Drake, Ed Peck.

5. 16 October 1965
One of the Wounded
Director: Paul Henreid.
Writer: Rod Serling.
Cast: Anne Baxter, Lane Bradford,
Paul Richards.

7. 30 October 1965
Widow on the Evening
Stage
Director: Joe Pevney.
Writer: Rod Serling.
Cast: Katherine Ross, Tom Stern.

8. 6 November 1965
The House Rules at Mrs
Wayne's
Director: Allen Miner.
Writer: Rod Serling.
Cast: Nancy Gates.

9. 13 November 1965
The Sheriff at Fetterman's
Crossing
Director: Don Taylor.
Writer: Rod Serling.
Cast: Allan Sherman, Harold Peary,
Dub Taylor, Robin Hughes.

10. 20 November 1965
The Homecoming of
Lemuel Stove
Director: Joe Pevney.
Writer: Rod Serling.
Cast: Brock Peters, Russ Conway,
Don Keefer, John Pickard.

11. 27 November 1965
Westward The Shoemaker
Director: Joe Pevney.
Writer: Rod Serling.
Cast: David Opatoshu, Warren
Stevens.

12. 4 December 1965
The Oath
Director: Alex March.
Writer: Rod Serling.
Cast: Barry Sullivan.

18. 15 January 1966
A Little Stroll to the End
of the Line
Director: Norman Foster.
Writer: Rod Serling.
Cast: Dan Duryea, Robert
Emhardt.

19. 22 January 1966
The Trial in Paradise
Director: Allen Reisner.
Writer: Rod Serling.
Cast: Robert Lansing, Edward
Binns.

21/22. 5 & 12 February
1966
The Mourners for Johnny
Sharp
Director: Joe Pevney.
Writer: Rod Serling.
Cast: Beau Bridges, James
Whitmore, Pat Hingle.

(The following episodes were not
written by Rod Serling and are
provided here for reference
purposes only: 6. *The Flight of the
Arctic Tern*; 13. *Escort for a Dead
Man*; 14. *Hunt the Man Down*; 15.
The Ordeal of Bud Windom; 16. *To
the West of Eden*; 17. *Mantrap*; 20.
A Question of Guilt; 23. *Incident in
the Middle of Nowhere*; 24. *Pick Me
Another Time To Die*; 25. *The
Burden of the Badge*; 26. *To Hang a
Dead Man*.)

Lux Video Theater
(CBS)

4. 23 June 1952
Welcome Home, Lefty
Producer/Director: Dick McDonagh.
Writer: Rod Serling.
Cast: Chester Morris.

7. 18 August 1952
You Be the Bad Guy
Producer/Director: Dick McDonagh.
Writer: Rod Serling.
Cast: Macdonald Carey.

10. 3 November 1952
The Face of Autumn
Producer/Director: Dick McDonagh.
Writer: Rod Serling.
Cast: Pat O'Brien, Tony Canzoneri.

11. 24 November 1952
The Hill
Producer/Director: Dick McDonagh.
Writer: Rod Serling.
Cast: Mercedes McCambridge.

12. 26 January 1953
The inn of Eagles
Producer/Director: Dick McDonagh.
Writer: Rod Serling.
Cast: Macdonald Carey, Brian Keith.

13. 2 March 1953
A Time for Heroes
Producer/Director: Dick

McDonagh.
Writer: Rod Serling.
Cast: Dennis O'Keefe

22. 29 October 1953
The Return of Socko Renard
Producer/Director: Dick McDonagh.
Writer: Rod Serling.
Cast: Broderick Crawford.

Matinee Theater (NBC)

53. 12 December 1955
O'Toole from Moscow
Producer/Director: Albert McCleery.
Writer: Rod Serling.
Cast: Leo Durocher, Chuck Connors.

63. 12 May 1958
The Cause
Producer/Director: Albert McCleery.
Writer: Rod Serling.
Cast: Sidney Blackmer, Richard Crenna, Kent Smith, Lois Smith.

Modern Romances
(NBC)

40. February 1955
A Great Man Lay Dying
Producers: Wilburg Stark, Jerry Layton.
Director: James Sheldon.
Writer: Rod Serling.
Note: Exact dates of broadcast unknown.

41. 21–25 March 1955
A Long Time Till Dawn
Producers: Wilburg Stark, Jerry Layton.
Director: Tom Reynolds.
Writer: Rod Serling.

Motorola Television Hour (ABC)

26. 15 December 1953
At Ease
Producer: Herbert Brodkin.
Writer: Rod Serling.
Cast: Horace MacMahon, Brian Donlevy, Madge Evans.

31. 23 February 1954
The Muldoon Matter
Producer: Herbert Brodkin.
Director: Donald Richardson.
Writer: Rod Serling.
Cast: Charles Ruggles, Ed Begley, Frank McHugh, Kent Smith.

185. 22 September 1969
The New People (pilot)
(ABC)
Producer: Aaron Spelling.
Writer: Rod Serling.
Regular Cast: Tiffany Bolling, Zoey Hall, David Moses, Peter Ratray, Dennis Olivieri, Jill Jaress.
Cast: Richard Kiley, Parley Baer, Lee Jay Lambert.

1970–73
Night Gallery (NBC)
187–221 (see Programme Guide)

The Oath (ABC)

222. 26 August 1976
Sad and Lonely Sundays
Producers: Aaron Spelling, Leonard Goldberg.
Director: James Goldstone.
Writer: Rod Serling.
Cast: Jack Albertson, Will Greer.

On Stage (NBC)

184. 12 September 1968
Certain Honorable Men
Producer: Alan Landsburg.
Director: Alex Segal.
Writer: Rod Serling.
Cast: Peter Fonda, Van Heflin

Philip Morris Playhouse (CBS)

30. 18 February 1954
A Walk in the Night
Writer: Rod Serling.
Cast: Chester Morris.

Playhouse 90 (CBS)

58. 4 October 1956
The Forbidden Area
Producer: Martin Manulis.
Director: John Frankenheimer.
Writer: Rod Serling.
Based on the book by Pat Frank.
Cast: Charlton Heston, Tab Hunter, Vincent Price, Diana Lynn, Jackie Coogan, Charles Bickford, Victor

Jory.

59. 11 October 1956
Requiem for a Heavyweight
Producer: Martin Manulis.
Director: Ralph Nelson.
Writer: Rod Serling.
Cast: Jack Palance, Keenan Wynn, Kim Hunter, Ed Wynn, Max Baer, Maxie Rosenbloom.

60. 14 February 1957
The Comedian
Producer: Martin Manulis.
Director: John Frankenheimer.
Writer: Rod Serling.
Story: Ernest Lehman.
Cast: Mickey Rooney, Edmond O'Brien, Mel Torme, Kim Hunter, Constance Ford.

61. 19 September 1957
The Dark Side of the Earth
Producer: Martin Manulis.
Director: Arthur Penn.
Writer: Rod Serling.
Cast: Earl Holliman, Kim Hunter, Dean Jagger, Van Heflin.

62. 28 November 1957
Panic Button
Producer: Martin Manulis.
Director: Franklin J. Schaffner.
Writer: Rod Serling.
Cast: Robert Stack, Vera Miles, Leif Erickson, Marion Seldes, Lee J. Cobb.

64. 22 May 1958
Bomber's Moon
Producer: Martin Manulis.
Director: John Frankenheimer.
Writer: Rod Serling.

Cast: Robert Cummings, Hazel Court, Martin Balsam, Rip Torn, Larry Gates.

65. 19 June 1958
A Town Has Turned to Dust
Producer: Martin Manulis.
Director: John Frankenheimer.
Writer: Rod Serling.
Cast: Rod Steiger, William Shatner, Fay Spain, James Gregory.

68. 22 January 1959
The Velvet Alley
Producer: Herbert Brodkin.
Director: Franklin J. Schaffner.
Writer: Rod Serling.
Cast: Art Carney, Jack Klugman, Leslie Nielsen, Katherine Bard, Bonita Granville, George Voskovec, Alexander Scourby.

69. 28 May 1959
The Rank and File
Producer: Herbert Brodkin.
Director: Franklin J. Schaffner.
Writer: Rod Serling.
Cast: Van Heflin, Luther Adler, Harry Townes, Charles Bronson, Cameron Prud'homme, Carl Benton Reid.

94. 18 May 1960
In the Presence of my Enemies
Producer: Peter Kortner.
Director: Fielder Cook.
Writer: Rod Serling.
Cast: Charles Laughton, Arthur Kennedy, Susan Kohner, Oscar Homolka, George Macready, Sam Jaffe, Robert Redford, Otto Waldis.

Pursuit (CBS)

67. 17 December 1958
Last Night in August
Writer: Rod Serling.
Cast: Dennis Hopper, Cameron Mitchell, Franchot Tone.

Star Tonight (ABC)

47. 16 June 1955
Strength of Steel
Producer/Director: Harry Herrmann.
Writer: Rod Serling.
Cast: Frederick Tozere, Wyatt Cooper, Jim Holden.

Stars Over Hollywood (NBC)

1. 1950
Grady Everett for the People
Writer: Rod Serling.
Note: Accounts indicate Serling did sell this script to this show, but production records fail to indicate when, or even if, it was actually broadcast.

2. 1951–52
The Storm (WKRC)
Producer/Director: Robert Huber.
Writer: Rod Serling.
Note: Serling reportedly sold 21 scripts (?) to this local, half-hour anthology show. The exact dates of broadcast are unknown. Sources differ as to the titles of the episodes

identified as having been written by Serling. The Museum of Broadcasting lists twelve titles: *No Language But a Cry*; *A Machine to Answer Questions*; *Over the Rhine*; *The Cause*; *Train West*; *The Mind's Eye*; *The Steel Casket*; *Exodus*; *Last Performance*; *The Quest*; *The Air is Free* and *Ward Eight*. Gordon F. Sander also lists twelve episodes, but with different titles: *The Last Waltz*; *The Keeper of the Chair*; *The Sands of Tom*; *No Gods to Serve*; *The Machine That Talks*; *The Tennessee Waltz*; *The Twilight Hounds*; *Aftermath*; *Law Nine Concerning Xmas*; *Phone Call from Louie*; *Sight Unseen* and *Vertical Deep*.

Studio One (CBS)

24. 23 November 1953
Buffalo Bill is Dead
Producer: Felix Jackson.
Director: Franklin J. Schaffner.
Writer: Rod Serling.
Cast: Anthony Ross.

29. 1 February 1954
Herman Came by Bomber
Producer: Felix Jackson.
Director: Franklin J. Schaffner.
Writer: Rod Serling.
Cast: Paul Lasngton, Gwen Anderson.

32. 7 June 1954
The Strike
Producer: Felix Jackson.
Director: Franklin J. Schaffner.

Writer: Rod Serling.
Cast: James Daly, Frank Marth, Bert Freed, Roy Roberts, William Whitman, Wyatt Cooper, Douglas Taylor, William Leicester, George Brenlin, Cy Chermak, Bill Townsend.

34. 6 September 1954
U.F.O.

Producer: Felix Jackson.
Director: Mel Ferber.
Writer: Rod Serling.
Cast: Parker Fennelly, Dorothy Sands, Jack Warden.

52. 28 November 1955
The Man Who Caught the Ball at Coogan's Bluff

Producer: Felix Jackson.
Director: Franklin J. Schaffner.
Writer: Rod Serling.
Cast: Alan Young, Gisele MacKenzie, Horace MacMahon, Henry Jones.

54. 9 April 1956
The Arena

Producer: Felix Jackson.
Director: Franklin J. Schaffner.
Writer: Rod Serling.
Cast: Wendell Corey, Leora Dana, Chester Morris, John Cromwell.

Suspense (CBS)

19. 18 August 1953
Nightmare at Ground Zero

Producer/Director: Bob Stevens.
Writer: Rod Serling.
Cast: O. Z. Whitehead, Louise Larabee.

1959-1964
The Twilight Zone (CBS)

70–80, 81–93, 95–147, 149–55, 157–9, 161–4, 166. (see Programme Guide)

United Nations Special

167. 28 December 1964
A Carol For Another Christmas

Producer/Director: Joseph L. Mankiewicz.
Writer: Rod Serling.
Cast: Sterling Hayden, Robert Shaw, Steve Lawrence, Pat Hingle, Ben Gazzara.

The United States Steel Hour (ABC)

44. 12 April 1955
The Rack

Director: Alex Segal.
Writer: Rod Serling.
Cast: Marshall Thompson, Wendell Corey, Keenan Wynn.

50. 23 November 1955
Incident in an Alley

Director: Sidney Lumet.
Writer: Rod Serling.
Cast: Farley Granger, Alan Hewitt, Larry Gates, Lori March, Peg Hillias, Don Hammer.

56. 25 April 1956
Noon on Doomsday

Director: Daniel Petrie.
Writer: Rod Serling.

Cast: Everett Sloane, Jack Warden, Lois Smith, Philip Abbott, Albert Salmi.

Westinghouse-Desilu Playhouse (CBS)

66. 24 November 1958
The Time Element
Producer: Bert Granet.
Director: Allan Reisner.
Writer: Rod Serling.
Cast: William Bendix, Martin Balsam, Darryl Hickman, Jesse White.

Radio:

Grand Central Station (CBS)

1949
A Little Guy Named Johnny O'Neil
Writer: Rod Serling.
Note: Serling reportedly sold at least one more script to this show, title unknown.

Books:

1. Patterns: Four Television Plays
(Simon & Schuster, 1955).
2. Stories From the Twilight Zone
(Bantam, 1960).
3. More Stories from the Twilight Zone
(Bantam, 1961).

4. New Stories from the Twilight Zone
(Bantam, 1962).
5. Requiem for a Heavyweight
(Bantam, 1962).
6. From the Twilight Zone
(selection of stories from 2, 3 & 4, Bantam, 1962).
7. The Season to be Wary
(Little, Brown, 1967).
8. Night Gallery
(Bantam, 1971).
9. Night Gallery 2
(Bantam, 1972).
10. Stories from the Twilight Zone
(reprints 2, 3 & 4, Bantam, 1986).

Edited by Rod Serling:

1. Rod Serling's The Twilight Zone
(Tempo, 1963).
2. Rod Serling's The Twilight Zone Revisited
(Tempo, 1964).
3. Rod Serling's Triple W: Witches, Warlocks and Werewolves
(Bantam, 1964).
4. Rod Serling's Devils and Demons
(Bantam, 1967).
5. Rod Serling's Other Worlds
(Bantam, 1978).

6. Rod Serling's The Twilight Zone
(reprints 11& 12, 1984).

7. Rod Serling's Night Gallery Reader
(edited by Martin H. Greenberg and Carol Serling) (1987).

Miscellaneous:

Host:
The Liar's Club (1969).

Narrator:
The Undersea World of Jacques Cousteau (1968–74); Deadly Fathoms (1973); The Outer Space Connection (1975); Encounter With The Unknown (1975).

Guest Star:
The Jack Benny Show (1963); Ironside: Bubble, Bubble, Toil And Murder (1972).

Reference Books:

1. The Twilight Zone Companion
Marc Scott Zicree (Bantam, 1982)

2. Rod Serling: The Dreams and Nightmares of Life in the Twilight Zone
Joel Engel (Contemporary Books, 1989)

3. Serling: The Rise and Twilight of Television's Last Angry Man
Gordon F. Sander (Dutton, 1992)

Spotlight: Buck Houghton

(Producer, *The Twilight Zone*)

This interview was conducted in 1986 by Randy Lofficier and originally appeared, in a different format, in Starlog *No. 115. It is reproduced here by permission.*

Houghton was born in 1919 in Denver, Colorado. After graduating from UCLA, he landed a job as a reader for director Val Lewton, then worked as story editor for David O. Selznick at Selznick International. After the war, Houghton teamed up again with Lewton at RKO, where he was involved in the production of such classics as *Curse of the Cat People* (1944) – a sequel to Lewton's own *Cat People* (1942), directed by Robert Wise – *The Body Snatcher* (1945) and *Bedlam* (1946), the latter two starring Boris Karloff. After four years at RKO, Houghton moved to MGM where he eventually story-edited the first year of *The Schlitz Playhouse of the Stars*, one of the more prestigious anthology shows of the Golden Age of Television, which went on to last eight seasons from 1951 to 1959.

His first producing experience was *China Smith*, a 1952 syndicated television series starring Dan Duryea as an Irish detective in Singapore. After that, Houghton produced *Wire Service* (1956), starring George Brent, Dane Clark and Mercedes McCambridge as a trio of journalists; *Meet McGraw* (1957), about a disgruntled detective played by Frank Lovejoy; *Yancy Derringer* (1958), a beautifully polished Western starring Jock Mahoney as a former Confederate Officer based in New Orleans; and finally *Man with a Camera* (1958), starring Charles

Bronson as Mike Kovac, a globe-trotting paparazzo. Then came *The Twilight Zone* in 1959. When Serling's series almost lost its sponsors after its third season in 1962, Houghton was forced to move to Four-Star Productions, where he produced *The Richard Boone Show* (1963–4) with famous playwright Clifford Odets.

Houghton then went on to produce many more famous television series, including *Blue Light* (1966), *The High Chaparral* (1967–70), *Hawaii Five-O* (1970–74), *Harry O* (1974–5), *Executive Suite* (1976–7) and *Dynasty* (1981–8). In 1986, Houghton also produced a low-budget horror film entitled *The Wraith*.

Question: How did you get involved with *The Twilight Zone*?

Buck Houghton: CBS hired me to work with Rod Serling, who was someone that they put a great deal of store by. They wanted Rod to be working in tandem with somebody that they knew, instead of somebody that he knew. I guess that's a comment on their wish to control matters a little bit. Actually, Rod had somebody else in mind to be the producer, but he was not somebody with whom they were comfortable. So, with Rod's agreement – he did ask if they didn't have a shorter producer, since Rod was quite short and found me rather tall – but other than that little stroke of humour, why, everything went along fine, and we became very close friends very quickly.

Q: Did you become more interested in science fiction while working on *The Twilight Zone*?

BH: Well, yes, of course, because it is a provocative genre. But I must say it was more provocative in Rod's hands than in most other people's. A lot of the science fiction that I have read really doesn't draw me very strongly. For instance, we found very few stories we could turn into *Twilight Zones*. And yet, we canvassed the magazines and collections. I don't mean to scorn that body of work, but so often it was either hardware, which *The Twilight Zone* didn't have any of, or it took place on a planet not merely far way, but very far, too far, away. I'll put it another way. Rod always wrote about people and circumstances that you knew. Then he twisted it. So, in a sense, it was not really science fiction. It was a kind of imaginative fiction, which is a very different thing. I think it would be hard to find many *Twilight Zone*s that you could call science fiction as such. 'What if there was a man who could walk through walls?' That's not really science fiction. Science fiction should involve real science. . .

Q: Did you get involved in coming up with ideas for story episodes?

BH: Not particularly, no. Rod and I would walk around the lot and talk about 'what if?' type of situations. More often than not, my function was more to water the plant than to be the plant. I have the feeling that there were a lot of stories that would not have gotten finished if I hadn't watered the plant! Still, I was not the plant. There's a hell of a lot of difference between being the asparagus and being the guy that just waters it! I think I encouraged a lot, but no, I never went to Rod and said, 'Hey, what if we had a plot where the world was all bald,' or anything like that.

Q: How was Rod Serling to work with?

BH: Very good, very easy. He was a very nice man. Very stern about the standards with which he looked at his work, and everybody else's work, including mine, and so forth. But he always comprehended the difference between what he imagined and what became reality. This is something every writer has to absorb sometime or other. What you dream of as a picture, and the actual picture itself, are never quite that silken. So, he was well aware of the difference between what he imagined it might be and what came out. Quite often, it was as good or better than he thought. But then, once in a while, there was a disappointment. When you write, you work with the ideal actors, the ideal directors, the ideal lighting, the ideal weather, and the ideal this and that. And sometimes, things didn't come off as well as he thought.

Q: Since he was such a creative person, did he have trouble keeping 'hands off' when someone else was writing a script?

BH: No, he was very good about that. Hands off indeed! When a script came in that was ill, that just didn't work – there weren't many of them. I did 110, or 115, and Rod did eighty of those, so there wasn't a lot to deal with. But, once in a while, a script would come in that just wasn't right, and Rod really could not rewrite it. He was so subjective about his work that he would say, 'Well, Buck, I can start over and do that story, but I can't polish it, or change that sequence in the middle, because I wouldn't have started there, or be there by that time, or finish there, from my concept.' So, he never interfered with the other writers.

Q: What happened when the script would come in and need to be polished, if he couldn't do it?

BH: He'd set it aside and not do it. That didn't happen much. We didn't work with that many people.

Q: Do you have favourite episodes?

BH: I have some that I'm rather more pleased with than others. I think *Walking Distance*, which is about the man who went back to his childhood and met his parents, and found out that he couldn't interfere with the life of the little boy that he was, is about as moving an episode as we made. I thought that *Time Enough At Last*, the one with Burgess Meredith losing his glasses at the end was very good. To my mind, there are very few that I didn't appreciate and like in varying degrees, to be sure. It was awfully well put by one writer. 'What did he set out to do, did he do it, and was it worth doing?' Ninety per cent of the time I felt affirmative about those three qualifications on

The Twilight Zone episodes. They were awfully well done. The crew was good. The casting directors were excellent. Start with that good material and you'll come out fine.

Q: *The Eye of the Beholder* was an outstanding episode. . .

BH: That was Doug Hayes who directed that one. I always tried to get Doug to do it when I had a difficult pictorial problem, because he was very ingenious with a camera, in getting it to help tell a story. I think an awful lot of the audience saw that picture and didn't realise that they were not seeing any faces until it was too late, and by then we had 'em. They said, 'That's looking kind of peculiar, the camera movements are odd,' but they didn't realise they hadn't seen any faces. Yes, it was very cleverly shot, and a tremendous challenge to shoot. It was quite a trick, but the cameraman helped a lot. The crews loved this work too, because they were constantly being challenged to do something they hadn't done before. You can imagine the cameraman meeting with Doug and hearing we weren't going to be seeing any faces for three days. He was immediately having fun with how to get by hospital screens just before the nurse turned her face, and that sort of business. The cameraman was having a ball making the picture.

One day, the art director came running to me with a script that said, ' "Int. Limbo." Where the heck's that, Buck? What does that look like?' I said, 'Well, that's for you to come back and tell me.' So, the crew was constantly being stimulated by the need to come up with devices. The special effects people had a wonderful time.

Q: Were you for or against the move to one-hour episodes?

BH: I'd left the show then, so that's how much I disagreed with that. Not in a revolutionary way, or carrying a banner, but I felt it was a big mistake. I didn't want to see it fall on its face, and so, there were other things to do. . . I was getting along fine with Rod. Rod didn't want to go to one-hours either, for that matter. The suspension of disbelief is very tricky, and when you try to hold on to it for too long, people tend to say, 'Well, come on. Okay, so the guy can walk through walls, so what?' To say to somebody, anecdotally, 'Now, just stick with me for a minute. Don't worry about a thing, but outside this building there's nothing, just a vacuum. . .' People will pretend, but they'll only pretend for so long, then they start to lose interest. They want something else to come popping out. You try to tell an imaginative story over a great length of time socially, or to anybody else, and you'll find your audience getting away from you quickly.

Q: An hour seems to be an awkward time limit.

BH: Well, *The Outer Limits* did an awfully good job of it. *The Twilight Zone* series had three or four excellent ones, then they had some that were just pumped full of air and were boring before they got finished. Boy, that's fifty-five minutes thundering away one minute at a time, and if you don't change the ground rules a little bit. . . One of the fatal things to do with imaginative fiction is to have more than one miracle per customer. If you've got a guy that can walk through walls and can also foretell the future, you've blown it. People won't believe it. You're stretching them too far. So, I was against it. I didn't think the hours would work, and indeed, they didn't.

Q: You weren't interested in going back to the half hours?

BH: I wasn't available then. I was doing *The Richard Boone Show*, which was another anthology that I was very much engaged in, and very fond of, and enjoyed. So, no I didn't go back. I wouldn't have been unwilling, but I was too busy.

Q: Are you surprised at the status *The Twilight Zone* has acquired over the years?

BH: Of course! I'm amazed! That doesn't happen very often. One has a feeling that, when one's doing something, that however good that something may be, that it's only good for the moment. Fine, then on to the next thing. So, yes, I was completely surprised as to the longevity. It didn't rate that well. It wasn't a resounding success by any means. We waited for renewal every year with the same anxiety as anybody else, because we weren't overpoweringly successful. I don't know. I have a feeling it was largely a matter of luck. CBS turned around and started rerunning them right away. If they'd waited a little while it might never have caught on. I don't know what made it work.

Spotlight: Richard Matheson

(Writer, The Twilight Zone, The Twilight Zone: The Movie)

This interview is made up of two interviews conducted in 1979 and 1982 respectively by Jean-Marc and Randy Lofficier, which originally appeared, in a different format, in L'Ecran Fantastique *No. 11 and* The Twilight Zone Magazine, *Volume 3, Number 4. They are reproduced here by permission.*

Born in 1926, Matheson has delighted generations of fiction lovers since the publication of his first, and most-remembered story, *Born of Man and Woman*, in the Summer 1950 issue of *The Magazine of Fantasy and Science-Fiction*.

Almost from the start, Matheson's writing career was intermeshed with Hollywood. His first novel, *I Am Legend* (1954), was filmed twice: once in 1964 as *The Last Man on Earth* (starring Vincent Price) and then again in 1971, by Boris Sagal, as *The Omega Man* (starring Charlton Heston).

In 1956, Universal approached Matheson to adapt his novel, *The Shrinking Man*. The film, entitled *The Incredible Shrinking Man*, was directed by Jack Arnold and launched Matheson's screen career.

Starting in 1960, the author entered into a profitable collaboration with film-maker Roger Corman, which gave birth to a long line of films based on Edgar Allen Poe's stories: *The Fall of the House of Usher* (1960), *The Pit and the Pendulum* (1961), *Tales of Terror* (1962), *The Raven* (1963), etc. Matheson also kept up his television work, working with Gene

217

Roddenberry on *Star Trek* (*The Enemy Within*), with Rod Serling again on *Night Gallery*, and with Steven Spielberg, for whom he wrote the 1971 telefilm *Duel*, which starred Dennis Weaver as a driver relentlessly pursued by a mysterious truck. For *Dark Shadows* director Dan Curtis, Matheson made the first two telefilms, *The Night Stalker* (1972) and *The Night Strangler* (1973), which launched the *Kolchak: The Night Stalker* series, a new version of *Dracula* (starring Jack Palance) (1973) and *Trilogy of Terror* (1975) (with William F. Nolan), a series of three truly terrifying vignettes, starring actress Karen Black.

He himself adapted his later novels, *Hell House* (1971) and *Bid Time Return* (1975), for the screen, the latter being shot in 1979 as *Somewhere in Time* by *Night Gallery* alumnus Jeannot Szwarc, starring Christopher Reeve and Jane Seymour.

Question: How did you become a television writer?

Richard Matheson: Charles Beaumont and I knew each other. We got this agent at the same time, in 1959 I think it was. They made appointments for us, and one of the first appointments that they made, if not the first, was to see the pilot of *The Twilight Zone*. We saw it, and then went in and pitched ideas and started writing for it. I knew nothing about television. This was the first experience either one of us had had in really going in and pitching ideas. We had no feelings about it one way or another. I don't know whether Charles Beaumont did. I certainly didn't. Certainly, none of us foresaw what was going to happen to it, that it would still be running on television twenty-five years later.

Q: Tell us about your contribution to *The Twilight Zone*, in particular the hour-long episodes.

RM: I just used two novelettes of mine, but it just wasn't *The Twilight Zone*. I think the hour-long format was a very bad form. For original half-hour stories, it's okay, but they expected more in a story for an hour. It's almost like they wanted a movie in 48 minutes. Whereas, with a half-hour, you can just sort of play around with a little tiny premise, almost anecdotal, with a little point to it. That really was *The Twilight Zone*. The hour just was not the form, although *Death Ship* turned out quite well.

Q: What are your favourite episodes of *The Twilight Zone*?

RM: I have a few favourites, but no single favourite. I like *Nick of Time* and *Steel* quite a bit. *The Last Flight* is kind of fun. Another one I liked was *A World of Difference*. What surprises people is that the ones that are most well-known, I like not the least, but less. I thought what Bill Shatner did in *Nightmare at 20,000 Feet* was wonderful, but I didn't like the monster on the wing. Everybody always talks about that one with Agnes Moorehead, *The Invaders*. Even now, I see it and think, 'Gee, that's slow!' I just saw it recently and I thought, 'Get on with that opening!' She's sitting there cutting vegetables, cutting. What the heck is this, Julia Child's cooking show in outer space? And the little spacemen waddle. They look like those things they used to have in cartoons. Or from the men on street corners selling little dolls that walk around. In my script, I indicated that you hardly ever saw them. Just a sudden movement here and there. It was hard to believe that she was terrified by these things with little buzzing guns!

Q: How was writing for *The Twilight Zone* budget-wise?

RM: I never considered budget. I just wrote. The type of stories *I* wrote by and large, I think the type of stories that we *all* tended to write, were not high budget type of things. Especially, I tended to write about normal people. I had hundreds and hundreds of ideas that were absolutely fascinating, but you couldn't resolve them, and I don't believe in doing that. A lot of writers do. You just create this wonderful fascinating situation and you have no answer for it. So you just don't give them an answer, you just let it hang. And very often, you just get away with it.

But I just don't like it.

Q: How were you approached to do the script for *The Twilight Zone: The Movie*?

RM: Spielberg called me and asked if I was interested. He said that I was the most likely one to work on it. Probably because I was the only survivor outside of George Clayton Johnson. I had lunch with Spielberg, John Landis and Joe Dante, and we discussed it and the general format of the picture. It would be either three stories within the context, or four. We discussed whether to use the actual voice of Rod Serling in the narration, or an imitation of the same, and I think it was decided at that time that it was not a good idea.

Q: Had you worked with Steven Spielberg before?

RM: Not directly with him. I wrote *Duel*, which was the television film he directed, which was also released theatrically in Europe. I think that gave him a boost up in his career. But I only spoke to him briefly during the shooting and afterwards.

Q: What was it like to be involved again with *The Twilight Zone* after all these years?

RM: It was entirely different. It was a film project. I was not involved with Rod or Chuck Beaumont, or Buck Houghton, or Herb Hirschman, or Bert Granet, or any of the people. It was an entirely different kettle of fish.

Q: How were the particular segments that were remade chosen?

RM: I have no idea whatever. They chose one of mine, Landis did his own original and a little teaser segment to open it. Originally Spielberg wanted me to write something for him, a Halloween story about a not-nice young man who went out and tormented these kids while they were trick-or-treating. Then all the things that were make-believe began to become real and turn against him as a sort of cosmic punishment. It ended up like a painting by Hieronymus Bosch. I don't know whether they didn't like it or what, I think it was a very good script. I think one thing that they did say is that it would cost too much money, and I can see the truth in that. Beyond that, I don't know. That was replaced by *Kick The Can* by George Clayton Johnson, which I adapted.

Q: Would you have liked to remake other stories?

RM: I really don't know. Probably if I were going to make the film I would not have remade any of them, since they've been run so many times. I probably would have done nothing but originals in the tone of *The Twilight Zone*.

Q: How did you go about bringing a new dimension to each of these original stories, while maintaining the original structure of each story?

RM: In the case of the one for Joe Dante, the original story, *It's A Good Life* by Jerome Bixby, is wonderful but one key, in that it starts off with a very bad situation for the characters, which doesn't improve. Joe Dante and I agreed that it would probably be better to have that situation come on gradually, rather than start right there in the lower depths and stay there. Start on a more or less normal level and then work through the story to the horrendous situation through revelation of it.

On *Nightmare at 20,000 Feet*, I went back to my story in the sense that it was one man alone. They told me at the time that they were seriously considering getting Gregory Peck to play the part. So, I wrote my screenplay to fit him. I had the same type of problem on *Jaws 3-D*. It was requested that I custom-write a role for Mickey Rooney, which I did so successfully that when Mickey Rooney turned out not to be available, the whole part was pointless. In this case, Gregory Peck was apparently not available. So, my approach didn't work. It would have been like the character from that aeroplane picture he was in, *Twelve O'Clock High*, where he played a bomber leader who cracked up from being in an aeroplane again, but with a gremlin on the wing. In this case, he knew about gremlins from the war, and yet he wasn't believed. He was having no mental problems. It was simply the problem that the aeroplane might be ruined by this thing, and nobody could see it but him. So that was my approach, much more low key. Then George Miller did a rewrite on my script, which made it a different type of person. It's still basically the same story, the same basic things happen, but the tenor is different.

On George Clayton Johnson's script, *Kick The Can*, they had ideas on it and I incorporated their ideas, which had to do with bringing an outsider into the rest home where these old people are, who would talk them into the idea of becoming young again. And also incorporating an idea that George had, which was that you stayed with the story after the old people had become young and had to face the consequences of what it would really be like for them in that circumstance.

Q: Did you find working on original scripts, especially from other writers, a help or a handicap?

RM: I didn't even use the script on the story by Jerome Bixby, I used the story itself. On George Clayton Johnson's, I saw a cassette of his programme in Spielberg's office and I read the script and I tried to be as faithful as I could in keeping with the changes.

Q: How did you work with each of the four directors?

RM: I worked very closely with Joe Dante on the Jerome Bixby story. We worked together on the script, he, his associates and I, all through it. With Spielberg I worked less closely, although I did work with him on the script. We had a good relationship. He has always been very nice to me, very pleasant, and we have gotten along extremely well. He is an enormously talented young man and I like him very much. With Miller, I didn't work with him much at all, although I did go in one day when he was preparing to shoot, and sat with him. I admired how he worked with the performers and I admired his visual sense of what he wanted. He storyboarded the whole context just as Spielberg always does. Joe Dante I liked very much. He's a very bright young man, and I hear that his segment is really good. I enjoyed very much working with him. I had a little problem with George Miller on his first rewrite of my script. I didn't like it, but then his second rewrite was quite good and I didn't object to it at all. John Landis, I only saw peripherally and not on a creative basis, since he wrote his own piece and directed it, and I had nothing to do with it.

Q: Were there any significant changes made during production?

RM: I have no idea. I went and watched Joe Dante shoot one day and he seemed pretty much to be shooting what I had written. I didn't watch *Kick The Can*, so I don't know. I know that Melissa Mathison, under her pen-name Josh Rogan, did revisions on it. George Miller, as I said, did some changes on my script for *Nightmare at 20,000 Feet*. The monster I preferred, and of course the technical expertise that George Miller applied. But I didn't like the almost hysterical note on which it began. I thought that John Lithgow was fantastic, but a little too frenetic. There were a lot of small things I didn't like. I didn't like the little girl or the fat man. I enjoyed talking to a few of the actors who had been in earlier things that I'd done. For instance, the man who played the doctor in *The Incredible Shrinking Man*, William Schallert, was in the film, and Kevin McCarthy was in it. It was interesting to meet all these people again.

Spotlight: Frank Marshall

(Executive Producer, The Twilight Zone: The Movie)

This interview was conducted in 1982 by Randy Lofficier soon after the set accident. It was originally intended for publication in The Twilight Zone Magazine, *Volume 3, Number 4, but was withdrawn at Mr. Marshall's request.*

Executive Producer Frank Marshall began his career in film making working as director Peter Bogdanovitch's assistant on the low-budget, cult classic *Targets* (1968). His relationship with Bogdanovitch continued with Marshall as a fully-fledged producer on films like *The Last Picture Show* (1971), *What's Up, Doc?* (1972), *Paper Moon* (1973), *Daisy Miller* (1974), *At Long Last Love* (1975) and *Nickelodeon* (1976), until he decided to leave Bogdanovitch and pursue his own path as an independent producer. In 1979, Marshall produced Walter Hill's *The Warriors*.

Soon afterwards, he teamed up with Steven Spielberg – through editor Verna Fields who had cut *Daisy Miller* – and was hired to produce *Raiders of the Lost Ark* (1981). On the set he met Kathleen Kennedy, who was to become his wife and producing partner. The pair partnered Spielberg under the aegis of Amblin Entertainment and went on to produce every subsequent Spielberg picture, including *Poltergeist* (1982), *E.T.* (1982), *The Twilight Zone: The Movie* (1983), *Gremlins* (1984), *Indiana Jones and the Temple of Doom* (1984), *The Color Purple* (1986), *Who Framed Roger Rabbit?* (1988), *Indiana Jones and the Last Crusade* (1989), as well as the television series *Amazing Stories*.

In 1989, Marshall decided to leave Amblin and strike out on his own as director. He has since directed *Arachnophobia* (1990) and *Alive* (1993).

Question: Why do *The Twilight Zone: The Movie*?

Frank Marshall: I know, for myself, that I remember with great fondness Rod Serling's original TV series. *The Twilight Zone* had wonderfully simple stories, yet they were always exciting. They were very unique in their treatment of short stories and I loved the O'Henry twists. The challenge for us was to try to create that same excitement with the new technology and advances that have been made in movie making, as well as to apply the ability we have to create on a larger scale than television. I think that Steven is one of the only directors around who has done a movie that could be called a *Twilight Zone* kind of movie: *Duel*. So he was a natural to be involved in the project.

Q: Do you feel that Steven chose to do *The Twilight Zone: The Movie* now, because he felt more commercially secure as a director after his previous successes, but that he has really wanted to do it for a long time?

FM: I don't think Steven looks at things that way. He's been a fan of *The Twilight Zone* since its TV days. He even worked on Rod Serling's *Night Gallery*. I think he really was attracted to the idea to try to maintain the integrity and wonderful feeling of the original series. It's perfect timing, since we were able to fit it in between *E. T.* and *Indiana Jones and the Temple of Doom*, and he only had to direct one quarter of the movie. For Steven, as a director, it was a wonderful exercise in film making. He was able to do a short story, but on a large scale which is not a frequent opportunity. He shot it in six days. Everybody that I know and who is involved with the project, loved Rod Serling and the series. We are very faithful to the show. Our picture is almost an homage to it.

Q: When did the project first get under way?

FM: Warner Bros had had the title for three or four years. They'd been trying to do a movie, but hadn't been able to come up with a good story. So, when Terry Semel mentioned it to Steven, he was delighted to try. Steven's idea was to make it in three or four episodes and string them together with some sort of transition. Then Steven said he would put together a list of directors. That was in June of 1982.

Q: What did you do on *The Twilight Zone: The Movie*?

FM: My position on the film was that of Executive Producer. As such, I was the coordinator of the four episodes. For example, I made sure that everybody was shooting the same aperture, so we didn't have one segment in Panavision and one in 1.85. I made sure that each segment would be finished on time so that, at the end, we could put them all together as one movie. I've been following post-production closely, keeping the four editors and cutting rooms communicating, and laying out the schedule for scoring, dubbing, etc. Although each segment had its own production unit and associate producer to do the line producing, I actually did the line producing on the George Miller segment.

Q: Were all these different schedules schizophrenic for you?

FM: Yes. A little bit, because there's a lot of psychology involved in day-to-day stuff. You have to treat each segment, and each director, differently. The Landis segment, for example, was shot very early on, because he was going to be doing another movie. It was really done all out of his production office at Universal, very much as an independent movie. The next three were done out of Warner Bros. We tried to keep the same crew on these three segments as much as possible, because we were shooting with practically no break in between. We had the same art director, the same first assistant director, etc. It was shot much like television. We shot for ten days on Joe Dante's, then we shot for fourteen days on George Miller's, then we shot six days on Steven's. There were only one or two days in between each one, where the crew would adjust to the new set.

Q: Did each unit share the same pre-production facilities, such as storyboards, etc.?

FM: What happened was that we set a certain cost limit for each segment, so there were actually four budgets on the movie. Then we had what I call the 'umbrella budget', which encompassed the above-the-line costs and the post-production costs. So there were really five budgets. As regards storyboards, it varied. Steven didn't do any. Joe did some, and George did a lot. Each director was free to pick their own creative units.

Q: Did you dub in some of Rod Serling's unused dialogue?

FM: No. There were several ideas discussed, and that was one of them. But we are not going to do it. We will have someone who will be a narrator. Our feeling is that to get a 'Rod Serling Imitator' cheapens the movie and is in bad taste. We want to maintain the integrity of the old show. We may reprise the idea of a narration that led you into and out of each episode, with someone who is well respected. We will not imitate Rod, we're not doing a send-up.

Q: Was there any input from people that had worked on the TV series, other than Richard Matheson?

FM: Oh yes. Carol Serling has been very important in all phases of the movie. She's been involved from the very start and been helpful in that she's read all the scripts, she's made suggestions, helped us here in post-production. She's made teleplays and unpublished stuff of Rod's available to us. She's been really great. George Clayton Johnson was involved with us on Steven's segment. Several of the actors in Joe's segment had played roles in the series. Jerry Goldsmith, who did the music on many shows is scoring the film. Buck Houghton, the original producer, came and talked to us, and he's in Joe's segment. We tried to maintain, and be faithful to the original series as much, and in as many ways, as possible.

Spotlight: Joe Dante

(Director, The Twilight Zone: The Movie)

This interview was conducted in 1982 by Randy Lofficier and originally appeared, in a different format, in The Twilight Zone *Magazine, Volume 3, Number 4. It is reproduced here by permission.*

Joe Dante, one of the four directors who contributed a segment (*It's A Good Life*) to *The Twilight Zone: The Movie*, started his movie career as a trailer editor for Roger Corman's New World Pictures. In the course of his work, he and his friends Jon Davison (producer of *Airplane*) and Allan Arkush managed to persuade Corman to let them try their hand at film making. The result was *Hollywood Boulevard* (1976), a mixed-bag comedy which has become something of a cult classic. After that, Dante went on to do *Piranha* (1978), a low-budget horror picture intended to cash in on the success of *Jaws*, which became one of New World's most profitable films.

Dante then moved to Avco-Embassy, where he made *The Howling* (1981). This remarkable werewolf picture, which starred Patrick Macnee, and was highlighted by outstanding Bottin special effect work, made Dante one of the hottest directors in Hollywood. Dante was eventually contacted by Steven Spielberg to direct *Gremlins* (1984). However, *The Twilight Zone: The Movie* was, at the time, entering production, and Dante was tapped to be one of the four directors on that film.

Following the colossal success of *Gremlins*, Dante's career took a nose-dive with *Explorers* (1985), a shaggy-dog science fiction picture which bombed at the box office. Sadly, none of Dante's subsequent pictures, *Innerspace* (1987), *The Burbs* (1989), *Gremlins 2: The New Batch* (1990), seemed to exhibit the whimsical charm for which he had become famous, nor did they perform particularly well commercially. It is only with *Matinee* (1993), a charming homage to 1950s monster movies, that Dante regained some of his lustre.

Question: How did you become involved in *The Twilight Zone: The Movie*?

Joe Dante: Accidentally. One day, I got a call from Steven Spielberg's office. They were interested in my possibly doing a different picture than *The Twilight Zone*. I had never met Spielberg. The first thing I did when I met him was to apologise for ripping off *Jaws*. But he told me that one of the reasons he had called me in was that I had done the best *Jaws* rip-off, which was a nice thing to hear. At the time, *The Twilight Zone* was in an embryonic stage of development. Steven and John Landis were working on exactly what they were going to do. How many directors there were going to be, who they were going to be, etc. I think John put in a plug for me. There I was and, suddenly, I was a part of it. Which is even truer in George Miller's case. George happened to be at a meeting at the studio one day. Steven met him and said, 'Well, why don't we have George do one?' It's the way things happen in Hollywood.

Q: When you came in, had the stories been chosen?

JD: When I came in, the film was at the point where everybody seemed to know what they wanted to do. John knew what he wanted to do. Steven wanted to do the episode that I ended up doing, and then he changed his mind. So I inherited that episode, which didn't bother me because I had always liked the original *It's A Good Life*.

Q: Why was Richard Matheson called in?

JD: The studio felt that since Rod Serling wasn't around anymore, they needed someone who knew the series first-hand. Matheson had probably written more of them than anybody else. Charles Beaumont had done a lot but he wasn't around anymore. So Richard seemed to be the best choice for the job.

Q: Would the tone of the film have been the same without Matheson's collaboration?

JD: Possibly. Everything is a guess. You can guess what you think everything is going to be like. But you don't know what the actual tone is going to be until you see it. My episode, for example, might have seemed a little more horrific than it actually turned out to be. I think, in fact, that the whole movie moved a little further away from being a horror movie per se than might possibly have been expected. In fact, it's a little more like the TV show really was, as opposed to perhaps what people's memories of the show might be. The attempt was made to be as faithful as possible to the spirit of the programme because, during the years it was on, especially the first three, I think it was the best dramatic show on television. Yet, the stories have been changed. And that's good, because you can't give people the same stories they saw on TV, with no changes. They would all be ahead of us. What we tried to do is to sort of reinterpret these stories for a present-day movie audience. There are spectacle values in a movie that you can't have in a TV show. The trick is to make sure that those values don't outweigh the drama.

Q: How did you approach the retelling of the original TV episode?

JD: Richard and I worked on the script for a while. We originally went back to the Jerome Bixby short story. I hadn't read it in a long time, and I wondered what might have been left out. It was written in 1950. In it, the kid has awesome mental powers, origin unknown. He doesn't like technology, so he does away with electricity, cars and modern conveniences in general, forcing everybody into a kind of pioneer existence. Once their remaining resources are used up, that's it, unless they can convince this kid that things can be different. In 1950, this was a fascinating premise, but we figured that a modern kid would probably use such powers in a different way. So, our kid reshapes his world into more of a reflection of the life that a frightened, lonely kid of today might find appealing. H.G. Wells's *The Man Who Could Work Miracles* operates on much the same premise – the person who can have anything he wishes for, except what he really needs.

One thing we dropped was the kid's ability to read minds. In the original, the characters always had to say and think nice things because of this. In our story, that was a needless complication. Also, we didn't want to tell the same story. There was something vaguely funny about the way people always said how nice everything was in the original TV episode. I think that, if you ran it in a theatre today, you might get some bad laughs in the wrong places, because people might just find the reactions to the kid a bit too much. One thing we kept, however, is that, in the old story, the kid literally made television. There wasn't any electricity, but he would put images on it and the characters would all have to sit down and look at it. I found that to be an interesting piece of the story to develop a little more.

Q: What are the differences between your segment and the original *Twilight Zone* episode?

JD: I read Rod's script, and I watched the show again. It was as good as I remembered it. But it was kind of bleak and hopeless, ending where it started, with this child in control of all these people. In that, it's a rather atypical *Twilight Zone*. Most of them have a moral, and some sort of redemption takes place within the individuals. In this particular story, no one changes. The characters just realise that there's no escape. In fact, Rod Serling's last comment in his narration of the episode is that he has no comment: 'No comment here, no comment at all.' Our segment, on the other hand, is not just the slice of life that the original story was. It's a little more of a story, with a regular beginning, middle and an end.

The way that our story wound up developing was that we added a heroine to it. This was another *Twilight Zone* element that was not in the original. The original story took place in the *Twilight Zone*, and nobody escaped, whereas most *Twilight Zones* usually start with somebody from the outside going into the *Twilight Zone*. Our story is not initially about the little boy at all. It's about a school teacher who encounters the kid and the world that he lives in. It enabled us to tell the story from a different viewpoint. The kid finds this woman and takes her home with him. She goes inside his house, which is a little Victorian house, and there are these three people there who are the kid's ostensible uncle, mother and father, etc. In fact, they're actually people that he's brought in as surrogate parent figures and won't let leave. The thrall with which he holds these people in his power is sort of slowly demonstrated through the story so that, at the beginning, you don't know whether the adults are crazy and the kid is being held captive against his will in the house, or if it's the other way around.

In the house, everything is centred around the television. The kid makes everybody else watch cartoons, whether they want to or not. The inside of the house is, in fact, made to look like a cartoon. The result is somewhat like an off-Broadway cartoon designed by Chuck Jones. I talked to Chuck about this, and asked his advice and invited him to visit the set. We used a lot of Warner Brothers cartoons throughout the picture. This makes it more personal for me, because I love cartoons. If I had my way, I wouldn't mind having a channel that had nothing but cartoons and no commercials. This is where my segment perhaps breaks tradition with other *Twilight Zones*. In the middle of the story, it's maybe a little bit more about cartoons than it is about people.

Q: In all your films, you put in some in-jokes or references. Did you do the same here?

JD: Yes, I tried to put in some *Twilight Zone* references. *The Howling* was full of werewolf movie references. Whatever I'm doing, I may as well acknowledge what has come before. It adds perspective, and it's something that I always appreciate in movies. But it only works as long as it doesn't get in the way of the story. Anyway, there are a lot of references to old *Twilight Zone*s. There are a lot of actors from the show. Carol Serling, Rod Serling's widow, was supposed to be in mine but she had to go out of town, so she's in George's. But Buck Houghton, *Twilight Zone*'s original producer, is in mine, as are Billy Mumy, who starred in the original TV episode, Patricia Barry, William Schallert and Kevin McCarthy.

Q: How long did the shooting take?

JD: Maybe fourteen days. It's interesting that it was only a 30-minute episode and it took more time to shoot than my whole first feature. It would have taken less time if we had made it in the summer, but in the winter, when you have a kid, you can only use him for so many hours. In the summer, he doesn't have to go to school. But I was very happy, I used every possible minute they gave me. When you think that the original TV shows were done in three and four days, it's astounding. Admittedly, they had access to standing sets and things like that.

Q: Can you tell us some anecdotes that happened during the filming?

JD: I had a great time shooting this, because the actors were lots of fun. For example, as part of the plot, the characters have to eat a lot of junk food and act like they love it. The kid makes all the junk food because that's what he likes. Of course, our heroine, Kathleen Quinlan, finds all this rather odd. These people are just digging into candied apples, potato chips, burgers – just horrible food. The kind I eat. I told you, I identify with this kid. We have so many takes of these people scoffing down this stuff. I'd call 'Cut!' and Kevin McCarthy would keep eating! And I'd say 'Stop!' and he'd mumble, 'Oh, okay, okay,' and stop. Then, I'd look again and, in-between shots, when I was setting something up, Kevin would be eating jelly beans, anything that was around. It was just astounding! It was like, 'Kevin, come on, this stuff is cold now!' I don't know how he did it. I think we gave him some cold candied apples on his way out, just as a memento of *The Twilight Zone*.

Spotlight: Philip DeGuere

(Executive Producer, The New Twilight Zone)

This interview was conducted in 1985 by Randy Lofficier and originally appeared, in French, in L'Ecran Fantastique *No. 62. It is reproduced here by permission.*

Writer/producer Phil DeGuere's television credits include the hit series *Baa Baa Black Sheep* and *Simon and Simon*. But by the time he was asked by CBS to head the production of *The New Twilight Zone*, DeGuere was no stranger to SF and fantasy. He had also produced the short-lived *Whiz Kids*, a telefilm adaptation of Marvel Comics' *Doctor Strange*, the pilot *Otherworld* (which led to a disappointing SF series) and worked on an aborted dramatisation of Arthur C. Clarke's classic novel *Childhood's End*.

Question: Why are you producing a new *Twilight Zone* television series?

Philip DeGuere: Because it's there. Probably for the same reason that people climb Mount Everest. CBS owns *The Twilight Zone*, and had intended to revive the show for quite a while. Why I'm fortunate enough to be able to do it is a happy accident of timing. But I think it's an idea whose time has come. Luckily CBS has the rights to it, so consequently, we're doing it.

Q: What do you have in mind for *The New Twilight Zone*?

PDG: The new show is going to be considerably different from the original, I think. Obviously, for one reason: it's in colour.

Secondly, the original show had one single story in every half an hour, whereas the new one will have a number of stories in an hour. So, the format is different. And the way I've always thought about it is that *The Twilight Zone* is a territory, and Rod Serling was the first person that opened up the door to this territory. He came back with some maps, and we are now going back into that territory again, and we're going in to make new maps. We're not going to take his old maps, we're going to go into some unexplored areas of *The Twilight Zone*. The reason I think this is going to be a comfortable experience is that in the course of the last 25 years, the idea, the concept is understood by everybody. I think it's the concept itself that is viable. What we're going to do is go out and see what we can find.

Q: What is going to be the overall 'vision' of the series?

PDG: I don't think there's going to be a specific vision. The last thing I would ever try to do would be to step into Rod Serling's shoes. So, instead of that, what I've tried to do is to put together a collection of the finest writers that we can find in America, and the best directors and the best actors, and create a collection of self-contained stories. Some of them are very grim, some of them are very funny, some of them are optimistic and some of them are not. Every hour of *The Twilight Zone,* consequently, is going to be a collection of the things that you go to the theatre for. You laugh, you cry, you get a little scared, maybe you get a little message. You know that these elements are going to be present every time that you tune into the show. You may not know which is going to come when. You might be scared in the first one week, and the next week you might not be scared until the end of the show.

For me, more than anything else, it's really the chance to create a situation in which the best film makers and the best storytellers in the United States get together. What we're trying to do is a combination between film making and storytelling. If all goes well and the show's a success, I think the breakthrough that it's going to represent is the opportunity for film makers to express themselves on a more limited canvas than the big time feature film, which obviously takes more time and money.

Q: Creating an anthology series must be different from your point of view, than doing a series like *Whiz Kids* or *Baa Baa Black Sheep*, for example. . .

PDG: Oddly enough, it isn't taking the two that you just mentioned, because those particular shows were really murder to produce. *Whiz Kids* was completely impossible to produce, because 90 per cent of the people that worked on the show didn't understand computers. Consequently, they didn't know how to deal with them properly. You can imagine with *Baa Baa Black Sheep*, having to put those old World War II aircraft in the air and flying around all the time. The logistics of doing a show like this are somewhat difficult. The advantages are that people approach it with such a high degree of enthusiasm.

I don't think there's anybody who has come on to this show from the beginning, including myself, who did it just because it's a job. In Hollywood – this is the dream factory and we stamp out movies like sausages – it's very hard, especially in television, to get the best talent to come and work enthusiastically, and to come and do it under the kinds of time tables, and in a certain sense financial restrictions, that television offers. Obviously we don't spend as much money as you spend on feature films. But luckily, and I think also because it's *The Twilight Zone* and it's really held in high esteem by everybody involved, the fact is we have the best that is available. That has made it much easier to overcome the difficulties that this kind of a show presents.

Spotlight: Wes Craven

(Director, The New Twilight Zone)

This interview was conducted in 1985 by Randy Lofficier and originally appeared, in French, in L'Ecran Fantastique *No. 62. It is reproduced here by permission.*

Wes Craven's first film, *Last House on the Left* (1972) was produced for £40,000 and filmed in 16mm in three weeks. The picture turned heads and churned stomachs, becoming an instant cult classic, but did not open any doors. 'The phone never rang,' remembers Craven. 'The picture was so upsetting to the establishment that I had only one call in two years, even though it was a big hit.' Craven's second film, *The Hills Have Eyes* (1977), was also an independent picture, made again in 16mm in five weeks on a limited budget. That film, too, made money. This time, Hollywood began to take notice. Craven's next film was a tele-film entitled *Stranger in our House*, released theatrically overseas as *Summer of Fear* (1978).

Craven's subsequent projects were mostly a succession of mediocre, low-budget projects: *Deadly Blessing* (1981), *Swamp Thing* (1982), an adaptation of DC Comics' popular character, and *The Hills Have Eyes, Part II* (1983), probably the nadir of Craven's career.

Things took a turn for the better when the director's next film, *A Nightmare on Elm Street* (1984), proved to be a runaway hit. *Nightmare* not only created the popular character of dream demon Freddy Krueger, but spawned numerous sequels and a television show. It also gave Craven what had so far eluded him: commercial respectability in Hollywood. His next film was *Deadly Friend* (1986), a moving variation on the Frankenstein theme. It was at that time that he was tapped to direct several episodes of *The New Twilight Zone*.

Since then, Craven has directed several other theatrical and television films, the more interesting being *The Serpent and the Rainbow* (1988) and *Shocker* (1989) in which he tried, unsuccessfully, to create a new Freddy.

Question: How did you get started on *The New Twilight Zone*?

Wes Craven: Phil DeGuere, the executive producer, is one of my old supporters. We also share the same agent. I heard that he was doing this so I dropped some hints, and he offered me a job directing two of them. So I came in and directed *A Little Peace and Quiet* and *Word Play*.

Q: Tell us a little of the story of the two episodes.

WC: *Word Play* is the story of a middle of the road salesman, played by Robert Klein, whose very life is supported by his use of words. He's a wordsmith, as we say in English. He's able to speak very quickly and cleverly, and one day he wakes up and the entire English language is changing. Words that used to mean one thing mean something entirely different. For instance, the word 'lunch' suddenly is 'dinosaur'. When someone says, 'Do you want to meet for dinosaur today,' he has no idea what they mean. Within a few more scenes, much more of the language has changed, so by the end of the day, he's not able to understand a single word anybody is saying. This runs parallel to a real family crisis that takes place. His young son becomes terribly ill. It examines in a rather humorous, loving way, the way language is wrapped into the very fabric of our intelligence and our conception of reality. It's a heart-rending love story and comedy, and is quite touching.

A Little Peace and Quiet is very strange, because it starts out very funny and ends up extremely sober and moving. It's the story of a woman who is surrounded by noise. The noise of aeroplanes, the noise of her children screaming, the noise of her husband, her dishwasher which is not working correctly. She finds something that will allow her to freeze everything and silence everything, so that she's able to move through the world at will with nobody doing anything, everybody frozen in place. She thinks she has found her most fond wish, and at the end she finds that there is a terrible price attached to this. It's sort of a shocking ending, and suddenly it moves out from being a story about a family, to being a story of the whole family of man. It's a segment that sort of takes you off guard and leaves people with their mouths open, it's so powerful. A tremendous performance by Melinda Dillon.

Q: How many episodes have you done?

WC: I came in originally to do two segments of *The New Twilight Zone*. But I had so much fun, and they so much liked what I did, that I directed six. They just kept giving me one more to do, then one more. The feature film that I was going to do just kept being delayed, so I figured I was having such a good time and the work seemed to be so good, that I stayed and did six.

Q: How many days did you have to shoot each segment?

WC: They varied. I think the most that I've ever shot was about four-and-a-half days. Some were in two days. They're very quick schedules.

Q: What kind of stories do you most want to do?

WC: The interesting thing was that all of them were things that I've typically not done before. I've done a love story, I've done comedy, I've done science fiction. I really haven't, except for *Swamp Thing*, done anything that was like science fiction. So, I really enjoyed each one immensely, because they gave me a chance to expand and show that I was able to direct things that I never had a chance to do before. I think if I had to choose a favourite, at this point, it would be *A Little Peace and Quiet*, although some of the new shows aren't cut yet, and I haven't seen how good or bad they are.

Q: What is the spirit of *The New Twilight Zone*?

WC: Well, the spirit of the new certainly includes the old. There's a feeling on everybody's part that, in a way, we're treading on sacred ground, to be going back in and doing new classics. Or, doing a show that has become a classic. There's a great feeling of being in Rod Serling's shadow, and people on the crew walking around and whistling *The Twilight Zone* theme. On the other hand, there's a great exuberance that we're going to do better, that we have a lot more technical facilities that they didn't have then, and that we are young and full of ideas ourselves, and that we are going to outdo them, and make something a little more special. It's a great feeling of happiness and excitement.

Spotlight: Alan Brennert

(Executive Story Consultant, *The New Twilight Zone*)

This interview was conducted in 1987 by John Peel. It is reproduced here by permission.

Alan Brennert was already an accomplished science fiction writer – having sold two novels, *City of Masques* (1978) and *Kindred Spirits* (1984) as well as stories to *Analog*, *The Magazine of Fantasy and Science Fiction* and *Galaxy* – before moving to Hollywood and breaking into television.

He eventually landed on *Wonder Woman* after story editor Anne Collins bought an idea from him. *Wonder Woman* provided a 'fairly nice training ground' in the constraints and frustrations of television writing. Brennert then went on to *Buck Rogers*, which he calls another 'particularly ghastly experience'. The turning point came in 1981 when he did a story entitled *Closed Circuit* for *Darkroom*, a short-lived anthology series, which was nominated for a Writers' Guild Award. That led to a writing job on the hit detective show *Simon and Simon* where Brennert met Philip DeGuere, who was later to become Executive Producer on *The New Twilight Zone*.

After his experience on *The New Twilight Zone*, Brennert went on to become Supervising Producer of *L A Law*, writing several episodes and collecting an Emmy Award.

Question: How did you come to work on *The New Twilight Zone*?

Alan Brennert: It was offered to me because I had worked with Phil DeGuere on *Simon and Simon*, and he knew my work. I came aboard the same week that Harlan did. In fact, I was the catalyst for that. I had read *Shatterday*, and wanted to adapt it for the show, unless Harlan wanted to do it himself. I just thought we should do the story. Phil talked to him, and that's how Harlan got involved in the show. My story, *Her Pilgrim Soul,* was actually the first story purchased for *The New Twilight Zone*. It was bought by Jim Crocker over lunch in Studio City in August, 1984. Phil was in Paris, shooting a two-hour *Simon and Simon*, and mine was the first meeting with a freelancer – I believe – that Jim Crocker took. This was even before they had offices, so we did it over lunch. I pitched him about four or five stories, and he bought *Her Pilgrim Soul*. Then when they started staffing the show, Harlan and I came on at about the same time. Rock O'Bannon came in about a month later.

Q: Who decided which stories to adapt?

AB: Phil had bought one or two stories before I came on staff, like *Nightcrawlers*. But it was my background in fantasy and science fiction that led me to go to my old bookshelf and to all those old stories that I had always loved and say, 'Why don't we try these?' That was how *A Message from Charity* came about. I'd been wanting to do that for fourteen years; I read it when I was seventeen years old. When Harlan came on, he also had favourite stories that he suggested. It just evolved naturally. It always seemed to make perfect sense to me and to everyone else on the show that there was a wealth of literature out there that we could draw from. Why settle for half-baked original ideas when you could go back and get classic stories, or sometimes wonderful but overlooked stories from the literature of SF and fantasy, and adapt them?

Q: How did you choose the stories? For example, Ray Bradbury's *The Burning Man*?

AB: J. D. Feigelson had actually adapted that for a two-hour CBS pilot called *Strange Dimensions*. The pilot never got off the ground, and we read the script and bought *The Burning Man* and *The Little People of Killany Woods* from it. The latter was one that Jim Crocker and I basically rammed through because we thought it was terrific. I mean, no one had ever done a story connecting leprechauns and UFOs and I thought it was so unpredictable, with such a lovely ending. That was J. D.'s baby every step of the way. He saw it through all the way to post-production, and approved all the special effects; I thought it came out very, very nicely. We also had some writers bring us stories. Steven Barnes brought us Robert Silverberg's *To See the Invisible Man*; David Gerrold suggested Sturgeon's *A Saucer of Loneliness*, and so on.

Q: As Executive Story Consultant, how did you share responsibilities with Rockne S. O'Bannon and Harlan Ellison?

AB: There really wasn't a great deal of difference in our titles, except in terms of our individual deals. You see, I had turned down every staff position I had been offered for five years after the disaster of *Buck Rogers*, and Phil had lured me in by telling me I could work at home, and needn't come into the studio every day; I hate commuting. So I tended, during the writing process, not to be up at the studio every day. I would work here at home, then go to the studio a couple of days a week. Once a script went into production, of course, I'd have to be up there for pre-production, casting, rehearsals, and all the rest of it. On a day-to-day basis, though, Rock was the – excuse the expression – the solid rock! He was the one who was there every day, who rewrote the bulk of the scripts. He worked on *Dreams for Sale*, *Children's Zoo*, *Teacher's Aide*, and *Opening Day*, for example. Sometimes massive rewrites, sometimes simple production changes. Like when the production unit says, 'We can't shoot this thing on a vacant lot. We've got to shoot it in a store front.' That doesn't sound like a big change, but if you've got dialogue that makes reference to the location, you've got to make adjustments. Rock was basically the person who did the day-to-day stuff.

I did some of that myself, but it was mainly limited to writers that I had brought into the show. That was part of my deal also. I was told, 'You can hire who you want, buy stories without prior permission, but, ultimately, if you bring in a writer, you're responsible for him. They mess up, you have to rewrite them.' Often they did fine, but I still had to do rewrites for production. So I did little rewrites on *The Wish Bank*, *Ye Gods*, and so on, mostly just production details. Rock shouldered the load of the major rewrites.

Q: It seems that writers were given a good deal of freedom in terms of seeing their stories through production.

AB: Yes. Phil, being a writer/producer himself, believes that it's the writer's story, and in many cases, the writer is the only one who has a clear overview of the episode.

We had rehearsals, which is a luxury most dramatic shows don't have. It was nice to go into those and see the scripts get up on their own legs, so to speak. If something worked, fine. If it didn't, then you could go back and rewrite it before shooting started the next day. Casting, pre-production, rehearsals, post-production: these are all things that Phil allowed us access to. I'm very grateful to him for that, because it taught me a whole new set of skills. I never knew that I was good at editing film until I sat there in the editing room and did it. Now I wouldn't have it any other way. When I started on the show, I never thought that I would be a producer. I never thought I had the temperament for it, or the skills for it. The show taught me an enormous amount about production, and also that I enjoyed it and was good at it. It wasn't just me; Harlan once told me that he'd learned more writing for this show than he had in 20 years of writing for television. He was on the inside for the first time. He had access to the process. He was not shut out, as writers usually are, so he was able to contribute and collaborate.

Q: Harlan Ellison has a notorious record of disagreeing with producers. How was working with him?

AB: Harlan likes to define himself as a gadfly, which to a certain extent he was. He was one of the main forces responsible for maintaining the level of the writing and ideas on the show. Phil and Jim are terrific writers and terrific producers, but they didn't have the background in fantasy and science fiction that Harlan and I did. Harlan and I could look at a story and say, 'This was done in *Planet Stories* in 1939.' Harlan more than I; his knowledge of the field goes back two decades further than mine.

Harlan has very high standards, and he brought those standards to the show. He's also a terrific story man. If there's something in a story that he thinks is really worthwhile, but is buried amidst bad plotting, bad dialogue or bad characterisation, he can find a way to make it work. One story he made excellent contributions to was *Teacher's Aide*. One of the reasons that that story seems fragmented now is that ultimately about twelve minutes were cut out of it. It was scheduled badly, in the wrong hour. That story had to suffer, unfortunately; the longer version was much better. The other thing that Harlan did was fight for stories, to get them on to the air. For instance, at one time Phil was considering not having closing narration on *Wordplay*. We all felt that this was a mistake, that it needed the closing narration. Harlan was the point man: he wrote the closing narration and fought it through. He was very valuable as far as the narrations go. For the first half of the first season, most of the narrations were written by Harlan or me. It sort of fell to us because we were the prose writers on staff, I suppose.

Harlan also fought for *Profile in Silver*, which was a story that I bought. He put his weight behind it. The same with *Tooth and Consequences*. (That was one of those stories that when the original writer pitched it to us, we looked at each other and said, 'This is kind of silly, but what the hell!') He also worked very hard on *Red Snow*. There are many things that Harlan did behind the scenes that are not apparent on the screen. For example, in *Quarantine*, he didn't like my original ending. He thought it didn't work. So I asked him what he'd do. He thought a moment and said, 'How about having one of the characters say: "You're one of us now because you share our guilt in what we had to do today"?' That was exactly what the scene needed. That was just something that he came up with on the spur of the moment. It really formed the lynch-pin of that scene. He really was a vital part of the creation of *The New Twilight Zone*.

Q: Could you tell us why Harlan resigned his position of Creative Consultant?

AB: The behaviour of CBS Program Practices was just totally inexcusable. Harlan had had production greenlighted on a story entitled *Nackles*, slotted for the Christmas episode, which he had intended to direct himself. It was about a white bigot, played by Ed Asner, who tells black children that Santa Claus did not come for them. Then CBS pulled the rug out from under him. To cancel a script when you're two days into prep for shooting is irresponsible in the extreme.

The story had already been cast, and Harlan was set to direct it when they cancelled. That was inexcusable behaviour. I can understand their reservations, but it was a very poor way to go about handling the situation. None of us blamed Harlan at all for quitting; in his position, we would have done the same thing. I have to point out that CBS Program Practices on the West Coast approved the story, nor did CBS Programming have any problems with it. Only Alice Henderson in New York decided that it was not acceptable viewing.

The only other thing that really stands out as far as Program Practices and censorship was in the episode *Need to Know*, where the guy who went to Tibet and found the secret of the universe turns to the main character and says, 'Do you know what God is?' That was what drove him insane, the knowledge of what God is, because it's not the sort of thing that a human mind can encompass. They did not want to touch this with a ten-foot crucifix! They said, 'Forget this!' We tried everything, saying, 'Well, God is such grandeur and so infinite that human beings cannot assimilate the concept.' But they didn't buy that. They wound up changing it to 'Do you know what the meaning of life is?' Bleugh.

Networks get apoplectic when you start talking about God. Religion terrifies them. It's the one subject guaranteed to create problems. The Network was so nervous about what had happened on *Need to Know*, we even had problems in *The Library*, with the books of people's lives. I was amazed we got *Dead Run* through. My friend Greg Bear came up with that story, which was published in *Omni*. I showed it to the staff, and we got CBS to approve it, but I honestly don't know how we got it past Program Practices. They took out one Biblical quote when the Executive – played by John DeLancie – is arguing his case, but that was basically it. We had to do one or two little changes in it that were totally innocuous.

As we got into production, though, Programming started getting increasingly nervous about it. They were worried about the ending, about the gay character. They *hated* the gay character. They kept saying, 'I think you should come up with something else.' And I would say, 'No, I don't think so, I like the character.' Then, when we cast the actor for the part – he turned out to be the best actor for it – it turned out he was also an acting student in the course given by our Network liaison, Tony Barr! How could he complain? I was very proud of *Dead Run*. It was one of the few socially conscious episodes that we did.

Q: One of the hallmarks of the old series was Serling's on-screen narration. How did you face the question of whether you would emulate this or not?

AB: It was difficult. The final decision wasn't made until just a few months from the first air date. At one point we thought we'd get an on-screen narrator. Then, we thought we wouldn't. Through sheer inertia, we wound up putting off the decision until we started shooting the episodes and, by then, it was too late to put anybody on-screen. I think that, at the back of all our minds, we knew it would be a mistake to have an on-camera narrator. There was even some question as to whether or not we would have any narrator at all. I always thought that was a very important point, and fought to have one. That's what set *The Twilight Zone* apart from all the other anthology series. There was a certain literary content to it; the narration provided a context and a commentary on the action. Charles Aidman turned out to be the very best of all the people that we tested.

At one point Phil and Harlan had both auditioned for the narrator. Harlan would have been quite interesting, but for some reason, it just never got past the trials. Harlan was actually pushing for a woman narrator, because he felt that that would be the best way to set us apart from the old show. It was an interesting idea, but ultimately Aidman was the best choice.

Q: Can you tell us more about your own story, *Her Pilgrim Soul*?

AB: As I said, that was the first story bought for *The New Twilight Zone*. It's my favourite of all the ones that I did. It's also very personal, because it's about a very close friend of mine who died much too young. The details of Nola's life are not anything like the details of her life, but the feeling is there. Anne Twomey was brilliant. Anne managed, somehow, to really capture the essence of both the character, and the woman who inspired it. Anne was a joy to work with. She and Kris Tabori were both wonderful; they're the kind of actors who really bring something extra to the material. There are many quotes from Yeats in the story, and Kris had gone out and gotten a volume of Yeats's poetry. He told me one day, 'You know, Alan, doing the show is worth it if only for the fact that I discovered this poem.' He was reading *The Lake Isle at Innesfree*. In the script, I had him stop at a certain point. It goes: *I will arise and go now, and go to Innesfree, / And a small cabin build there, of clay and wattles made / Nine bean-rows will I have there, a hive for the honeybee, / And live alone in the bee-loud glade.* And Kris said he wanted to read the next line also, *And I shall have some peace there*, because that's what he's looking for, and that's what she gives him. That's the kind of insight and attention both he and Anne brought to the roles. They really brought the story to life.

The title for the episode comes from another of Yeats's poems, *When You Are Old*: *How many loved your moments of glad grace, / And loved your beauty with love false or true, / But one man loved the pilgrim soul in you, / And loved the sorrows of your changing face.* I wouldn't say Yeats was one of my favourite poets. I'm familiar with his works, but mainly it was serendipity. I ran across that poem about the same time that I was coming up with *Her Pilgrim Soul*. The poem fit the story so well. I had read it in college, but re-reading it made me realise that it was perfect for the story.

Q: A few stories were remade from the original show – such as *Shadow Play*, *Dead Man's Shoes* and *The After Hours*. What were the feelings about this?

AB: There was a little apprehension about this, but it was something that CBS definitely wanted to do. We tried to pick episodes – at least early on – that had not been done terribly well, one way or another, on the original show. For example, *Night of the Meek*. Art Carney had given a terrific performance, but it was originally shot on video tape. This had produced a lot of limitations in the shooting. If you look at the episode, you can see the picture blur, as it did when you moved an early video camera. We felt we could certainly improve on that technically. *Dead Man's Shoes*, we did a sort of transsexual arrangement of the old show. We took the basic idea and came up with a different story. So our original idea was to do remakes sparingly, and to do them only when we departed in some way from the original. We didn't simply want to do a remake that would parrot the original. *Shadow Play* was similar to the original, but the rest were not.

For instance, I wanted for the second season to do a remake of *It's A Good Life*, and really do the short story. CBS wouldn't approve it, because it had been done in the movie. In the end, we wound up doing a better story for us, which was *The Toys of Caliban*. Overall we weren't really too nervous about the remakes. I mean, *Alfred Hitchcock Presents* every week was simply a remake of the old show. We knew we weren't going to do that, and that overall it would be a very small fraction of our overall production. The response was quite good to them all.

Q: One story that worked well was the adaptation of Arthur C. Clarke's classic short story, *The Star*.

AB: That was something I brought in. I knew we were going to be doing a Christmas show, and the components were going to be *Night of the Meek*, Harlan's story *Nackles* and another story which Phil had in the works called *Santa's Little Helper*, which I did not care very much for. So I suggested doing *The Star* instead. It was probably naive on my part, but I had always thought of *The Star* as having an implicit message that was not explicit in the story. I brought that out in my teleplay. When it aired, reaction was of two different camps. Either people loved the ending, thought it was wonderful, or they wanted to string me up and gut me with a Bowie knife! Because I had changed the ending.

The Star was originally published in *Infinity Science-Fiction*, and it turned out that a woman named Betsy Curtis had written a story that was a sort of a reply to Clarke's story. I had never read it, never even heard of it, but Harlan had read it. It turned out that a lot of her arguments that she had put forth were things that I later picked up on, on my own, implicit, as I say, in Clarke's story. Harlan was misremembering both stories as one, and that's why he didn't start jumping up and down and accusing me of changing the story. He genuinely thought my ending was the ending of the original story. Also, we had sent Arthur Clarke a copy of the script, and I figured that if he had any objections to it, he'd let us know. But we never heard a word from him. I stand by what I did. I like the episode a great deal, and I'm proud of it. I can see how people can take exception to what I did, but I can't argue that. They're right: it does differ from the original story.

Spotlight: Paul Chitlik and Jeremy Bertrand Finch

(Story Editors, *The New Twilight Zone*, Syndicated)

This interview was conducted especially for this book in 1994 by Jean-Marc Lofficier.

Paul Chitlik and Jeremy Bertrand Finch first met on *Guilty or Innocent*, a television show starring the famous trial lawyer, Melvin Belli. 'We decided that, after working in a pressure cooker like that, that if we hadn't taken up sharp objects and tried to gouge each other's eyes out, we probably should try to work together,' says Finch. *Aqua Vita* (episode no. 26b of the CBS *Twilight Zone*) was their first major sale to a network television series. They then went on to become prolific comedy writers for a variety of prime-time sitcoms such as *Brothers*, *Small Wonder*, *Who's the Boss*, *Amen*, *Perfect Strangers*, etc. They were eventually called back into *The Twilight Zone* by producer Marc Shelmerdine to become part of a new story editing team.

Question: How did you get started on *The New Twilight Zone*?

Paul Chitlik: We got the job in 1987 when Marc Shelmerdine called us. We had written two stories for the CBS *Twilight Zone*, *Aqua Vita* and a short one which was supposed to be only ten minutes long, but which fell through when the show didn't get renewed. We almost did it for ours, but it turned out to be too short, and wouldn't have worked as a half-hour episode. Marc had viewed all 35 hours of the CBS *Twilight Zone* and he'd picked several episodes which he liked. He came to us and said, 'You guys know how to write a story, I'd like you to work on my show.' He handed us a document – I wouldn't even call it a bible, more like a set of guidelines for the direction he wanted the show to take – and asked us for our comments. Jeremy and I developed a bible out of that. The other story editor, J. Michael Straczynski, developed his own version too. We then melded those and came up with the final words to the wise.

Q: How did all three story editors interface?

PC: It was clear early on that Joe Straczynski had his way of doing things, and that we had ours. So we made a deal with Marc. If Joe brought in a writer, he'd work with that writer in developing that episode. If we brought in a writer, we'd work with him. And if somebody came in 'neutral', if you wish, then Marc would assign who would work with that person. All this had nothing to do with whether or not that episode was going to be produced. That decision was made almost immediately every time after a writer walked out of the room. Marc, Joe, Jeremy and I would decide instantly whether or not we wanted to do his story.

Jeremy Bertrand Finch: In preparation for the show, we had to become familiar with all the original *Twilight Zone*s, as well as all the CBS ones, and keep all those in mind so that we didn't buy the same stories over again. On top of that, we had to come up on our own with new takes on the same old shows. When some writer would come in and say, 'This is a great story, it could be an *Alfred Hitchcock*, an *Outer Limits* or a *Twilight Zone*,' we knew immediately that there was almost no point in hearing the rest of what he had to say, because *Twilight Zone* is *Twilight Zone*, and not *The Outer Limits*. These are very different shows. But it was quite a challenge.

Q: Did you inherit any unproduced material from the CBS *Twilight Zone*?

JBF: We were given access to the archives which, at the time, were kept at the CBS Studio City lot. We went through a lot of files. They were located in a basement underneath a sound stage. There was chain link fence chaining off these cubicles, and lights that hung a little bit too low, casting a real harsh glare. Everything looked like it was in black and white. And there were these big, black filing cabinets with all those records that had just been shoved down there. It was truly like going through a newspaper morgue. There were hundreds and hundreds of stories in there.

PC: *The Cold Equations* came from there. One of Harlan Ellison's scripts, *Nackles*, was there too. We could have done it had we liked the script. The CBS International people were not the same people as the Network people. But we decided that it didn't work out for our show. Marc particularly felt so. There were other stories we dug out. They had bought a huge number of stories. We rescued *Memories*, and also *Extra Innings*. Jeremy and I worked on that one extensively because it was about twenty pages too long, but it worked out very well. Its writer went on to become executive producer on *Murphy Brown*.

Q: Why was there little attempt to develop scripts based on short stories?

JBF: We did look at some short stories that were submitted. George Clayton Johnson submitted one that we liked, but somehow it didn't get made. Some of the stories that we read were almost like vignettes, or too deeply internal. We could have dramatised them, but then the real power of the story would have been lost.

PC: Generally, our mandate was not to do short stories, unless they were something exceptional. *The Cold Equations* was the only one we did really. We were told to stay away from short stories, because they didn't fit in the mould of our *Twilight Zone*.

Q: Let's talk about some of your episodes: *Aqua Vita,* for example.

PC: That one started as a funny idea we were just kicking around at the time. We were walking around in Venice and we wondered: what if some old lady had a crush on one of these young guys, and he likes her a lot, he visits her every day, but she's 75 and there isn't much of a relationship. Then, one day, she takes a drink from one of these bottles of water that a new delivery man brings, and it makes her young and good-looking again. And she goes after the young guy. What then? That's the story we brought to Phil DeGuere. One of them, actually, because we brought a dozen stories. And Phil said that he liked the idea of the bottled water making someone young, but he wanted more than that.

JBF: So we came up with the reporter idea. By that time, we'd reached the development stage where there had to be some higher stakes. The way we'd envisioned it originally was simply as a funny love story. But we had to deepen it as the stakes kept getting higher. So we started to take a good, hard look at what the human motivations and ramifications might be. We still liked the element of love and ageing, but we had to work them together to make it more dramatic.

PC: Another element that became important was that the water was addictive. It stood in for cocaine, drug abuse, anything you want. The first dose is free, the next one, big shock, costs you $5,000! It was as blatant as we could make it. In this case, she paid not because she had to look young, nor because she was really addicted to the water, but because she had to keep her husband, and she had to keep her job. Or so she thought.

Q: Were you happy with the way the story was shot?

PC: Yes, right up to final moment.

JBF: We tried to put a little flourish on the end, in the spirit of *The Twilight Zone*: not just a twist ending, but a little something extra. We had it set up so that we leave Marc and Christie just after Marc has said, 'I'm going to do the only thing there is to do', and he grabs a glass of water.

PC: You don't know if he's going to drink it, or she's going to drink it. You just don't know what's going to happen afterwards.

JBF: Then we dissolve to a scene in the park, and we see two young people kissing. We wanted the viewer to assume they were Marc and Christie, before we'd reveal slowly that actually they are sitting on a bench as old people watching this. That was our flip ending. Then, we had the touching speech which they retained.

PC: But they didn't do it as a slow reveal. Instead, they showed Mark and Christie almost right away. We wanted not to see them until the last minute, after a delay of maybe ten or twenty seconds. But outside of that, we were extremely pleased with the episode. We were on the set, the actors came up and discussed the story with us. Christopher McDonald, who played the Delivery Man, was very funny. He's gone on to play the husband in *Thelma and Louise*.

Q: Tell us about *The Hunters*.

PC: That was a vision that I had. I saw cave drawings moving in my mind and I said to myself, wouldn't it be great if these cave drawings moved? Everything came from there.

JBF: We kick a story around until everything falls into place. We call it 'greenlight thinking'. There are no wrong ways for a story to go. We just free-associate with it. We can correct one another, run through 'What if this happens instead of that?' scenarios, then build on it. One of us will suggest an idea, and we'll go off and explore every possibility, until we're all done with that exploration phase. Then, we'll choose the best parts and put those together to build a story.

Q: What about *The Trunk*?

PC: *The Trunk* was a story that we'd previously tried to sell to the CBS *Twilight Zone*. We talked about it, turned it every which way, and somehow, it didn't fly. We were left with this story but we'd talked about it so much, and worked on it so much, that it was very close to our hearts. So we wanted to do it and we got that chance when we became story editors.

Q: Were your stories adapted faithfully?

PC: Yes. When they did our stories, they didn't generally screw around on the set. Every once in a while, they'd write some extra dialogue, which would annoy us, like during the writers' strike, but most of the time, they shot them as written. On *The Hunters*, they did some great animation. The creatures on the wall were exactly what I had in mind when we were coming up with that story. Some of the others didn't work out quite as well. The acting was kind of flat, or the production values were not always there. . .

Q: *Room 2426* was reminiscent of the episode *The Chimes of Big Ben* from *The Prisoner* television series, except of course for the teletransportation angle. Was that intentional?

PC: Really? No, I was completely unaware of it. I'd love to see that sometime. No, we primarily thought of political prisoners, in any country. The way that came about was that we thought of teletransportation first. We asked ourselves if there had ever been any *Twilight Zone* episode about teletransportation. We found there hadn't been. So we proposed it to Marc who said that it was a very interesting idea, particularly in the way we had chosen to connect it with the concept of fighting for political freedom. We did this because there had to be a reason for teletransportation to come into play. At that time, there was a lot of interest in what was happening in East Germany, behind the Iron Curtain, so that was a natural connection. Also, I had lived in Spain under Franco when I was younger. So that's where the idea came from.

JBF: There is a seductiveness about freedom when you don't have it. Anyone who's ever been behind bars, literally or figuratively, knows that there is no sweeter word than freedom. We wanted to explore what a person would be willing to do, would be capable of doing, to reach freedom.

Q: Can you tell us about *Father and Son Game*?

PC: That one came up because my father was very ill. He was in the hospital and he became known at that time, at least to Jeremy and me, as The Man God Could Not Kill. The doctors were giving him only a few more months to live – in actuality, he lived on for six more years – but I started thinking about organ replacements, and at what stage someone stops being 'human'. If you replace the heart, you're still human, especially if it's someone else's heart. But what if it's mechanical? You can similarly replace the liver, the stomach, the lungs, the limbs – we already do that – but at what stage do you stop being human and become a machine? That was the issue at stake here, because they'd replaced *everything* including the brain. What makes the brain human? What if we can duplicate all of a person's memories and store them electronically? We can't do it now, but we'll certainly be able to do it twenty or thirty years in the future. Is that person still a human being then? And if he isn't human anymore, according to most standards that we currently follow, then it follows that he's dead. If he's dead, who inherits?

Father and Son Game was nominated for a WGA award. Another episode which we story-edited, *The Hellgramite Method*, also won a Scot Newman Award. We bought a script from Bill Selby who is a very good writer, but we ended up tossing virtually everything out but one line. We got it down to the bug! We brought Bill back and we told him, 'We're sorry, we've thrown out everything you've written, but we're going to make sure you get a story out of this.' We started right then and there and, together, we rebuilt the story in that room.

JBF: We're really proud of what Bill came up with. When he won that Scot Newman Award, he was very kind to us and he had us sit next to him when he received it. I'm particularly proud of that experience because we tried to be as humane as could be, maybe to pay the debts of the past. When Bill came in and told us that complicated, lavish story, we knew he had something there. But one of the things he said scared me, and that was that he'd been through that kind of experience, this healing from alcoholism. And I know what happens when you get into people's personal experiences that obviously carry a lot of emotional importance to them. You're likely never to get a good script out of them, because they get attached to things that were memories of theirs. They're committed to directions for the story to go that are inappropriate, or don't work dramatically, but they'll tell you that that's the way it really happens.

PC: For other series, this emphasis on reality wouldn't necessarily be bad but *The Twilight Zone* is a show where reality is bent, changed in some ways, and that person's reality is not going to fit in with the show. You've got to amend reality, so we worked with Bill and solved the problems so he could make the story work, and it did.

INDICES

Legend

NG (#): Rod Serling's Night Gallery (episode number)
SS (#): The Sixth Sense (episode number, episode titles only)
SHOTZ (#): The Twilight Zone (Showtime version)
TZ (#): The Twilight Zone (episode number)
TZCBS (#): The New Twilight Zone – CBS (episode number)
TZLC (#): The Twilight Zone: Rod Serling's Lost Classics (episode number)
TZMV (#): The Twilight Zone: The Movie (segment number)
TZSYN (#): The New Twilight Zone – Syndicated (episode number)

Index: Episode Titles

Academy, The **NG**(11d)
Act Break **TZCBS**(8a)
Act Of Chivalry, An **NG**(18c)
Acts Of Terror **TZSYN**(11)
After Hours, The **TZ**(34), **TZCBS**(28a)
And Scream By The Light Of The
Moon,
The Moon **SS**(22)
And When The Sky Was Opened
TZ(11)
Appointment On Route 17 **TZSYN**(15)
Aqua Vita **TZCBS**(26b)
Arrival **TZ**(67)
Back There **TZ**(49)
Bard, The **TZ**(120)
Beacon, The **TZCBS**(11a)
Bewitchin' Pool, The **TZ**(156)
Big, Tall Wish, The **TZ**(27)
Big Surprise, The **NG**(15c)
Black Leather Jackets **TZ**(138)
Boy Who Predicted Earthquakes, The
NG(8a)
Brain Center At Whipple's, The
TZ(153)
Brenda **NG**(14b)
Burning Man, The **TZCBS**(8b)
But Can She Type? **TZCBS**(13b)
Button, Button **TZCBS**(20b)
Caesar And Me **TZ**(148)
Call, The **TZSYN**(9)
Camera Obscura **NG**(19b)
Card, The **TZCBS**(32a)
Cat And Mouse **TZSYN**(24)
Caterpillar, The **NG**(29a)
Cavender Is Coming **TZ**(101)
Cemetery, The **NG**(1a)
Certain Shadows On The Wall **NG**(4b)
Chameleon **TZCBS**(2c)
Changing Of The Guard, The **TZ**(102)
Chaser, The **TZ**(31)
Children's Zoo **TZCBS**(3b)
Class Of '99, The **NG**(9c)
Clean Kills And Other Trophies **NG**(5b)
Coffin, Coffin, In The Sky **SS**(15)
Cold Equations, The **TZSYN**(16)
Cold Reading **TZCBS**(18c)
Come Wander With Me **TZ**(154)

Convict's Piano, The **TZCBS**(30)
Cool Air **NG**(19a)
Crazy As A Soup Sandwich
TZSYN(29)
Crossing, The **TZSYN**(3)
Curious Case Of Edgar Witherspoon,
The **TZSYN**(1)
Dark Boy, The **NG**(17a)
Day In Beaumont, A **TZCBS**(24a)
Dead Man, The **NG**(2a)
Dead Man's Shoes **TZ**(83)
Dead Run **TZCBS**(19b)
Dead Weight **NG**(26c)
Dead Woman's Shoes **TZCBS**(9a)
Dealer's Choice **TZCBS**(8c)
Dear Departed, The **NG**(18b)
Dear Joan, We Are Going To Scare You
To Death **SS**(16)
Death At The Top Of The Stairs **SS**(6)
Death In The Family, A **NG**(9a)
Death On A Barge **NG**(41)
Death Ship **TZ**(108)
Death's-Head Revisited **TZ**(74)
Deliveries In The Rear **NG**(26a)
Devil Is Not Mocked, The **NG**(13b)
Devil's Alphabet **TZCBS**(22b)
Diary, The **NG**(15a)
Die Now, Pay Later **NG**(45)
Different Ones, The **NG**(21a)
Doctor Stringfellow's Rejuvenator
NG(16c)
Doll, The **NG**(6c)
Doll Of Death, The **NG**(43)
Dream Me A Life **TZSYN**(5)
Dreams For Sale **TZCBS**(2b)
Dummy, The **TZ**(98)
Dust **TZ**(48)
Echo Of A Distant Scream **SS**(10)
Elegy **TZ**(20)
Elevator, The **TZCBS**(16a)
Encounter, The **TZ**(151)
Escape Clause **TZ**(6)
Escape Route, The **NG**(1c)
Examination Day **TZCBS**(6a)
Execution **TZ**(26)
Extra Innings **TZSYN**(2)
Eye Of The Beholder, The **TZ**(42)

263

Eye Of The Hunted **SS**(9)
Eyes **NG**(1b)
Eyes That Would Not Die, The **SS**(26)
Face Of Ice **SS**(13)
Father And Son Game **TZSYN**(30)
Fear, The **TZ**(155)
Fear Of Spiders, A **NG**(11a)
Feast Of Blood, A **NG**(23b)
Fever, The **TZ**(17)
Finnegan's Flight **NG**(38)
Five Characters In Search Of An Exit **TZ**(79)
Five Women Weeping **SS**(24)
Flip Side Of Satan, The **NG**(10c)
Four O'Clock **TZ**(94)
Four Of Us Are Dying, The (**TZ**13)
Fright Night **NG**(32)
From Agnes -- With Love **TZ**(140)
Fugitive, The **TZ**(90)
Funeral, The **NG**(22b)
Gallows In The Wind **SS**(25)
Game Of Pool, A **TZ**(70), **TZSYN**(20)
Ghost Of Sorworth Place, The **NG**(24b)
Gift, The **TZ**(97)
Girl I Married, The **TZCBS**(35b)
Girl With The Hungry Eyes, The **NG**(31)
Grace Note **TZCBS**(23b)
Gramma **TZCBS**(18a)
Grave, The **TZ**(72)
Green Fingers **NG**(22a)
Hand Of Borgus Weems, The **NG**(8c)
Hatred Unto Death **NG**(44a)
He's Alive **TZ**(106)
Healer **TZCBS**(3a)
Heart That Wouldn't Stay Buried, The **SS**(2)
Hell's Bells **NG**(16d)
Hellgramite Method, The **TZSYN**(7)
Her Pilgrim Soul **TZCBS**(12a)
Hitch-Hiker, The **TZ**(16)
Hocus-Pocus And Frisby **TZ**(95)
House, The **NG**(4a)
House -- With Ghost **NG**(16a)
House That Cried Murder, The **SS**(4)
Housekeeper, The **NG**(2b)
How to Cure The Common Vampire **NG**(44b)
Howling Man, The **TZ**(41)
Hundred Yards Over The Rim, A **TZ**(59)

Hunt, The **TZ**(84)
Hunters, The **TZSYN**(4)
I Am The Night -- Color Me Black **TZ**(146)
I Did Not Mean To Slay Thee **SS**(21)
I Do Not Belong To The Human World **SS**(1)
I Dream Of Genie **TZ**(114)
I Of Newton **TZCBS**(12b)
I Shot An Arrow Into The Air (**TZ**15)
I Sing The Body Electric **TZ**(100)
I'll Never Leave You -- Ever **NG**(27a)
If I Should Die Before I Wake **SS**(23)
If She Dies **TZCBS**(5a)
In His Image **TZ**(103)
In Praise Of Pip **TZ**(121)
Incredible World Of Horace Ford, The **TZ**(117)
Invaders, The **TZ**(51)
It's A Good Life **TZ**(73), **TZMV**(3)
Jeopardy Room, The **TZ**(149)
Jess-Belle **TZ**(109)
Joy Ride **TZCBS**(33a)
Judgment Night **TZ**(10)
Junction, The **TZCBS**(32b)
Jungle **TZ**(77)
Junior **NG**(11b)
Keep In Touch -- We'll Think Of Something **NG**(17b)
Kentucky Rye **TZCBS**(3c)
Kick The Can **TZ**(86), **TZMV**(2)
Kind Of Stop Watch, A **TZ**(124)
King Nine Will Not Return **TZ**(37)
Lady, Lady, Take My Life **SS**(3)
Last Defender Of Camelot, The **TZCBS**(24b)
Last Flight, The **TZ**(18)
Last Laurel, The **NG**(7a)
Last Night Of A Jockey, The **TZ**(125)
Last Rites For A Dead Druid **NG**(25b)
Last Rites Of Jeff Myrtlebank, The **TZ**(88)
Late Mr. Peddington, The **NG**(23c)
Lateness Of The Hour, The **TZ**(44)
Leprechaun-Artist, The **TZCBS**(19a)
Library, The **TZCBS**(22c)
Lindemann's Catch **NG**(23a)
Little Black Bag, The **NG**(3b)
Little Boy Lost **TZCBS**(4a)
Little Girl Lost **NG**(29b)
Little Girl Lost **TZ**(91)

Little Peace And Quiet, A **TZCBS**(1b)
Little People, The **TZ**(93)
Little People Of Killany Woods, The **TZCBS**(14b)
Living Doll **TZ**(126)
Logoda's Heads **NG**(21c)
Lone Survivor **NG**(6b)
Lonely, The **TZ**(7)
Long Distance Call **TZ**(58)
Long Live Walter JamesOn **TZ**(24)
Long Morrow, The **TZ**(135)
Lost And Found **TZCBS**(28b)
Love Is Blind **TZSYN**(28)
Make Me Laugh **NG**(5a)
Man In The Bottle, The **TZ**(38)
Man Who Died At Three And Nine, The **SS**(5)
Many, Many Monkeys **TZSYN**(25)
Marmalade Wine **NG**(11c)
Masks, The **TZ**(145)
Matter Of Minutes, A **TZCBS**(15c)
Matter Of Semantics, A **NG**(15b)
Memories **TZSYN**(6)
Merciful, The **NG**(9b)
Message From Charity, A **TZCBS**(6b)
Messiah On Mott Street, The **NG**(20a)
Midnight Never Ends **NG**(14a)
Midnight Sun, The **TZ**(75)
Midnight Visit To The Neighborhood Blood Bank, A **NG**(16b)
Mighty Casey, The **TZ**(35)
Mind And The Matter, The **TZ**(63)
Mind Of Simon Foster, The **TZSYN**(23)
Miniature **TZ**(110)
Miracle At Camafeo, The **NG**(24a)
Mirror, The **TZ**(71)
Mirror Image **TZ**(21)
Misfortune Cookie, The **TZCBS**(14c)
Miss Lovecraft Sent Me **NG**(8b)
Monsters **TZCBS**(15a)
Monsters Are Due On Maple Street, The **TZ**(22)
Most Unusual Camera, A **TZ**(46)
Mr. Bevis **TZ**(33)
Mr. Denton On Doomsday **TZ**(3)
Mr. Dingle, The Strong **TZ**(55)
Mr. Garrity And The Graves **TZ**(152)
Mute **TZ**(107)
Nature Of The Enemy, The **NG**(3c)
Need To Know **TZCBS**(21a)

Nervous Man In A Four-Dollar Room **TZ**(39)
New Exhibit, The **TZ**(115)
Nice Place To Visit, A **TZ**(28)
Nick Of Time **TZ**(43)
Night Call **TZ**(139)
Night Of The Meek **TZ**(47), **TZCBS**(13a)
Nightcrawlers **TZCBS**(4c)
Nightmare As A Child **TZ**(29)
Nightmare At 20,000 Feet **TZ**(123), **TZMV**(4)
Nightsong **TZCBS**(27b)
Ninety Years Without Slumbering **TZ**(132)
No Time Like The Past **TZ**(112)
Nothing In The Dark **TZ**(81)
Number Twelve Looks Just Like You **TZ**(137)
Obsolete Man, The **TZ**(65)
Occurrence At Owl Creek Bridge, An **TZ**(142)
Odyssey Of Flight 33, The **TZ**(54)
Of Late, I Think Of Cliffordville **TZ**(116)
Old Man In The Cave, The **TZ**(127)
On Thursday We Leave for Home **TZ**(118)
Once And Future King, The **TZCBS**(25a)
Once Upon A Chilling **SS**(19)
Once Upon A Time **TZ**(78)
One For The Angels **TZ**(2)
One Life, Furnished In Early Poverty **TZCBS**(11b)
One More Pallbearer **TZ**(82)
Opening Day **TZCBS**(10c)
Other Way Out, The **NG**(37)
Our Sylena Is Dying **TZSYN**(8)
Painted Mirror, The **NG**(20b)
Paladin Of The Lost Hour **TZCBS**(7b)
Pamela's Voice **NG**(6a)
Parallel, The **TZ**(113)
Passage For Trumpet, A **TZ**(32)
Passage On The Lady Anne **TZ**(119)
Passerby, The **TZ**(69)
Penny For Your Thoughts, A **TZ**(52)
People Are Alike All Over **TZ**(25)
Perchance To Dream **TZ**(9)
Person Or Persons Unknown **TZ**(92)
Personal Demons **TZCBS**(18b)

Phantom Farmhouse, The **NG**(12a)
Phantom Of What Opera?, The **NG**(8d)
Piano In The House, A **TZ**(87)
Pickman's Model **NG**(18a)
Prime Mover, The **TZ**(57)
Printer's Devil **TZ**(111)
Private Channel **TZCBS**(33c)
Probe 7 -- Over And Out **TZ**(129)
Professor Peabody's Last Lecture **NG**(15d)
Profile In Silver **TZCBS**(20a)
Purple Testament, The **TZ**(19)
Quality Of Mercy, A **TZ**(80)
Quarantine **TZCBS**(17b)
Queen Of The Nile **TZ**(143)
Question Of Fear, A **NG**(13a)
Quoth The Raven **NG**(19c)
Rare Objects **NG**(33)
Red Snow **TZCBS**(21b)
Rendezvous In A Dark Place **TZSYN**(26)
Return Of The Sorcerer, The **NG**(30)
Ring With The Red Velvet Ropes, The **NG**(35)
Ring-A-Ding Girl **TZ**(133)
Rip Van Winkle Caper, The **TZ**(60)
Rivière Du Hibou, La **TZ**(142)
Road Less Travelled, The **TZCBS**(31)
Room 2426 **TZSYN**(22)
Room For One Less **NG**(46)
Room With A View **NG**(3a)
Satisfaction Guaranteed **NG**(47)
Saucer Of Loneliness, A **TZCBS**(25b)
Self-Improvement Of Salvadore Ross, The **TZ**(136)
Seventh Is Made Up Of Phantoms, The **TZ**(130)
Shadow In The Well **SS**(12)
Shadow Man, The **TZCBS**(10a)
Shadow Play **TZ**(62), **TZCBS**(23a)
Shatterday **TZCBS**(1a)
She'll Be Company For You **NG**(39)
Shelter, The **TZ**(68)
Shelter Skelter **TZCBS**(33b)
Short Drink From A Certain Fountain, A **TZ**(131)
Showdown With Rance McGrew **TZ**(85)
Silence, The **TZ**(61)
Silent Snow, Secret Snow **NG**(12b)
Since Aunt Ada Came To Stay **NG**(10a)

Sins Of The Fathers, The **NG**(28b)
Sixteenth mm Shrine, The **TZ**(4)
Small Talent For War, A **TZCBS**(15b)
Smile, Please **NG**(48)
Something In The Walls **TZSYN**(19)
Something In The Woodwork **NG**(40)
Song Of The Younger World **TZCBS**(35a)
Sounds And Silences **TZ**(147)
Special Service **TZSYN**(27)
Spectre In Tap-Shoes **NG**(34)
Spur Of The Moment **TZ**(141)
Star, The **TZCBS**(13c)
Static **TZ**(56)
Steel **TZ**(122)
Still Life **TZCBS**(14a)
Still Valley **TZ**(76)
Stop At Willoughby, A **TZ**(30)
Stop Killing Me **NG**(26b)
Stopover In A Quiet Town **TZ**(150)
Storyteller, The **TZCBS**(27a)
Strangers In Possum Meadows **TZSYN**(17)
Street Of Shadows **TZSYN**(18)
Take My Life... Please! **TZCBS**(22a)
Teacher's Aide **TZCBS**(7a)
Tell David... **NG**(21b)
Theatre, The **TZLC**(1)
There Aren't Any More MacBanes **NG**(27b)
There Was An Old Woman **TZSYN**(13)
They're Tearing Down Tim Riley's Bar **NG**(7b)
Thing About Machines, A **TZ**(40)
Third From The Sun **TZ**(14)
Thirty-Fathom Grave, The **TZ**(104)
Through A Flame, Darkly **SS**(20)
Time And Teresa Golowitz **TZCBS**(34a)
Time Enough At Last **TZ**(8)
Time Out **TZMV**(1)
To See The Invisible Man **TZCBS**(16b)
To Serve Man **TZ**(89)
Tooth And Consequences **TZCBS**(16c)
Toys Of Caliban, The **TZCBS**(29)
Trade-Ins, The **TZ**(96)
Trance, The **TZSYN**(10)
Trouble With Templeton, The **TZ**(45)
Trunk, The **TZSYN**(14)
Tune In Dan's Cafe, The **NG**(22c)
Twenty-Two **TZ**(53)

Twenty/Twenty Vision **TZSYN**(12)
Two **TZ**(66)
Two Hour Streets **SS**(14)
Uncle Devil Show, The **TZCBS**(10b)
Uncle Simon **TZ**(128)
Valley Of The Shadow **TZ**(105)
Voices In The Earth **TZCBS**(34b)
Waiting Room, The **NG**(25a)
Walking Distance **TZ**(5)
Wall, The **TZSYN**(21)
Welcome To Winfield **TZCBS**(17a)
What Are Friends For? **TZCBS**(26a)
What You Need **TZ**(12)
What's In The Box? **TZ**(144)
Where Is Everybody? **TZ**(1)
Where The Dead Are **TZLC**(2)
Whisper **NG**(42)
Whisper Of Evil **SS**(11)
Whole Truth, The **TZ**(50)
Will The Real Martian Please Stand Up?
TZ(64)

Wish Bank **TZCBS**(4b)
Witch, Witch, Burning Bright **SS**(8)
Witches' Feast, The **NG**(9d)
With Affection, Jack The Ripper **SS**(18)
With Apologies To Mr. Hyde **NG**(10b)
With This Ring, I Thee Kill **SS**(7)
Witness Within **SS**(17)
Wong's Lost And Found Emporium
TZCBS(9b)
Wordplay **TZCBS**(2a)
World Next Door, The **TZCBS**(28c)
World Of Difference, A **TZ**(23)
World Of His Own, A **TZ**(36)
Ye Gods **TZCBS**(5b)
You Can Come Up Now, Mrs. Millikan
NG(36)
You Can't Get Help Like That Anymore
NG(28a)
You Drive **TZ**(134)
Young Man's Fancy, A **TZ**(99)

Index: Creative Personnel

Legend:

AP: Associate Producer
CC: Creative Consultant
D: Director
DP: Director of Photography
EP: Executive Producer
ESC: Executive Story Consultant
M: Music Composer
P: Producer
PD: Production Designer
S: Story Author
SC: Story Consultant
SE: Story Editor
SP: Supervising Producer
SPFX: Special Effects
W: Writer (screenplay)

Abroms, Edward M. **D** NG(40)
Addiss, Justus **D** TZ(54, 60, 112)
Ahern, Lloyd **DP** NG

Aidman, Charles **Narrator TZCBS**
(also see ACTORS)
Aiken, Conrad **S** NG(12b)
Aiken, Joan **S** NG(11c)
Aldridge, Virginia **W** TZCBS(32b)
Alexander, Jeff **M** TZ(45)
Almeida, Laurindo **M** TZ(97)
Arkush, Allan **D** TZCBS(14c)
Arnold, Chuck **DP** TZCBS(20, 21, 22b, 23a, 29, 32b, 35)
Asher, William **D** TZ(33)
Astin, John **D** NG(4a, 11a, 17a) (also see ACTORS)
Astle, Tom J. **W** TZSYN(13)
Badham, John **AP** NG(1); **D** NG(8a, 19b, 22a, 31, 36, 43)
Bare, Richard **D** TZ(14, 19, 43, 57, 89, 90, 144)
Barker, Lynn **W** TZCBS(4a, 9a)
Barkin, Haskell **W** TZCBS(8a, 16c), **TZSYN**(1, 15); **S** TZSYN(1)
Barnes, Steven **W** TZCBS(7a, 16b)
Batcheller, Richard **DP** NG(1)
Bateson, Garrie **W** NG(22c)
Bear, Greg **S** TZCBS(19b)

Beascoechea, Frank P. **DP TZCBS**(12b, 13b, 15, 16a, 16b, 17, 18b, 18c, 19)

Beaumont, Charles **W TZ**(9, 20, 24, 28, 41, 56, 57, 58, 62, 77, 83, 90, 92, 103, 105, 110, 111, 115, 119, 126, 137, 143); **S TZ**(9, 20, 41, 77, 103, 111, 119, 137); **TZCBS**(9a, 23a)

Beck, Virgil **SPFX TZ**

Benedict, Richard **D NG**(6a)

Benison, Peter **DP TZSYN**(15, 17, 18)

Bettman, Gil **D TZCBS**(33a)

Betts, Harry **M TZCBS**(11b)

Biberman, Abner **D TZ**(98, 117, 137, 146)

Bierce, Ambrose **S TZ**(142)

Bilson, Bruce **D TZCBS**(17a)

Bissell, James D. **PD TZMV**

Bixby, Jerome **S TZ**(73), **TZMV**(3)

Black, Noel **D TZCBS**(16b, 35a)

Blackwood, Algernon **S NG**(6c)

Bloch, Robert **W NG**(21c)

Bochco, Stephen **S TZCBS**(17b)

Bofferty, Jean **DP TZ**(142)

Bogner, Ludek **DP TZSYN**(1, 4, 5)

Bolt, Ben **D TZCBS**(22b)

Bonnière, René **D TZSYN**(1, 15, 26)

Bottin, Rob **SPFX TZMV**(3)

Bradbury, Ray **W TZ**(100), **TZCBS**(16a); **S TZ**(100), **TZCBS**(8b)

Bradshaw, Randy **D TZSYN**(10, 20, 27, 30)

Brahm, John **D TZ**(8, 10, 13, 21, 28, 55, 62, 92, 99, 115, 134, 143)

Brand, Christianna **S NG**(28b)

Brennert, Alan **ESC TZCBS**; **W TZCBS**(1a, 6b, 9b, 11b, 12a, 12b, 13c, 15b, 17b, 19b, 34a, 34b); **TZSYN**(16); (under the pseudonym of Bryant, Michael) **W TZCBS**(3a)

Bryant, Michael (see Brennert, Alan)

Bugajski, Richard **D TZSYN**(6, 18, 22, 25)

Butler, Artie **M TZCBS**(18c)

Butler, David **D TZ**(120)

Butler, Robert **D TZ**(148, 151)

Carren, David Bennett **W TZCBS**(5a)

Carter, Benny **M NG**

Cassutt, Michael **W TZCBS**(4b, 21b,

32a)

Cates, Gilbert (under the pseudonym of Smithee, Alan) **D TZCBS**(7b)

Chambers, John **Make-up NG**

Champion, Madeline **S TZ**(15)

Chetwynd-Hayes, R. **S NG**(40)

Chitlik, Paul **SE TZSYN; W TZCBS**(26b), **TZSYN**(4, 14, 17, 22, 30)

Clarke, Arthur C. **S TZCBS**(13c)

Claxton, William **D TZ**(18, 77, 93, 100)

Cleave, Van **M TZ**(9, 12, 20, 23, 66, 75, 100, 109, 122, 124, 138, 140)

Clemens, George T. **DP TZ**(1-13, 15-73, 75, 77-87, 89, 91, 93-104, 106, 111, 114, 115, 117-122, 125, 130, 131, 133-136, 138-141, 144-153, 156)

Cobb, Ron **W TZCBS**(33b); **S TZCBS**(33b)

Collier, John **S TZ**(31)

Collins, Anne **W TZCBS**(5b, 22c)

Collins, Robert **DP TZCBS**(33a, 33b, 34b)

Constant, Marius **M TZ** (Theme)

Cook, R. C. **S NG**(22a)

Cook, Oscar **S NG**(29a)

Coolidge, Martha **D TZCBS**(13a, 17b, 33b)

Copper, Basil **S NG**(19b)

Corey, Jeff **D NG**(4b, 11d, 18b, 19c, 21b, 23a, 23c, 26a, 28a, 32) (also see ACTORS)

Crais, Robert **W TZCBS**(15a)

Craven, Wes **D TZCBS**(1a, 1b, 2a, 2c, 8c, 12a, 31)

Crocker, James **SP TZCBS**(1-18); **CC TZCBS**(19-24); **W TZCBS**(1b, 2c, 23a); **S TZCBS**(19a, 30)

Crosland, Alan **D TZ**(113, 127, 130, 133)

Dante, Joe **D TZMV**(3), **TZCBS**(10a)

Daviau, Allen **DP TZMV**(2, 4)

Davison, Jon **AP TZMV**(4)

Day, Price **S TZ**(94)

De Vorzon, Barry **M TZCBS**(3a)

Debney, John **M TZCBS**(27b)

Dedrick, Christopher **M TZSYN**(5)

DeFord, Miriam Allen **S NG**(9a)

DeGuere, Phil **EP TZCBS; W TZCBS**(4c, 6a); **S TZCBS**(17b); **D**

TZCBS(24a, 35b)

DeMatteis, J.M. **W TZCBS**(35b)

Derleth, August **S NG**(16a, 17a, 21c)

DeRoy, Richard **W TZ**(132)

DiMarco, Steve **D TZSYN**(14)

Doniger, Walter **D NG**(5b)

Donner, Richard **D TZ**(123, 140, 147, 149, 153, 154)

Dorn, Rudi **D NG**(6c)

Downey, Robert **D TZCBS**(3b, 16c)

Drasnin, Robert **M TZ**(84), **TZCBS**(3b, 4a, 7b, 23b)

Dresner, Hal **W NG**(3a); **S NG**(3a, 10c, 26b)

Duke, Bill **D TZCBS**(32b)

Duke, Daryl **D NG**(7a)

Dunaway, Don Carlos **D TZCBS**(11b)

Duncan, Chip **W TZCBS**(3c)

Egoyan, Atom **D TZSYN**(21)

Eisenstein, Phyllis **S TZCBS**(28b)

Ellison, Harlan **CC TZCBS**(1-18); **W TZCBS**(7b, 18a), **TZSYN**(29); **S TZCBS**(1a, 7b, 11b)

Elston, Logan **Sculptures NG**

Ely, David **S NG**(11d)

Enloe, Les **W TZCBS**(17a)

Enrico, Robert **W TZ**(142); **D TZ**(142)

Erbe, Micky **M TZSYN**(13, 16)

Fairman, Paul W. **S TZ**(25)

Feigelson, J.D. **W TZCBS**(8b, 14b); **D TZCBS**(8b, 14b)

Finch, Jeremy Bertrand **SE TZSYN**; **W TZCBS**(26b), **TZSYN**(4, 14, 17, 22, 30)

Finnell, Michael **AP TZMV**(3)

Finnerman, Gerald Perry **D NG**(39, 44a); **DP NG**

Fletcher, Lucille **S TZ**(16)

Flicker, Theodore J. **W NG**(13a, 16d); **D NG**(11b, 16d); **TZCBS**(8a) (also see ACTORS)

Florey, Robert **D TZ**(9, 17, 135)

Folk, Robert **M TZCBS**(20b, 25b, 28a, 33c, 34b, 35a)

Folsey, Jr., George **AP TZMV**(1)

Fox, Frederic Louis **S TZ**(85, 95)

Frand, Harvey **P TZCBS**

Frazier, Shamus **S NG**(22c)

Freeman, Jerrold **W NG**(11c); **D NG**(3a, 9d, 10c, 11c, 15d, 16c)

Fresco, Robert **DP TZSYN**(19, 22, 23, 29)

Friedberg, Rick **D TZCBS**(4b)

Friedkin, William **D TZCBS**(4c)

Fritch, Charles E. **S TZCBS**(14c)

Froug, William **P TZ**(125, 126, 129, 132-35, 137, 138, 140, 142-144, 146-149, 151- 156); **W TZSYN**(25)

Furia, Jr., John **W TZ**(114)

Galfas, Timothy **D NG**(26c, 29b, 45)

Gannon, Joe **W TZCBS**(2b)

Ganzer, Alvin **D TZ**(12, 16, 29, 35)

Garriguenc, René **M TZ**(22, 119, 121, 141)

Gebr, Jaroslav **Paintings NG**(1)

Geiger, Milton **S NG**(44a)

Gerrold, David **W TZCBS**(24a, 25b)

Gilbert, Kenneth **D TZCBS**(12b)

Gilford, C. B. **S NG**(24a)

Girard, Bernard **D TZ**(131)

Gist, Robert **D TZ**(114)

Glass, Paul **M NG**

Glouner, Richard C. **DP NG**

Gluskin, Lud **M TZ**(19, 22, 119, 121, 141, 143)

Godwin, Parke **S TZCBS**(34a)

Godwin, Tom **S TZSYN**(16)

Goldenberg, William **M NG**(1)

Goldsmith, Jerry **M TZ**(13, 27, 29, 39, 48, 49, 51); **M TZMV**

Goldsmith, Jon **M TZSYN**(19, 21)

Goldsmith, Martin **W TZ**(144, 151)

Goldstein, William **M TZCBS**(12a, 32a, 34a)

Graham, Gerrit **W TZCBS**(3b, 10c, 14a) (also see ACTORS)

Granet, Bert **P TZ**(113, 115, 116, 118, 119, 121-124, 127, 128, 130, 131, 136, 139, 141, 145, 150)

Grateful Dead, The **M TZCBS**(Theme, 1b, 2, 3c, 4b, 4c, 5b, 6a, 8c, 10a, 12b, 13b, 14c, 17a, 19b, 22a, 22b, 23a)

Grauman, Walter E. **D TZ**(110)

Gray, Arthur **S TZCBS**(22b)

Gray, Dulcie **NG**(23b)

Greene, David **D TZ**(87)

Grubb, Davis **S NG**(7a)

Gunnarsson, Sturla **D TZSYN**(17)

Guss, Jack **W NG**(43)

Haldeman, Joe **S TZCBS**(12b)

Hale, William **D NG**(10a, 15a, 16b)

Hall, Stephen **S NG**(27b)

Haller, Daniel **D NG**(27a)

Hamner Jr., Earl **W TZ**(84, 87, 109, 133, 134, 138, 150, 156)

Hancock, John **D TZCBS**(3c, 5a, 20a, 22c, 25b)

Hanus, Otta **D TZSYN**(13)

Harrington, Curtis **D TZCBS**(34b)

Hart, Mickey **M TZCBS**(1a, 18a)

Hatch, Wilbur **M TZ**(76)

Hebb, Brian R. R. **DP TZSYN**(20, 21, 30)

Herrmann, Bernard **M TZ**(1, 5, 7, 42, 91, 126, 132)

Heyes, Douglas **W NG**(2a); **D TZ**(11, 20, 31, 34, 39, 41, 42, 48, 51), **NG**(2a); (under the pseudonym of Howard, Matthew) **W NG**(2b, 14b)

Hickox, S. Bryan **P TZLC**

Hirschman, Herbert **P TZ**(103-112, 114, 117, 120)

Hoch, Edward D. **S NG**(35)

Holtz, Lou **S TZ**(131)

Hora, John **DP TZMV**(3)

Horowitz, Lawrence **EP TZLC**

Houghton, Buck **P TZ**(1-102)

Howard, Matthew (see Heyes, Douglas)

Hubbell, Chris **W TZCBS**(3b, 10c, 14a)

Hunter, Robert **W TZCBS**(22b)

Ichac, Marcel **P TZ**(142)

Idelson, William **W TZ**(58)

Immel, Jerrold **M TZCBS**(5a)

Jackson, Doug **D TZSYN**(2, 23)

Jameson, Malcolm **S TZ**(116)

Johnson, George Clayton **W TZ**(52, 70, 81, 86), **TZMV**(2), **TZSYN**(20); **S TZ**(13, 26, 57, 132)

Johnson, Lamont **D TZ**(68, 79, 81, 82, 86, 94, 95, 119)

Jones, James Earl **Host & Narrator TZLC**

Kane, Artie **M TZCBS**(30)

Kaplan, Elliot **M TZCBS**(21b, 24b)

Kay, Roger **D TZ**(132)

Kearney, Gene **W NG**(8d, 9d, 11b, 12b, 13b, 15b, 16a, 17b, 20b, 34, 37); **D NG**(8b, 8d, 12b, 13b, 16a, 17b, 20b, 37, 38) (also see ACTORS)

Keats, Bob **Make-up TZ**

Kempel, Arthur **M TZCBS**(16a, 18b, 19a)

Kennedy, Kathleen **AP TZMV**(2)

King, Allan **D TZSYN**(5)

King, Stephen **S TZCBS**(18a)

Kirk, Russell **S NG**(24b)

Knight, Damon **S TZ**(89)

Kornbluth, Cyril M. **S NG**(3b)

Korologos, Mike **S TZ**(152)

Korven, Mark **M TZSYN**(25)

Kroeker, Allan **D TZSYN**(19)

Krzemien, Richard **W TZCBS**(3c)

Kulik, Buzz **D TZ**(37, 45, 56, 59, 63, 70, 80, 109, 118)

Kuttner, Henry (under the pseudonym of Padgett, Lewis) **S TZ**(12)

Lafferty, Perry **D TZ**(103, 104, 105)

Laird, Jack **P NG**; **S NG**(34); **W NG**(8b, 9b, 10b, 15d, 16b, 18c, 19c, 23c, 26b, 26c, 27a, 44b, 45, 46, 47, 48); **D NG**(13a, 15b, 18a, 18c, 44b, 46, 48) (also see ACTORS)

Landis, John **P TZMV; W TZMV**(1); **D TZMV**(1)

Langelaan, George **S NG**(8c)

Langford, Michael **S TZSYN**(19)

Lanoe, Henri **M TZ**(142)

Larner, Stevan **DP TZMV**(1)

Larry, Sheldon **D TZCBS**(15c)

LaSelle, Joseph **DP TZ**(1)

Laskus, Jacek **DP TZLC**

Lava, William **M TZ**(78)

Lavut, Martin **D TZSYN**(16)

Lawrence, Anthony **SP TZCBS**(25-35); **W TZCBS**(35a)

Lawrence, Nancy **SP TZCBS**(25-35); **W TZCBS**(35a)

Leader, Anton **D TZ**(24, 75)

Lee, William M. S. **TZCBS**(6b)

Leiber, Fritz **S NG**(2a, 31)

Leisen, Mitchell **D TZ**(4, 6, 25)

Levinson, Shelley **D TZCBS**(13b, 34a)

Levitt, Gene **D NG**(6b)

Lewis, Bryan **S NG**(13a)

Lindon, Lionel **DP NG**

Lopes, Carlos **M TZSYN**(7, 14, 28)

Love, Robin **W TZCBS**(33b)

Lovecraft, H. P. **S NG**(18a, 19a)

Lucas, John Meredyth **D NG**(2b, 8c, 21a, 22b)

Lupino, Ida **D TZ**(145) (also see ACTORS)

Lynch, Paul **D TZCBS**(6a, 6b, 9b, 21a,

23a, 27a, 28c), **TZSYN**(3, 4, 29)
MacMillan, Michael **EP TZSYN**
Malkin-Remal, Gary **M TZCBS**(26b)
Malmuth, Bruce **D TZCBS**(28a)
Mandl, Fred **DP TZ**(154, 155)
Margulies, William **DP NG**
Maritano, Bryce **S TZCBS**(25a)
Markowitz, Robert **D TZLC**(1,2)
Marmorstein, Malcolm **W NG**(10c)
Marshall, Frank **EP TZMV**
Martin, George R. R. **SE TZCBS**(25-35);

W TZCBS(24b, 25a, 28b, 29, 31)
Marx, Christy **W TZSYN**(24)
Mason, Aidan **TZSYN**(7, 14, 28)
Matheson, Richard **W TZ**(18, 23, 36, 43, 51, 78, 91, 99, 107, 108, 122, 123, 139, 141); **NG**(15c, 22b); **TZMV**(2, 3, 4); **TZLC**(1); **S TZ**(11, 14, 91, 107, 108, 122, 123, 139); **NG**(15c, 22b), **TZCBS**(20b); (under the pseudonym of Swanson, Logan) **W TZCBS**(20b)
Mathison, Melissa (under the pseudonym of Rogan, Josh) **W TZMV**(2)
Matz, Terry **S TZCBS**(29)
Maurois, André **S NG**(4a)
May, Bradford **D TZCBS**(18a, 27b, 32a); **DP TZCBS**(1-11, 12a, 13a, 13c, 14, 16c, 18a, 25-31, 32a, 33c, 34a)
McBride, Jim **D TZCBS**(25a)
McCammon, Robert **S TZCBS**(4c)
McCarthy, Dennis **M TZCBS**(17b, 22c, 31)
McCracken, Michael **SPFX TZMV**(4)
McDearmon, David Orrick **D TZ**(26, 40, 49)
McLean, Seaton **P TZSYN**
McLeod, Norman Z. **D TZ**(78)
McNeeley, Jerry **W TZ**(136)
Medak, Peter **D TZCBS**(5b, 9a, 14a, 18b, 20b, 23b, 33c)
Medford, Don **D TZ**(32, 38, 71, 74, 108)
Meik, Vivian **S NG**(43)
Mellé, Gil **M NG** (Theme)
Meredith, Burgess **Narrator TZMV** (also see ACTORS)
Messina, Patrice **W TZCBS**(23b, 30)
Milius, John **D TZCBS**(10c)

Miller, George **D TZMV**(4)
Miller, Robert Ellis **D TZ**(102)
Miller, Robin **DP TZSYN**(8, 12, 16)
Miner, Allen H. **D TZ**(97)
Mitchell, Gordon **W TZCBS**(22a)
Moe, David **PD/AP TZSYN**
Mooney, Hal **M NG**
Moore, Catherine L. (under the pseudonym of Padgett, Lewis) **S TZ**(12)
Morawack, Lucien **M TZ**(19, 143)
Morgan, Tommy **M TZ**(88, 95, 152)
Morley, Glenn **M TZSYN**(12)
Morris, Rene **S NG**(27a)
Murray, Lyn **M TZ**(32)
Natale, Louis **M TZSYN**(2, 4, 6, 8, 11, 17, 20, 23, 26, 29)
Nelson, Oliver **M NG**
Nelson, Ralph **D TZ**(36)
Neufeld, Sigmund **D TZCBS**(3a)
Neuman, E. Jack **W TZ**(45)
Newland, John **D NG**(27b)
Newman, Andrea **S NG**(39)
Newman, Joseph **M D TZ**(121, 125, 138, 156)
Nimoy, Leonard **D NG**(41) (also see ACTORS)
Norton, B.W.L. **D TZCBS**(7a, 15a)
Nyby, Christian **D TZ**(85, 101)
O'Bannon, Rockne S. **SE TZCBS**(1-24); **SC TZCBS**(25-35); **W TZCBS**(2a, 10a, 13a, 15c, 18b, 27a, 28a); (under the pseudonym of Rae, Steven) **W TZCBS**(14c)
O'Hara, Michael **EP TZLC**
O'Kun, Lan **W TZCBS**(28c)
Orieux, Ron **DP TZSYN**(2, 3, 14)
Oster, Emil **DP NG**
Oswald, Gerd **D TZCBS**(11a, 13c)
Padgett, Lewis (see Kuttner, Henry or Moore, Catherine L.)
Palmer, Tom **W TZSYN**(2)
Parr, Rebecca **SE TZCBS**(25-35); **W TZCBS**(11a, 13b, 18c)
Parrish, Robert **D TZ**(2, 30, 35)
Pasko, Martin **SE TZCBS**(25-25); **W TZCBS**(11a, 13b, 18c)
Petal, Marvin **S TZ**(79)
Phillips, Bob **AP TZLC**
Phillips, Ralph **W TZSYN**(3)
Pittack, Robert W. **DP TZ**(92, 105,

107-110, 112, 113, 116, 123, 124, 126-129, 132, 139, 141)

Pittman, Bruce **D TZSYN**(8)

Pittman, Montgomery **W TZ**(66, 72, 88); **D TZ**(64, 66, 72, 83, 88)

Plager, Joseph **AP TZLC**

Poledouris, Basil **M TZCBS**(6b, 15a, 20a)

Polk, Lee **S TZ**(98)

Post, Ted **D TZ**(23, 129, 152, 155)

Poulsson, Andreas **DP TZSYN**(6, 7, 9, 10, 11, 13, 24, 25, 26, 27, 28)

Presnell, Jr., Robert **W TZ**(31)

Prince, Robert **M NG**

Purdy, Jim **D TZSYN**(12)

Quinn, Seabury **S NG**(12a)

Rae, Steven (see O'Bannon, Rockne S.)

Ramin, Ron **M TZCBS**(21a, 27a)

Rawlins, David **D NG**(22c)

Rayfiel, David **W NG**(39, 42)

Reardon, Craig **SPFX TZMV**(4)

Reaves, Michael **W TZCBS**(27b), **TZSYN**(18)

Redford, J.A.G. **M TZCBS**(26a)

Redlich, Edward **W TZCBS**(33c)

Reisner, Allen **D TZ**(3), **NG**(3c, 14b)

Rich, David Lowell **D TZ**(116)

Rich, John **D TZ**(46, 124)

Ritch, OCee **W TZ**(83); **S TZ**(56)

Roby, Mary Linn **S NG**(45)

Rogan, Josh (see Mathison, Melissa)

Rolfe, Sam **S TZ**(80)

Rose, Reginald **W TZ**(117)

Rosenberg, Stuart **D TZ**(15, 106, 107)

Rosenman, Leonard **M TZ**(11)

Rosenquist, J. Wesley **S NG**(36)

Rosenthal, Michael D. **S TZ**(124)

Rubin, Lance **M TZCBS**(8a, 8b)

Sackheim, William **P NG**(1)

Safan, Craig **M TZCBS**(7a, 9, 10b, 10c, 16b, 16c)

Sagal, Boris **D TZ**(61, 67), **NG**(1a)

Sanford, Gerald **W NG**(10c, 21b, 22c)

Sapinsley, Alvin T. **W NG**(8c, 10a, 18a, 24b, 25b, 27b)

Sarafian, Richard C. **D TZ**(126)

Saunders, Merl **M TZCBS**(1b, 2, 3c, 4b, 4c, 5b, 6a, 8c, 10a, 12b, 13b, 14c, 17a, 19b, 22a, 22b, 23a, 28b, 28c, 29, 32b, 33a, 33b, 35b)

Sauter, Eddie **M NG**

Schnirring, Alice-Mary **S NG**(18b)

Scholz, Carter **W TZCBS**(15b)

Schulman, J. Neil **W TZCBS**(20a)

Schuster, Harold **D TZ**(84)

Scott, Jeffry **S NG**(26c)

Scott, Nathan **M TZ**(30, 99)

Seaman, Robert **DP TZCBS**(22a, 22c, 23b, 24)

Selby, William **W TZSYN**(7)

Self, William **P TZ**(1)

Senensky, Ralph **D TZ**(111), **NG**(24a, 24b)

Serling, Carol **Consultant TZMV; SP TZLC**

Serling, Rod **EP TZ**(1-36); **W TZ**(1, 2, 3, 4, 5, 6, 7, 8, 10, 11, 12, 13, 14, 15, 16, 17, 19, 21, 22, 25, 26, 27, 29, 30, 32, 33, 34, 35, 37, 38, 39, 40, 42, 44, 46, 47, 48, 49, 50, 53, 54, 55, 59, 60, 61, 63, 64, 65, 67, 68, 69, 71, 73, 74, 75, 76, 79, 80, 82, 85, 89, 93, 94, 95, 96, 97, 98, 101, 102, 104, 106, 112, 113, 116, 118, 120, 121, 124, 125, 127, 128, 129, 130, 131, 135, 145, 146, 147, 149, 152, 153, 155); **NG**(1a, 1b, 1c, 3b, 3c, 4a, 4b, 5a, 5b, 6a, 6b, 6c, 7a, 7b, 8a, 9a, 9c, 11a, 11d, 14a, 15a, 16c, 18b, 19a, 19b, 20a, 21a, 22a, 23a, 24a, 25a, 26a, 28a, 29a, 33, 36, 38, 40); **TZLC**(2); **S TZCBS**(13a, 28a); **TZLC**(1) **TZSYN**(8); **Host TZ, NG**.

Shear, Barry **D NG**(1c)

Sheldon, James **D TZ**(50, 52, 58, 73, 76, 100)

Sheldon, Mary **W TZCBS**(21a)

Sheldon, Sidney **S TZCBS**(21a)

Shelmerdine, Mark **EP TZSYN**

Shilton, Gilbert **D TZSYN**(7, 9, 28)

Shoenfeld, Bernard C. **W TZ**(140)

Shores, Richard **M TZ**(148)

Shragge, Lawrence **M TZSYN**(12)

Siegel, Don **D TZ**(128, 136)

Silverberg, Robert **S TZCBS**(16b)

Silverstein, Elliot **D TZ**(65, 69, 96, 141)

Sisk, Frank **S NG**(23c)

Skall, William **DP TZ**(55)

Slesar, Henry **S TZ**(127, 136), **TZCBS**(6a)

Smight, Jack **D TZ**(7, 44, 47, 53)

Smith, Clark Ashton **S NG**(30)

Smithee, Alan (see Cates, Gilbert)

Sohl, Jerry **W TZ**(115, 126, 143)

Solomon, Maribeth **M TZSYN**(13, 16)

South, Leonard J. **DP NG**

Spielberg, Steven **P TZMV; D NG**(1b, 5a), **TZMV**(2)

St. Clair, Margaret **S NG**(8a, 14b)

Steinberg, David **D TZCBS**(10b)

Steiner, Fred **M TZ**(37, 59, 69, 107, 110, 114, 120), **TZCBS**(24a)

Stevens, Leith **M TZ**(8)

Stevens, Morton **M TZCBS**(11a, 13a, 13c, 14b)

Stevens, Robert **D TZ**(1, 5)

Stewart, Paul **D TZ**(91)

Stills, Stephen **M TZCBS**(27b)

Stone, Richard **M TZCBS**(25a)

Straczynski, J. Michael **SE TZSYN; W TZCBS**(26a), **TZSYN**(5, 8, 9, 10, 11, 19, 21, 23, 26, 27); **S TZSYN**(1)

Strassfield, A.T. **W TZ**(148)

Straumer, E. Charles **DP NG**

Stuart, Jeff **W TZSYN**(10)

Sturgeon, Theodore **S TZCBS**(15c, 25b)

Swain, Jack **DP TZ**(70, 74, 76, 88, 90, 95)

Swanson, Logan (see Matheson, Richard)

Sweeny, Jr., Charles L. **S NG**(9b)

Szwarc, Jeannot **D NG**(3b, 9a, 9b, 9c, 10b, 12a, 14a, 15c, 19a, 21c, 23b, 25a, 25b, 26b, 28b, 29a, 30, 33, 34, 35, 42, 47); **TZCBS**(21b, 24b)

Taylor, Don **D NG**(7b, 20a)

Thackery, Bud **DP NG**

Thomas, R. L. **D TZCBS**(16a)

Till, Eric **D TZSYN**(24)

Todd, Donald **W TZCBS**(8c, 10b)

Tomerlin, John **W TZ**(137)

Tourneur, Jacques **D TZ**(139)

Trikonis, Gus **D TZCBS**(18c, 22a, 26a, 28b)

Tubb, E.C. **S NG**(29b)

Tucker, John **M TZSYN**(1, 18, 22)

Tucker, Paul **D TZCBS**(19b, 26b)

Turner, Brad **D TZSYN**(11)

Turner, Harry **S NG**(16d)

Turner, Ray **M TZ**(78)

Tuttle, William **Make-up TZ**(24, 34, 42, 64, 79, 95, 102, 122, 123, 145)

Underwood, Bob **W TZSYN**(6)

Van Elting, Kurt **S NG**(32, 37)

Van Vogt, A. E. **S NG**(10a)

Vanderlei, Phil **Sculptures NG**

Venable, Lynn **S TZ**(8)

Waddell, Martin **S NG**(42)

Walden, Robert **W TZSYN**(12)

Wallace, Penelope **S NG**(21b)

Wallace, Tommy Lee **W TZCBS**(19a); **D TZCBS**(2b, 4a, 19a)

Walter, Elizabeth **S NG**(11a)

Wandrei, Donald **S NG**(20b)

Wannberg, Ken **M TZCBS**(14a)

Ward, Robin **Narrator TZSYN**

Waxman, Franz **M TZ**(4)

Weill, Claudia **D TZCBS**(15b)

Weir, Bob **M TZCBS**(1a)

Weis, Don **D TZ**(122)

Welles, Halsted **W NG**(12a, 17a, 28b, 30, 41, 44a)

Welles, Orson **Narrator NG**(12b)

Wellman, Manly Wade **S TZ**(76), **NG**(13b)

Welsman, John **M TZSYN**(3, 9, 10, 15, 24, 27, 30)

Westmore, Bud **Make-up NG**

Wetherwax, Michael **M TZCBS**(27b)

Wheeler, Charles **DP TZ**(137, 143)

Whitmore, Stanford **W NG**(23b, 29b)

Wild, Harry **DP TZ**(14)

Wilkins-Freeman, Mary E. **S NG**(4b)

Williams, Patrick **M TZLC**

Willingham, Cal **W TZCBS**(33a), **TZSYN**(28)

Wilson, Anthony **W TZ**(154)

Winston, Ron **D TZ**(22, 27, 150)

Worrell, Everil **S NG**(41)

Wright, Thomas J. **D TZCBS**(29, 30); **Paintings NG**

Wu, William F. **S TZCBS**(9b)

Young, Christopher **M TZCBS**(15b, 15c)

Young, Robert Malcolm **W NG**(31, 32, 35)

Zelazny, Roger **S TZCBS**(24b)

Index: Actors

Abbott, Phillip **TZ**(58, 113)

Ackerman, Leslie **TZCBS**(28b)

Aclin, Bruno **TZCBS**(25b)

Adams, Casey **TZ**(73)

Adams, Dorothy **TZ**(48)

Adams, Julie **NG**(24a)

Adams, Lilliam **TZCBS**(21b)

Adams, Mary **TZ**(53)

Adams, Stanley **TZ**(78, 152)

Adams, Steve **TZSYN**(28)

Adano, Ralph **NG**(33)

Adelin, Louis **TZ**(142)

Adler, Jay **TZ**(77, 106)

Adler, Luther **TZ**(38)

Agar, John **TZCBS**(24a)

Agutter, Jenny **TZCBS**(24b, 34b)

Aherne, Brian **TZ**(45)

Aidman, Charles **TZ**(11, 91) (also see CREATIVE PERSONNEL)

Akins, Claude **TZ**(22, 93)

Albert, Eddie **TZSYN**(5)

Albertini Dow, Ellen **TZCBS**(21a, 27a)

Albertson, Jack **TZ**(68, 114); **NG**(26c)

Albright, Hardie **TZ**(89)

Alderson, John **NG**(23a)

Aletter, Frank **TZ**(113)

Alexander, Denise **TZ**(14)

Alexander, Wayne **TZCBS**(22b)

Alianak, Hrant **TZSYN**(10)

Alldredge, Michael **TZCBS**(14b, 32b)

Allen, Clark **TZ**(79)

Allen, Joan **TZCBS**(33b)

Allen, Liz **TZ**(34)

Allen, Marty **NG**(19c)

Allen, Todd **TZCBS**(1b)

Allison, Patricia **TZCBS**(27a)

Allman, Sheldon **TZ**(22)

Alloca, Frank **TZ**(12)

Allport, Christopher **TZCBS**(6a)

Alonso, John **TZ**(48)

Alu, Al **TZCBS**(3b)

Ambriz, Domingo **TZMV**(1)

Ames, Totty **TZ**(134)

Anderson, Barbara **NG**(32)

Anderson, Cheryl **TZCBS**(11a)

Anderson, John **TZ**(32, 54, 116, 127)

Andrade, Steven **TZSYN**(4)

Andre, E. J. **NG**(3b)

Andrei, Damir **TZSYN**(19)

Andrews, Dana **TZ**(112); **NG**(21a)

Andrews, Edward **TZ**(14, 134)

Andrews, Tod **TZ**(156)

Angarola, Richard **TZ**(110)

Annis, Richard **NG**(15d)

Anthony, Lee **TZCBS**(2b)

Anton, Billy **TZCBS**(27a)

Anton, Tony **TZCBS**(27a)

Antonio, Lou **TZ**(41)

Aranson, Jack **NG**(23a)

Archer, John **TZ**(64)

Arkin, Adam **TZCBS**(15c)

Armstrong, David **TZ**(96)

Armstrong, R.G. **TZ**(81)

Arnaz, Jr., Desi **NG**(9a)

Arnold, Frank **NG**(12a)

Arnold, Phil **TZ**(55)

Arnone, Lee **TZCBS**(2a)

Arthur, Maureen **NG**(18b)

Ash, Monty **TZCBS**(13a)

Ashe, Martin **NG**(12a)

Ashton, John **TZCBS**(2c)

Ast, Pat **TZCBS**(19b)

Astin, John **TZ**(59); **NG**(6a, 16d, 31) (also see CREATIVE PERSONNEL)

Astor, David **NG**(7b)

Atherton, William **TZCBS**(13a, 32a)

Atkinson, Steve **TZSYN**(21)

Atterbury, Malcolm **TZ**(3, 112)

Atwater, Barry **TZ**(22); **NG**(1a', 43)

Auberjonois, Rene **NG**(19b)

Aubrey, Renée **TZ**(147)

Aubuchon, Jacques **TZ**(105)

Audley, Eleanor **TZ**(16)

Austin, Karen **TZCBS**(15c)

Austin, Pamela **TZ**(137)

Avery, Val **TZ**(47)

Avnsoe, Shannon Lee **TZCBS**(25b)

Ayer, Harold **TZCBS**(21a)

Aykroyd, Dan **TZMV**(P)

Azarow, Martin **TZCBS**(16c)

Azzara, Candy **TZCBS**(22c)

Babcock, Barbara **NG**(14b)

Bacon, James **NG**(35)

Baddeley, Hermione **NG**(23b)

Badham, Mary **TZ**(156)

Baer, Parley **TZCBS**(27a)

Bagetta, Vince **TZ**(104)
Bailey, Raymond **TZ**(6, 49, 140)
Bain, Trevor **TZSYN**(11)
Bair, Douglas **TZCBS**(13b)
Baird, Jimmy **TZ**(102)
Baker, Diane **NG**(7b)
Baker, Penny **TZCBS**(18b)
Bakey, Ed **NG**(23a)
Ball, Robert **TZ**(114)
Ballard, Ray **NG**(12a); **TZCBS**(21a)
Ballard, Shirley **TZ**(92)
Balsam, Martin **TZ**(4, 115); **TZCBS**(18b, 34b)
Balter, Sam **TZ**(124)
Band, Neville **TZ**(151)
Bank, Douglas **TZ**(144, 146)
Bannister, Jeffrey **TZMV**(3)
Bannon, Jack **NG**(13a)
Barbeau, Adrienne **TZCBS**(7a)
Barber, Andrea **TZCBS**(5a)
Barclay, John **NG**(6c, 19b, 28b)
Bardette, Trevor **TZ**(82)
Barker, Lex **NG**(25a)
Barlow, John **TZCBS**(19b)
Barnes, Rayford **TZ**(80)
Barnes, Vickie **TZ**(88)
Barrett, Benjamin **TZSYN**(17)
Barrett, Leslie **TZ**(15)
Barrie, Barbara **TZ**(110)
Barron, James **TZSYN**(11)
Barron, Joanne **TZCBS**(13a)
Barrows, George **NG**(44a)
Barry, Gene **TZCBS**(34a)
Barry, Patricia **TZ**(31, 114); **TZMV**(3)
Barsi, Judith **TZCBS**(1b)
Bartell, Harry **TZ**(15)
Barth, Ed **TZ**(115)
Bartholome, Tricia **TZCBS**(10a)
Bartlett, Martine **TZ**(139)
Barton, Anne **TZ**(22, 62)
Barton, Larry **TZ**(122)
Basehart, Richard **TZ**(129)
Baseleon, Michael **NG**(17a)
Bass, Bobby **TZCBS**(4c)
Bass, Victoria **TZCBS**(28c)
Bassett, Joe **TZ**(11)
Bassett, Steve Howell **TZCBS**(2c)
Batanides, Arthur **TZ**(3, 71)
Bates, Jeanne **TZ**(73)
Baxley, Barbara **TZ**(107); **TZCBS**(20a)
Baxley, Paul **TZ**(18)

Baxter, George **TZ**(6)
Bean, Orson **TZ**(33)
Beck, Billy **TZ**(115)
Beck, John **TZSYN**(21)
Beck, Mary Ann **NG**(8d)
Becker, Terry **TZ**(146)
Beckley, William **NG**(6b)
Beckman, Henry **TZ**(40, 105); **NG**(7b)
Beecher, Bonnie **TZ**(154)
Bega, Leslie **TZCBS**(9a)
Behrens, Bernard **TZCBS**(2a)
Behrens, Frank **TZ**(101)
Beir, Fredrick **TZ**(108)
Beker, Jeanne **TZSYN**(10)
Belasco, Leon **TZ**(124)
Bell, Michael **NG**(22a)
Bellamy, Ned **TZCBS**(28a)
Bellamy, Ralph **TZCBS**(15a)
Bellin, Thomas **TZCBS**(18c)
Belliveau, Cynthia **TZSYN**(12)
Bellwood, Pamela **TZSYN**(24)
Bender, Russ **TZ**(16, 90, 118)
Benedict, Paul **TZCBS**(35a)
Benedict, William **TZ**(147)
Bennell, Nigel **TZSYN**(6)
Bennett, Deborah **TZCBS**(28a)
Bennett, Fran **TZCBS**(15b)
Bennett, Hywell **TZCBS**(22b)
Bennett, Marjorie E. **TZ**(31, 86, 112); **NG**(26a)
Bennett, Zachary **TZSYN**(13)
Benson, Anthony **TZ**(118)
Bently, Marc **TZCBS**(10a)
Benton, Gene **TZ**(89)
Beregi, Oscar **TZ**(60, 74, 107)
Bergen, Patrick **TZLC**(2)
Berkeley, Xander **TZCBS**(22a)
Berman, Shelley **TZ**(63)
Bernard, Barry **TZ**(10); **NG**(23b)
Bernard, Joseph **TZ**(68)
Bernarth, Shari Lee **TZ**(113)
Bernstein, Jaclyn **TZCBS**(3b)
Bernstein, Nat **TZCBS**(16c)
Best, James **TZ**(72, 88, 109)
Beswick, Martine **NG**(7a)
Betancourt, Anne **TZCBS**(2a)
Bettis, Paul **TZSYN**(8)
Betz, Carl **NG**(2a)
Bevans, Clem **TZ**(95)
Bevans, Philippe **TZ**(102)
Bieri, Raymond **TZCBS**(23a)

Bigelow, Pixie **TZSYN**(1)
Biggs, Richard **TZCBS**(29)
Biheller, Bob **TZ**(102)
Bikel, Theodore **TZ**(94)
Billings, Earl **TZCBS**(23a)
Billington, Shelby **TZCBS**(10c)
Binns, Edward **TZ**(15, 135)
Birk, Raye **TZCBS**(2a, 28b)
Birkett, Bernadette **TZCBS**(28c)
Birney, David **TZCBS**(16c)
Bishop, Rummy **TZSYN**(14)
Bishop, Stephen **TZMV**(1)
Bixby, Bill **TZ**(104); **NG**(25b, 30)
Blackwood, John **TZSYN**(24)
Blake, Ellen **NG**(27b)
Blake, Larry **TZ**(45); **NG**(19a)
Blakely, Susan **TZCBS**(32a)
Blanch, Jewel **NG**(6c)
Bliss, Lela **TZ**(8)
Block, Hayley Taylor **TZCBS**(11a)
Blodgett, Michael **NG**(2a)
Blondell, Joan **TZ**(144)
Bloomfield, Don **TZLC**(1)
Blossom, Roberts **TZCBS**(8b, 35a)
Bluhm, Brandon **TZCBS**(16a)
Blum, Jack **TZSYN**(21)
Blumenfeld, Alan **TZCBS**(22c)
Blyden, Larry **TZ**(28, 85)
Blyth, Ann **TZ**(143)
Bocaccio, Gerard **TZCBS**(20a)
Bochner, Lloyd **TZ**(89)
Bogosian, Eric **TZCBS**(3a)
Bohn, Merritt **TZ**(2, 122)
Bolender, Bill **TZLC**(2)
Boles, Jim **TZ**(67, 109); **NG**(23a, 41)
Bolt, John **TZ**(154)
Bonar, Ivan **NG**(13a)
Bond, David **TZ**(115)
Bondy, Chris **TZSYN**(15)
Bonnell, Vivian **TZCBS**(3a)
Bonney, Gail **NG**(12a)
Boone, Pat **NG**(11d)
Boone, Randy **TZ**(130)
Boone, Robert **TZ**(74, 107)
Booth, Billy **TZ**(30)
Booth, Nesdon **TZ**(6, 57)
Borden, Eugene **TZ**(83)
Boretski, Peter **TZSYN**(22)
Borrie, Alexandra **TZCBS**(29)
Bosley, Tom **NG**(1b, 5a)
Bostrom, Zachary **TZCBS**(32a)

Bottoms, Timothy **TZSYN**(7)
Bouchey, Willis **TZ**(145)
Boulting, Ingrid **TZCBS**(5b)
Bower, Antoinette **TZ**(129)
Boyd, Guy **TZCBS**(23a)
Boyd, Tanya **TZCBS**(32b)
Bradley, Brian **TZCBS**(2a)
Bradley, Leslie **TZ**(10)
Brahm, Roberta Carol **NG**(28a)
Brainard, Richard **TZCBS**(7a)
Brandon, Henry **NG**(43)
Brandt, Hank **NG**(13b)
Brannt, Janya **NG**(25b)
Bray, Robert **TZ**(130)
Brazell, Wolfe **TZ**(106)
Breitman, Larry **TZ**(95)
Breman, Lennie **TZ**(115)
Brenner, Eve **TZCBS**(15a, 34b)
Breslin, Patricia **TZ**(43, 112)
Brestoff, Richard **TZCBS**(15b)
Brinkley, Ritch **TZCBS**(19b)
Brittany, Morgan (see Cupito, Suzanne)
Britton, Bonnie-Campbell **TZCBS**(16b)
Britton, Robert **TZCBS**(27a)
Brocco, Peter **TZ**(13, 95); **NG**(26a); **TZMV**(2)
Broderick, James **TZ**(118)
Bronson, Charles **TZ**(66)
Brooke, Walter **TZ**(77, 131)
Brooks, Albert **TZMV**(P)
Brooks, Barry **TZ**(65)
Brooks, Joel **TZCBS**(18c)
Brooks, Martin E. **NG**(7a)
Brown, Barry **NG**(5b)
Brown, Beverly **TZ**(54)
Brown, Christopher **TZCBS**(31)
Brown, Clarence **TZCBS**(21a)
Brown, D.W. **TZCBS**(17b)
Brown, Dwier **TZCBS**(2a)
Brown, Helen **TZ**(99)
Brown, Johnny **NG**(44b)
Brown, Lew **TZ**(40, 49, 58, 130); **NG**(36)
Brown, Pamela **TZCBS**(3b)
Brown, Vanessa **TZCBS**(6b)
Brown Wyeth, Sandy **TZCBS**(3b)
Browning, James **TZ**(102)
Brubaker, Robert **TZ**(67)
Bruce, Carol **TZCBS**(9b)
Bruns, Philip **TZCBS**(3c)
Bryant, John **TZCBS**(7b)

Bryant, Joshua NG(18a)
Bryar, Claudia TZ(107); TZCBS(17a)
Bryar, Paul TZ(11)
Buchanan, Edgar TZ(88)
Buktenika, Ray TZCBS(22a)
Bullock, Earl TZCBS(29)
Bullock, Osmond TZCBS(22b)
Bundy, Brooke NG(41)
Buono, Victor NG(16b, 47)
Burgess, Cara NG(23b)
Burgess, Jane TZ(57)
Burgess, Michael TZLC(1)
Burke, Christine TZ(116)
Burke, Walter TZ(27); NG(26a)
Burkholder, Scott TZLC(1)
Burlingame, Brad TZCBS(3c)
Burnett, Carol TZ(101)
Burnett, Tannis TZSYN(15)
Burnham, Terry TZ(29)
Burns, Bart TZ(105)
Burns, Michael TZ(68)
Burns, Paul E. TZ(6)
Burroughs, Jackie TZSYN(25)
Burton, Jeff NG(22a)
Burton, Robert TZ(3)
Bush, Rebeccah TZCBS(33c)
Busia, Akosua TZCBS(28b)
Buza, George TZSYN(29)
Buzzi, Ruth NG(9d)
Byrd, Thomas TZMV(1)
Byron, Carol TZ(132)
Cabot, Cecil NG(16d)
Cabot, Sebastian TZ(28)
Cadeau, Lally TZSYN(19)
Caesar, Adolph TZCBS(15c)
Caine, Howard TZ(106)
Calder, King TZ(45, 105)
Calhoun, Jeff TZCBS(10a)
Caliri, Jonathan TZCBS(17a)
Call, Ed NG(11d)
Call, Tony TZ(104)
Callahan, James TZ(132)
Cambridge, Godfrey NG(5a)
Camp, Hamilton TZCBS(14b)
Camp, Wilson TZCBS(13a)
Campanella, Joseph NG(3c, 8b)
Campbell, Julia TZLC(2)
Campbell, Lee J. TZSYN(11)
Carbone, Tony TZ(71)
Carlin, George NG(44b)
Carlson, Charles S. TZ(45)

Carlson, Les TZSYN(4)
Carlson, Steve NG(18b)
Carlyle, Johny TZCBS(1a)
Carmen, Julie TZCBS(4b)
Carney, Art TZ(47)
Carradine, David NG(12a)
Carradine, John TZ(41); NG(15c);
TZCBS(14a)
Carradine, Robert TZCBS(14a)
Carrier, Albert TZ(101)
Carrigan, Douglas TZSYN(19)
Carroll, Christopher TZCBS(22b)
Carroll, Dee TZ(43)
Carroll, Janet TZCBS(18c)
Carroll, J. Winston TZSYN(2)
Carry, Lou TZCBS(18b)
Carson, Jack TZ(50)
Carson, Jean TZ(46)
Carson, Fred NG(14b)
Carter, Claire TZCBS(14c)
Carter, Conlan TZ(104)
Carter, Mitch TZCBS(25a)
Cartwright, Nancy TZMV(3)
Cartwright, Veronica TZ(100)
Carver, Brent TZSYN(22)
Carver, Mary TZ(117)
Cassel, Seymour TZ(136)
Cassidy, Jack NG(7a)
Catron, Jerry TZ(18)
Cavell, Marc TZ(19)
Cedar, Larry TZMV(4)
Cervenka, Exene TZCBS(4c)
Challee, William TZ(72); NG(3b)
Chambers, Joan TZ(110)
Chambers, Phil TZ(115)
Chandler, George TZ(50)
Chandler, Jeffrey Alan TZCBS(6a)
Chapman, Lonny NG(12b)
Chase, Eric NG(15c)
Chaykin, Maury TZSYN(20)
Chesney, Diana NG(15a)
Chevrier, Don TZSYN(2)
Cheylov, Milan TZSYN(14)
Chilcott, Barbara TZSYN(1)
Chiles, Linden TZ(94)
Christine, Virginia TZ(6)
Christmas, Eric NG(16a)
Christopherson, Peg TZSYN(24)
Christy, Al TZCBS(7a)
Christy, Ted TZ(144)
Clark, Dane TZ(57); NG(34)

Clark, Dort NG(38)
Clark, Eugene TZSYN(21)
Clark, Fred TZ(46)
Clark, Gage TZ(82)
Clark, Oliver TZCBS(16c)
Clarke, John TZ(4)
Classen, Joy TZCBS(26a)
Claudier, Annette TZMV(1)
Clayton, Melissa TZCBS(27a)
Cletro, Timmy TZ(33)
Cliff, John TZ(152)
Close, John TZ(28, 62)
Close, Pat TZ(102)
Cloud, Lisa TZCBS(19b)
Clute, Sidney NG(5a)
Coburn, James TZ(127)
Coca, Imogene NG(9b)
Cochran, Steve TZ(12)
Coco, James TZCBS(8a)
Coe, Peter TZ(38)
Coffey, Scott TZCBS(33c)
Coffin, Frederick TZCBS(14c)
Cohane, Suzanne NG(9c)
Colbin, Rod TZCBS(21b)
Cole, Gary TZCBS(12a); TZLC(1)
Colicos, John NG(6b)
Colley, Don Pedro NG(16c)
Collins, Burton TZCBS(30)
Collins, Jack NG(37)
Collins, Johnnie (III) NG(15d)
Collins, Jolina TZCBS(13b)
Collins, Patricia TZSYN(21)
Collins, Robert TZSYN(21)
Collins, Russell TZ(86)
Colmans, Edward NG(6b)
Comerate, Sheridan TZ(5)
Comi, Paul TZ(25, 54, 113)
Comiskey, Pat TZ(13)
Compton, Forrest TZ(104)
Connelly, Christopher NG(34)
Connolly, Norma TZ(53)
Connors, Chuck NG(35)
Conrad, Michael TZ(138)
Conroy, Burt TZ(153)
Conroy, Frances TZCBS(22c)
Considine, John TZ(104)
Constantine, Michael TZ(146); NG(8a)
Constanzo, Robert TZCBS(3a)
Conte, Richard TZ(9)
Convy, Bert NG(7b)
Conway, Curt TZ(106)

Conwell, John TZ(34)
Cook, Elisha TZCBS(17a)
Cooksey, Danny TZCBS(8b)
Coolidge, Phil TZ(87)
Cooper, Ben TZ(76)
Cooper, Clancy TZ(57)
Cooper, Gladys TZ(81, 119, 139)
Cooper, Jackie TZ(148)
Cooper, Jeanne TZ(3)
Cooper, Maxine TZ(11)
Corbett, Glenn NG(14b)
Corbin, Barry TZCBS(19b)
Corby, Ellen NG(32)
Cord, Alex NG(17b)
Cordell, Cathleen NG(2b, 47)
Corden, Henry TZ(97)
Corder, Sharon TZSYN(21)
Cordic, Regis J. NG(33)
Cordova, Margarita TZ(40)
Corey, Jeff NG(2a) (also see
CREATIVE
PERSONNEL)
Corey, Joseph TZ(5)
Cornaly, Anne TZ(142)
Cornthwaithe, Robert TZ(85, 112)
Cort, Bud TZSYN(14)
Court, Alyson TZSYN(23)
Court, Hazel TZ(155)
Cousins, Kay TZ(47)
Cowan, Jerome TZ(4)
Cox, Wally TZ(140); NG(11b)
Coyne, Kathleen TZCBS(10a)
Coyote, Peter TZCBS(23a)
Crane, Bob TZ(56); NG(16a)
Crane, Norma NG(1c)
Crane, Susan TZ(100)
Cravat, Nick TZ(123)
Craven, John TZ(127)
Craven, Wes TZCBS(3b) (also see
CREATIVE PERSONNEL)
Crawford, Broderick NG(28a)
Crawford, Eve TZSYN(1)
Crawford, Joan NG(1b)
Crawford, John TZ(59)
Crawford Brown, Pat TZCBS(14b)
Crockett, Karlene TZCBS(16b)
Cromwell, James TZCBS(6b)
Cron, Claudia TZCBS(33c)
Cronyn, Martha TZSYN(19)
Crosby, Gary TZ(154)
Crosby, Toria TZCBS(13a)

Cross, Ben **TZCBS**(22b)
Cross, Jimmy **NG**(18c)
Crothers, Scatman **TZMV**(2)
Crowder, Jack **TZ**(153)
Crowley, Patricia **TZ**(111)
Culley, Zara **NG**(21c)
Culver, Howard **TZ**(62)
Cumbuka, Ji-Tu **NG**(35)
Cummings, Robert **TZ**(37)
Cummings, Susan **TZ**(89)
Cunningham, Owen **NG**(13a)
Cunningham, Tracey **TZSYN**(2)
Cupito, Suzanne **TZ**(29, 105, 148)
Currie, Cherie **TZMV**(3)
Curtis, Billy **TZCBS**(18b)
Curtis, Craig **TZ**(115)
D'Antonio, Carmen **TZ**(97)
Dailey, Irene **TZ**(107)
Dale, Jennifer **TZSYN**(8)
Dallimore, Maurice **TZ**(101)
Daly, James **TZ**(30)
Daniels, Alex **TZCBS**(33c)
Danny, Pierre **TZ**(142)
Dano, Royal **NG**(27a)
Danova, Cesare **NG**(48)
Dantine, Helmut **TZ**(13b)
Danton, Mark **TZSYN**(14)
Danton, Ray **NG**(24a)
Danziger, Kenneth **TZCBS**(16b)
Darden, Severn **NG**(28a)
Darin, Bobby **NG**(26c)
Darrow, Henry **NG**(19a)
Darrow, Susannah **NG**(7b)
Darvas, Lili **TZ**(58)
Dauber, Lewis **TZCBS**(15a)
Davey, John **NG**(9c); **TZCBS**(3c)
David, Alan **TZCBS**(28a)
Davidson, James **NG**(22c)
Davies, Glynis **TZSYN**(10)
Davis, Brad **TZCBS**(20b)
Davis, Charles **NG**(6b, 35)
Davis, Jerry **TZ**(117)
Davis, Jim **NG**(25a)
Davis, Ossie **NG**(1a)
Davis, Roger **TZ**(141); **NG**(36)
Dawber, Pam **TZCBS**(13b)
Dawson, Hal K. **TZ**(85)
Dayton, June **TZ**(52)
De Camp, Rosemary **NG**(20b)
De Corsia, Ted **TZ**(4, 153)
De La Pena, Gilbert **TZCBS**(23a)

De Longis, Tony **TZCBS**(30)
De Marney, Terrence **TZ**(96)
De Vries, Mark **NG**(13b)
De Wilde, Brandon **NG**(9c)
De Witt, Jacqueline **TZ**(8)
Deacon, Richard **TZ**(153); **NG**(44b)
Dean, Floy **NG**(15a)
Dee, Sandra **NG**(21b, 34)
Defales, Francis **TZ**(147)
Dehner, John **TZ**(7, 77, 152)
DeLain, Marguerite **TZCBS**(19a)
DeLancie, John **TZCBS**(19b)
Delegall, Bob **TZCBS**(26b)
Delevanti, Cyril **TZ**(52, 61, 87, 119);
  NG(28b)
Demarest, William **TZ**(144)
DeMita, John **TZCBS**(3c)
DeMunn, Jeffrey **TZCBS**(3c)
Denomme, Kelly **TZSYN**(14)
Devine, Andy **TZ**(95)
Devon, Laura **TZ**(109)
Devon, Richard **TZ**(83)
Dewhurst, Colleen **TZSYN**(13)
Dexter, Alan **TZ**(35)
DeYoung, Cliff **TZCBS**(31)
Diamond, Robert **TZ**(121)
Diamond, Selma **TZMV**(2)
Diaz, Edith **TZCBS**(25b)
Dillaway, Dana **TZ**(2, 100)
Diller, Phyllis **NG**(6a)
Dillman, Bradford **NG**(18a)
Dillon, Brendan **NG**(6b, 19b)
Dillon, Melinda **TZCBS**(1b)
Dishy, Bob **TZCBS**(8a)
Divoff, Andrew **TZCBS**(21b)
Dixon, Donna **TZMV**(4)
Dixon, Glenn **NG**(2a)
Dixon, Ivan **TZ**(27, 146)
Dixon, Jo Ann **TZ**(55)
Dobo, Michael **TZCBS**(28a)
Dolan, Julie **TZCBS**(9a)
Dolan, Rudy **TZ**(98)
Donahue, Patricia **TZ**(30); **NG**(8c, 18b)
Donahue, Shawn **TZCBS**(10c)
Donald, John **NG**(8a)
Donath, Ludwig **TZ**(106)
Donno, Eddie **TZMV**(1)
Donoghue, Tim **TZCBS**(14b)
Donovan, KiNG **NG**(9b)
Doohan, James **TZ**(105)
Doran, Ann **TZCBS**(32b)

Dorn, Susan **TZ**(23)
Douglas, Donna **TZ**(42, 101); **NG**(25b)
Douglass, Diane **TZSYN**(12)
Doukas, Nike **TZCBS**(27a)
Dowling, Stuart **TZCBS**(22b)
Downey, Ferne **TZSYN**(13)
Downey, Robert J. **TZCBS**(2a)
Downs, Frederic **NG**(7b)
Doyle, Martin **TZCBS**(26b)
Doyle, Richard **NG**(9c)
Drake, Ken **TZ**(124)
Dreger, Reg **TZSYN**(23)
Dremann, Beau **TZCBS**(34a)
Dubbins, Don **TZ**(20)
Duckworth, Todd **TZSYN**(26)
Duff, Howard **TZ**(23); **NG**(27b)
Duffy, Thomas F. **TZCBS**(13a)
Dugan, Sue **TZMV**(1)
Duggan, Bob **TZ**(55, 56)
Duke, Patty **NG**(15a)
Dukes, David **TZCBS**(5b)
Dumbrille, Douglass **TZ**(136)
Dunn, Michael **NG**(28b)
Dunne, Murphy **TZCBS**(10b)
Dunsmore, Rosemary **TZSYN**(15)
Dupont, Dexter **TZ**(84)
Durand, Jean **NG**(43)
Durant, Don **TZ**(87)
Duryea, Dan **TZ**(3)
Duvall, Robert **TZ**(110)
Duvall, Shelley **TZCBS**(25b)
Dzundza, George **TZCBS**(21b)
Eaton, Gillian **TZCBS**(15b)
Eaton, Robert **TZ**(93)
Ebsen, Buddy **TZ**(57); **NG**(25a)
Edmonson, William **TZ**(12, 62)
Eiding, Paul **TZCBS**(25a)
Eilbacher, Beverly **TZCBS**(32a)
Eilbacher, Lisa **TZCBS**(27b)
Eilber, Janet **TZCBS**(23a)
Eiman, Johnny **TZ**(90)
Eisenmann, Christopher **TZMV**(2)
Elam, Jack **TZ**(64)
Eldredge, John **TZ**(49)
Elias, Jeannie **TZCBS**(13b)
Elias, Louie **TZ**(104)
Elic, Joseph **TZ**(65, 82)
Elliott, Bill **NG**(9a)
Elliott, Ross **TZ**(108, 121)
Ellis, Jill **TZ**(64)
Ellis, Judy **TZ**(12)

Ellis, June **TZ**(75)
Ellis, Monie **NG**(15b)
Emerson, Douglas **TZCBS**(16a)
Emhardt, Robert **TZ**(56)
Emille, Michelyn **TZSYN**(5)
English, Barbara **TZ**(28)
Ennis, Michael **TZCBS**(26a)
Erdman, Richard **TZ**(124)
Erickson, Leif **NG**(11d ,40)
Erlich, Phyllis **TZCBS**(13a)
Erway, Ben **TZ**(22)
Erwin, Bill **TZ**(3, 5, 64)
Evans, Douglas **TZ**(55)
Evans, Evans **TZ**(59)
Evans, Jeanne **TZ**(14, 89)
Evans, John Williams **NG**(9a)
Evans, Ross **TZCBS**(23b)
Fabares, Shelley **TZ**(138)
Falk, Peter **TZ**(71)
Farentino, James **NG**(10a, 31)
Farrell, Terry **TZCBS**(28a)
Faustino, David **TZCBS**(27a)
Fawcett, Bill **TZ**(88)
Faye, Herb **TZ**(124)
Fein, Bernard **TZ**(13, 106)
Felder, Clarence **TZCBS**(3c)
Fell, Norman **TZCBS**(30)
Fenmore, Tanya **TZMV**(2)
Ferdin, Pamelyn **NG**(14b)
Ferguson, Frank **TZ**(143)
Ferrell, Tyra **TZCBS**(9a)
Ferris, Adam **TZCBS**(3a)
Feury, Peggy **NG**(37)
Fey, Stephane **TZ**(142)
Fiedler, John **TZ**(47, 101)
Field, Logan **TZ**(11)
Field, Sally **NG**(42)
Fielding, Elizabeth **TZ**(11)
Filippone, Lucy **TZSYN**(6)
Filips, Jan **TZSYN**(25)
Fimple, Dennis **TZCBS**(17a)
Finnegan, Tom **TZCBS**(23b, 28c)
Fisher, Brad **TZCBS**(19b)
Fitch, Louise **TZCBS**(33c)
Fitzgerald, Margaret **TZMV**(4)
Fix, Paul **TZ**(146)
Flanagan, Deidre **TZSYN**(6)
Flanigan, Stephen **TZCBS**(18b)
Flavin, James **TZ**(32, 78)
Fleer, Harry **TZ**(65, 78)
Fletcher, Lester **TZ**(54)

Fletcher, Louise **TZSYN**(4)
Fletcher, Page **TZSYN**(24)
Flicker, Barbara **NG**(11b)
Flicker, Theodore **NG**(16d) (also see CREATIVE PERSONNEL)
Fluegel, Darlanne **TZCBS**(18a)
Flynn, Gertrude **TZ**(64); **TZCBS**(19b)
Flynn, Joe **TZ**(6); **NG**(22b)
Foley, Joan **TZCBS**(33c)
Foray, June **TZ**(126)
Ford, Constance **TZ**(128)
Ford, Corky **TZCBS**(7b)
Ford, Michael **TZ**(93)
Forest, Michael **TZ**(138)
Forrest, Mabel **TZ**(88)
Forrest, Stephen **TZ**(113); **NG**(25a, 44a)
Forsyth, Rosemary **NG**(26a)
Fortunato, Dean **TZCBS**(16b)
Foster, Donald **TZ**(77)
Foster, Jamie **TZ**(103)
Foster, Meg **TZCBS**(2b)
Foster, Ron **TZ**(130)
Foulger, Byron **TZ**(5)
Foulk, Robert **TZ**(84)
Foulkes, Ted **NG**(17a)
Fox, Bernard **NG**(16a)
Fox, Chuck **TZ**(74)
Fox, John J. **NG**(5a, 16d, 20a)
Fox, Michael **TZ**(29, 55, 147); **TZCBS**(6b)
Frakes, Jonathan **TZCBS**(13b)
Franciosa, Anthony **TZSYN**(29)
Francis, Anne **TZ**(34, 109)
Francis, Ivor **NG**(12a, 29b)
Franciscus, James **TZ**(10)
Frank, David **NG**(7b)
Franken, Steve **NG**(4a)
Frankfather, William **TZCBS**(32b)
Franklin, Camille **TZ**(111)
Franz, Eduard **TZMV**(4)
Frappier, Jill **TZSYN**(9)
Fraser, Aaron Ross **TZSYN**(19)
Freeman, Morgan **TZCBS**(8c)
Fresco, Davis **TZ**(97); **NG**(33)
Friedkin, Gary **TZCBS**(18b)
Frishman, Dan **TZCBS**(18b)
Frizzell, Lou **NG**(16c)
Frome, Milton **TZ**(13)
Frost, Alice **TZ**(4, 73)
Fudge, Alan **TZCBS**(17a)

Fujikawa, Jerry **TZ**(80)
Fuller, Jerry **TZ**(56)
Fuller, Lance **TZ**(88)
Furth, George **NG**(3b)
Gabor, Zsa Zsa **NG**(20b)
Gallagher, Jack **TZCBS**(16b)
Gallo, Lew **TZ**(16, 60, 118)
Galvin, Ray **TZ**(82)
Gammell, Robin **TZCBS**(21a)
Ganzel, Teresa **TZCBS**(16c)
Ganzer, Sandra **TZCBS**(34b)
Garber, Terri **TZSYN**(8)
Garber, Victor **TZCBS**(24a)
Garcia, David **TZ**(69)
Garcia, Margarita **NG**(24a)
Garde, Betty **TZ**(54, 75)
Gardenia, Vincent **TZCBS**(3a)
Gardiner, John **TZSYN**(25)
Garland, Beverly **TZ**(13)
Garner, Martin **TZMV**(2)
Garner, Shay **TZCBS**(21a)
Garrett, Hank **TZCBS**(23a)
Garth, Anabel **NG**(23a)
Garwood, Kelton **TZ**(79)
Gates, Larry **TZ**(68)
Gavin, James **TZ**(49)
Gazzaniga, Don **TZ**(148)
Geary, Richard **TZ**(72)
Gei, Angela **TZSYN**(18)
Gelman, Alan David **TZCBS**(15c)
Gemignani, Rhoda **TZCBS**(23b)
Genge, Paul **TZ**(48)
Geoffreys, Stephen **TZCBS**(16a)
Gerber, Jay **TZCBS**(22c)
Gershon, Gina **TZCBS**(34a)
Gerson, Betty Lou **TZ**(133)
Giambalvo, Louis **TZCBS**(20a)
Gibbons, Robert **NG**(11d)
Gibson, Henry **TZCBS**(17a)
Gierasch, Stefan **TZCBS**(15b)
Gilbert, Jody **NG**(16d)
Gilchrist, Connie **TZ**(121)
Gilgreen, John **NG**(38)
Gilleran, Tom **TZ**(138)
Gillespie, Larrian **TZ**(47)
Gilman, Kenneth David **TZCBS**(27b)
Gilvezan, Dan **TZCBS**(1a)
Ging, Jack **TZ**(50)
Giovi, Marlena **TZCBS**(18b)
Girard, Wendy **TZCBS**(12a)
Girling, Cindy **TZSYN**(28)

Glass, Everett **TZ**(61)
Glass, Ned **TZ**(32, 75); **NG**(25b)
Glass, Ron **TZCBS**(12b)
Glazer, Eugene Robert **TZSYN**(30)
Glover, Ed **TZ**(92)
Glover, John **TZCBS**(15b)
Goetz, Peter Michael **TZCBS**(15b)
Goldsmith, David **TZCBS**(10a)
Golm, Lisa **TZ**(38)
Gomez, Thomas **TZ**(6, 48)
Gordon, Don **TZ**(13, 136)
Gordon, Gerald **TZ**(121)
Gordon, Pamela **TZCBS**(1b)
Gordon, Susan **TZ**(90)
Gordon, William D. **TZ**(39, 42)
Gorman, Mari **TZCBS**(25b)
Gosch, Christopher **TZCBS**(10a)
Gosselaar, Mark-Paul **TZCBS**(26a)
Gossette, Lorne **TZSYN**(26)
Gottarelli, Gino **NG**(13b)
Gould, Elliot **TZCBS**(14c)
Gould, Harold **TZ**(129, 156)
Gould, Sandra **TZ**(101, 144)
Governick, Harry **TZCBS**(13a)
Gowans, John **TZCBS**(5a)
Gower, André **TZCBS**(8b)
Graham, Gerrit **TZCBS**(17a) (also see
CREATIVE PERSONNEL)
Granato, Sherry **TZ**(103)
Grant, Norah **TZSYN**(25)
Gray, Lorraine **NG**(39)
Gray, Vernon **TZ**(25)
Green, Austin **TZ**(69)
Green, Janice **TZSYN**(19)
Green, Joey **TZCBS**(19a)
Green, Johnny **TZCBS**(26a)
Green, Laurel **TZCBS**(34a)
Green, Seymour **TZ**(37)
Greene, Michael **TZCBS**(3c)
Greenleaf, Raymond **TZ**(49)
Greenlee, David **TZCBS**(29)
Greer, Dabbs **TZ**(95, 105)
Greer, Lenny **TZ**(127)
Greer, Will **NG**(45)
Gregg, Bradley **TZCBS**(19a)
Gregg, Virginia **TZ**(109, 145)
Gregory, Benjie **TZCBS**(13a)
Gregory, James **TZ**(1, 69); **NG**(26b)
Gregory, Mary **TZ**(22, 44, 68);
NG(21a)
Grey, Bethelynn **TZ**(98)

Grey, Duane **TZ**(31, 48)
Grey, Joel **NG**(27b)
Gries, Jonathan **TZCBS**(33b)
Griffin, Jennifer **TZCBS**(23)
Grimes, Scott **TZCBS**(4a)
Grinnage, Jack **TZ**(63)
Griswold, Claire **TZ**(110)
Grizzard, George **TZ**(31, 103)
Gronning, Pia **TZCBS**(9a)
Gross, Edan **TZCBS**(28a)
Grove, Christopher **TZCBS**(22b)
Gruber, John **NG**(11d)
Grumbach, Anthony **TZCBS**(1a)
Guadagni, Nicky **TZSYN**(16)
Guardino, Harry **NG**(24a)
Guastaferro, Vincent **TZCBS**(2b)
Guild, Lyn **TZ**(22)
Haas, Lukas **TZCBS**(26a)
Haase, Heather **TZCBS**(10a, 34a)
Hacker, Joseph **TZCBS**(26b)
Hackett, Joan **TZ**(87)
Hagen, Kevin **TZ**(20, 134)
Hagen, Uta **TZCBS**(22c)
Hagerthy, Ron **TZ**(83)
Hagman, Larry **NG**(2b)
Haid, Charles **TZSYN**(18)
Haigh, Kenneth **TZ**(18)
Hale, Barnaby **TZ**(106)
Hale, Diana **NG**(22b)
Hall, Grayson **NG**(4b)
Hall, Margie **NG**(7b)
Hall, Randy **TZCBS**(33a)
Hall Lovell, Andrea **TZCBS**(10c)
Hallahan, Charles **TZMV**(1)
Hallier, Lori **TZSYN**(15)
Hamill, Mark **NG**(27b)
Hamilton, Antony **TZCBS**(27b)
Hamilton, Bernie **TZ**(62)
Hamilton, Joe **TZ**(21)
Hamilton, Kim **TZ**(27)
Hamilton, Murray **TZ**(2); **NG**(16c)
Hammond, Reid **TZ**(58)
Hampton, Roger **TZCBS**(15a)
Hancock, John **TZCBS**(30)
Handzlik, Jan **TZ**(22)
Hanek, John **TZ**(134)
Haney, Anne **TZCBS**(29)
Hansen, Dion **TZ**(128, 153)
Hansen, J. Omar **TZCBS**(25b)
Hansen, William **NG**(8a)
Harcourt, Shelagh **TZSYN**(3)

Hardin, Jerry **TZCBS**(20a)
Hardwicke, Cedric (Sir) **TZ**(128)
Harlan, Laura **TZCBS**(25b)
Harling, Noelle **TZCBS**(7a)
Harmon, Deborah **TZCBS**(13b)
Harmon, John **TZ**(98, 116)
Harper, Banks **TZCBS**(25a)
Harper, Tess **TZCBS**(17b)
Harrell, Cindy **TZCBS**(28b)
Harris, Jonathan **TZ**(53, 61); **NG**(10a)
Harris, Joshua **TZCBS**(1b)
Harrison, Susan **TZ**(79)
Harrower, Elizabeth **TZ**(146)
Hart, Buddy **TZ**(102)
Hart, Michael **NG**(5a)
Hartford, Betty **TZ**(92)
Hartford, Dee **TZ**(156)
Hartley, Mariette **TZ**(135)
Hartman, Elizabeth **NG**(17a)
Hartman, Paul **TZ**(49)
Harvey, Irene **TZ**(138)
Harvey, Laurence **NG**(29a)
Haskins, Dennis **TZCBS**(34b)
Hastings, Bob **TZ**(114)
Hatcher, Tom **TZ**(73)
Hatton, Brian **TZCBS**(25a)
Haufrect, Alan **TZMV**(2)
Havard, Elven **TZCBS**(14c)
Haworth, Joe **TZ**(26)
Haydn, Richard **TZ**(40)
Hayes, Chad **TZCBS**(2c)
Hayes, Ryan **TZ**(30)
Hays, Kathryn **NG**(39)
Hayward, Brooke **TZ**(145)
Hayward, David **TZCBS**(2b, 25b)
Hayward, Louis **NG**(4b)
Heath, Dody **TZ**(24)
Hebert, Chris **TZCBS**(11b)
Hector, Jay **TZ**(55)
Hector, Kim **TZ**(156)
Hector, Pat **TZ**(88)
Hedaya, Dan **TZCBS**(8c)
Heffley, Wayne **TZ**(54, 138)
Heller, Chip **TZCBS**(17a, 28a)
Helmore, Tom **NG**(29a)
Helton, Jo **TZ**(68, 118)
Helton, Percy **TZ**(107, 152)
Hemblen, David **TZSYN**(12)
Hemsley, Sherman **TZCBS**(12b)
Henderson, Bill **TZCBS**(13a)
Hendler, Julia **TZCBS**(10a)

Hengen, Butch **TZ**(30)
Henkins, Paul **NG**(40)
Herbert, Charles **TZ**(100)
Herbert, Pitt **TZ**(101)
Herrman, Robert **NG**(7b)
Hertford, Whitby **TZCBS**(16b)
Heslov, Grant **TZCBS**(34a)
Hess, James **TZCBS**(19a)
Heyes, Douglas **TZ**(51) (also see CREATIVE PERSONNEL)
Heyes, Joanna **TZ**(42)
Heyes, Jr., Douglas **TZ**(48)
Heyman, Barton **TZ**(129)
Hickman, Bill **TZ**(133)
Hickox, Harry **NG**(22a)
Hicks, Chuck **TZ**(122, 132)
Hicks, Hilly **NG**(9c)
Hieu, Joseph **TZMV**(1)
Higgins, Joe **TZ**(92)
Higgins, Barry **NG**(27b)
Hiken, Gerald **TZCBS**(6b)
Hill, Carol **TZ**(79)
Hill, Ken **TZCBS**(20a)
Hillaire, Marcel **TZ**(46, 115)
Hingle, Pat **TZ**(117)
Hirt, Christianne **TZSYN**(16)
Hobart, Rose **NG**(18b)
Hobbs, Mary Gail **NG**(7b)
Hobbs, Peter **TZCBS**(16b)
Hodgins, Earl **TZ**(86)
Hoffman, Basil **TZCBS**(20b)
Hoffman, Bern **NG**(39)
Hogan, Michael **TZSYN**(4)
Hogan, Robert **TZ**(141); **NG**(14b)
Hole, Jonathan **TZ**(35)
Holland, John **TZ**(61)
Holliman, Earl **TZ**(1)
Hollis, Gary **TZCBS**(10c)
Holloway, Sterling **TZ**(144)
Holman, Rex **TZ**(69)
Holmes, Wendell **TZ**(6)
Honodel, Diane **TZ**(32)
Hope, Barclay **TZSYN**(16)
Hopkins, Bob **TZ**(13)
Hopper, Dennis **TZ**(106)
Horan, Barbra **TZCBS**(26b)
Horne, Geoffrey **TZ**(97)
Hornsby, Peter **TZ**(28)
Horton, Russell **TZ**(102, 121)
Horvarth, Charles **TZ**(27)
Hosea, Bobby **TZCBS**(32b)

Hotchkiss, Frank **NG**(9c)
Houghton, Jim **TZ**(88)
Houghton, Mona **TZ**(79)
House, Eric **TZSYN**(26)
Howard, Arliss **TZCBS**(3c)
Howard, Clint **NG**(8a)
Howard, Jennifer **TZ**(42)
Howard, Rance **NG**(8a)
Howard, Ron **TZ**(5)
Hoy, Robert **NG**(8c)
Hoyos, Rodolfo **TZ**(71); **NG**(24a)
Hoyt, Clegg **TZ**(56, 120)
Hoyt, John **TZ**(44, 64)
Hubbert, Cork **TZCBS**(19a)
Hubley, Season **TZCBS**(4a)
Huddle, Elizabeth **TZCBS**(13c)
Hudson, Deirdre **NG**(18c)
Hughes, David **TZSYN**(13)
Hughes, Jackson **TZCBS**(33c)
Hughes, Robin **TZ**(41)
Humphreys, Alf **TZSYN**(13)
Hunnicutt, Arthur **TZ**(84)
Hunt, Marsha **TZ**(141)
Hunter, Henry **TZ**(58)
Hunter, J. Michael **TZLC**(2)
Hunter, Kim **NG**(23c)
Huntington, Joan **NG**(8c)
Hush, Lisabeth **NG**(12b)
Hutchinson, Josephine **TZ**(100)
Hutton, James **TZ**(11)
Huxham, Kendrick **TZ**(10)
Hyde, Jack **TZ**(62)
Hyde-White, Wilfrid **TZ**(119)
Hyland, Diana **TZ**(141)
Hyland, Frances **TZSYN**(5)
Idelson, William **TZ**(23)
Idette, Patricia **TZSYN**(8)
Ingersoll, Mary **TZCBS**(25b)
Inness, Jean **TZ**(49)
Innocent, Harold **TZ**(65)
Ireland, Jill **NG**(24b)
Irvin, Greg **TZ**(55)
Irving, Amy **TZLC**(1)
Isaac, Vincent J. **TZMV**(1)
Ishimoto, Dale **TZ**(80)
Isler, Seth **TZCBS**(1a)
Ives, Burl **NG**(37)
Jackson, Elma Veronda **TZCBS**(1b)
Jackson, Harry **TZ**(13, 52)
Jackson, Sherry **TZ**(88)
Jacques, Ted **TZ**(136)

Jacquet, Roger **TZ**(142)
Jaeck, Scott **TZCBS**(3c)
Jaffe, Sam **NG**(1c)
Jagger, Dean **TZ**(56)
Jakub, Lisa **TZSYN**(18)
Jalbert, Pierre **NG**(6b)
Jameson, Joyce **TZ**(114)
Jamison, Richard **TZCBS**(16b)
Janiss, Vivi **TZ**(17, 38)
Jason, Harvey **NG**(22b)
Jefferson, Jr., Herbert **NG**(5b)
Jenkins, Paul **TZCBS**(19b)
Jenkins, Teryn **TZCBS**(15a)
Jillian, Ann **TZ**(107)
Johns, Larry **TZ**(72)
Johnson, Anthony **TZCBS**(3a)
Johnson, Arch W. **TZ**(56, 85)
Johnson, Arte **TZ**(50); **NG**(10c)
Johnson, Jason **TZ**(22, 44)
Johnson, Russell **TZ**(26, 49)
Johnston, John Dennis **TZMV**(4); **TZCBS**(32b)
Jolicoeur, Paul **TZSYN**(20)
Jones, G. Stanley **TZ**(101)
Jones, Henry **TZ**(33); **NG**(28a)
Jones, Jeff **TZCBS**(10c)
Jones, Kevin **TZ**(102)
Jones, Marilyn **TZCBS**(14a)
Jones, Miranda **TZ**(59)
Jones, Morgan **TZ**(64, 113)
Journeaux, Donald **TZ**(10)
Joy, Mark **TZLC**(2)
Joyce, Debbie **TZ**(10)
Jozefson, Jack **TZCBS**(9b)
Kanaly, Steve **TZSYN**(17)
Kane, Byron **TZ**(140)
Kania, Cynthia **TZCBS**(26b)
Karlan, Richard **TZ**(26, 71)
Karnes, Brick **TZCBS**(25b)
Karnes, Doris **TZ**(44)
Karnes, Robert **TZ**(67); **NG**(14a)
Karp, Gary **TZCBS**(11b)
Karr, Patti **TZCBS**(5b)
Kasdorf, Lenore **NG**(9c)
Kauffman, Cristen **TZCBS**(30)
Kay, Beatrice **NG**(19a)
Kaye, Danny **TZCBS**(7b)
Kaye, Evelyn **TZSYN**(12)
Keach, Sr., Stacy **TZCBS**(9b)
Keane, Valley **TZ**(44)
Kearney, Carolyn **TZ**(132)

Kearney, Gene **NG**(5a, 16d) (also see
CREATIVE PERSONNEL)
Keaton, Buster **TZ**(78)
Keaton, Diane **NG**(3a)
Keats, Steven **TZCBS**(3b)
Kechne, Virginia **TZCBS**(1b)
Keefer, Don **TZ**(73, 119, 140); **NG**(36)
Keen, Noah **TZ**(67, 96)
Keene, William **TZ**(57, 75)
Keenleyside, Eric **TZSYN**(28)
Keep, Michael **TZ**(92)
Kehoe, Jack **TZCBS**(11b)
Keith, Paul **TZCBS**(18c)
Keith, Robert **TZ**(145)
Kellaway, Cecil **TZ**(20, 119)
Kellin, Mike **TZ**(104)
Kelljan, Robert **TZ**(149)
Kellogg, Ray **TZ**(124)
Kelly, Stan **TZLC**(2)
Kelman, Ricky **TZ**(99)
Kelsey, Linda **TZCBS**(35b)
Kelton, Pert **TZ**(110)
Kemmer, Edward **TZ**(123)
Kemmerling, Warren **TZ**(69)
Kemper, Doris **TZ**(111)
Kendis, William **TZ**(17, 64)
Kenneally, Phillip **NG**(19b)
Kennedy, Madge **TZ**(118)
Kennedy, Mimi **TZCBS**(26b)
Kent, Carole **TZ**(17)
Kenyatta, Caro **NG**(44a)
Kenyon, Sandy **TZ**(54, 68, 105)
Kerlee, Dennis **TZ**(102)
Keymas, George **TZ**(42); **NG**(22a)
Khaner, Julie **TZSYN**(7, 9)
Kidnie, James **TZSYN**(6)
Kiel, Richard **TZ**(89)
Kiley, Richard **NG**(1c, 24b);
TZCBS(24b)
King, Charmion **TZSYN**(8)
King, Wright **TZ**(62, 116)
Kingston, Lenore **TZ**(73)
Kinsolving, Lee **TZ**(138)
Kipling, Ron **TZ**(64)
Kirk, Phyllis **TZ**(36)
Kiser, Virginia **TZCBS**(32a)
Kleeb, Helen **TZ**(109)
Klein, Robert **TZCBS**(2a)
Klein, Sally **TZCBS**(17a)
Klein, Sonny **NG**(5a)
Klemperer, Werner **NG**(22b)

Klenck, Margaret **TZCBS**(31)
Kline, Robert **TZ**(85)
Klugman, Jack **TZ**(32, 70, 108, 121)
Knapp, Charles **TZMV**(4)
Knepper, Rob **TZCBS**(33a)
Knight, Don **NG**(29a)
Knight, Keith **TZSYN**(27)
Knight, Ted **TZ**(7)
Knox, Terence **TZSYN**(16)
Kobe, Gail **TZ**(23, 103, 136)
Kober, Jeff **TZCBS**(13a)
Koetting, Tim **TZSYN**(8)
Kolb, Mina **TZCBS**(16c)
Konopka, Ken **TZ**(148)
Konrad, Dorothy **NG**(41)
Kopell, Bernie **NG**(8a)
Korkes, Jon **NG**(21a)
Kosleck, Martin **NG**(13b)
Kotto, Yaphet **NG**(20a)
Kovacs, Geza **TZSYN**(23)
Kove, Martin **TZCBS**(10c)
Kowanko, Peter **TZCBS**(35a)
Kozak, Heidi **TZCBS**(33a)
Krentzman, Chad **TZCBS**(30)
Krieger, Ed **TZCBS**(6a)
Kriesa, Christopher **TZCBS**(32b)
Kroger, John **TZ**(45)
Kruger, Fred **TZ**(12, 49)
Kudara, Elena **TZSYN**(14)
Kuenstle, Charles **TZ**(104)
Kulcsar, Mike **TZCBS**(21b)
Kulick, Daniel **TZ**(101, 118)
Kulp, Nancy **TZ**(90)
Kuluva, Will **TZ**(71, 115)
Kuter, Kay E. **TZCBS**(23b)
Kyes, Nancy **TZCBS**(4a)
La Roche, Mary **TZ**(36)
Lacey, Laara **NG**(22b)
Lagerfelt, Caroline **TZCBS**(14c)
Laird, Jack **NG**(10b, 16d, 22b) (also see
CREATIVE PERSONNEL)
Laird, Journey **NG**(16b)
Laird, Michael **NG**(17a, 32, 34)
Lamas, Fernando **NG**(44a)
Lamb, Gil **TZ**(78)
Lambert, Doug **TZ**(136)
Lambert, Jeffrey **TZMV**(4)
Lambert, Lee Jay **NG**(46)
Lambert, Paul **TZ**(37)
Lanchester, Elsa **NG**(22a)
Land, Peter **TZCBS**(4b)

Landau, Martin **TZ**(3, 149); **TZCBS**(11a)
Landers, Muriel **TZ**(87)
Landis, Andy **TZCBS**(19b)
Landon, Hal **TZCBS**(14b)
Landry, Karen **TZCBS**(32b)
Lane, Abbe **TZMV**(4)
Lane, Charles **TZ**(33)
Lane, Rusty **TZ**(35)
Langton, Paul **TZ**(118)
Lansing, Donna-Jean **TZCBS**(5a)
Lansing, Robert **TZ**(135)
Lanteau, William **TZ**(120)
Lantry, Virginia **TZCBS**(19b)
Lanyer, Charles **TZCBS**(20a)
LaPaglia, Anthony **TZCBS**(24b)
Larch, John **TZ**(9, 48, 73)
LaRoche, Mary **TZ**(126)
Larroquette, John **TZMV**(1)
Larsen, Anker **TZ**(142)
Larson, Darrell **NG**(27b)
Lascoe, Henry **TZ**(120)
Lasell, John **TZ**(49); **NG**(29b)
Lashly, James **TZCBS**(19b, 32b)
Lau, Wesley **TZ**(53, 90)
Launer, S. John **TZ**(11, 14, 19, 121)
Laurie, Piper **TZCBS**(8b)
Law, Christopher **NG**(28a)
Lawrence, Cesca **TZCBS**(34b)
Lawrence, Shawn **TZSYN**(18)
Lawrence, Steve **NG**(18b)
Lawson, Louise **NG**(15d)
Le Mat, Paul **TZSYN**(15)
Le May, John **TZCBS**(19b, 26b)
Leachman, Cloris **TZ**(73); **NG**(28a)
Leavitt, Norman **TZ**(152)
Leavy, Donna Lyn **TZCBS**(19b)
Leblanc, Serge **TZSYN**(3)
Ledebur, Frederic **TZ**(41)
Lederer, Francis **NG**(13b)
Lee, A'leshia **NG**(28a)
Lee, Michelle **NG**(10a)
Lee, Ruta **TZ**(131)
Lehman, Ted **TZCBS**(34b)
Leigh, Janet **TZSYN**(26)
Lembeck, Harvey **NG**(18b)
Lenehan, Nancy **TZCBS**(19b)
Lenney, Dinah **TZCBS**(28c)
Leong, Albert **TZMV**(1); **TZCBS**(14c)
Lerner, Ken **TZCBS**(32a)
Lerner, Michael **NG**(36)

Lester, Jaclyn-Rose **TZCBS**(31)
Leverington, Shelby **TZCBS**(13a)
Levey, Ed **TZCBS**(3a)
Levian, Lauren **TZCBS**(3a, 33b)
Levin, Charles **TZCBS**(13b)
Levin, Matt **TZCBS**(4c)
Levy, Marty **TZCBS**(9b)
Lewis, Al **NG**(5a)
Lewis, Art **TZ**(17, 46)
Lewis, Derrick **TZ**(104)
Lewis, Diana **TZCBS**(33b)
Lewis, Jenny **TZCBS**(5a)
Lewis, Mary Margaret **TZCBS**(15a)
Lewis, Monica **TZ**(21a)
Libby, Brian **TZCBS**(19b)
Libertini, Richard **TZCBS**(25b)
Licht, Jeremy **TZMV**(3)
Licon, Betsy Jane **TZCBS**(12a)
Lieb, Bob **TZ**(47)
Liggett, Huck **TZCBS**(20a)
Lincoln, Scott **TZCBS**(11a)
Lindine, Jack **TZCBS**(16c)
Lindsay, Barbara **TZCBS**(6b)
Lindsey, George **TZ**(146)
Linville, Joanne **TZ**(69)
Linville, Larry **NG**(11d)
Lipton, Sandy **TZCBS**(23b)
Lithgow, John **TZMV**(4)
Livingston, Jock **NG**(18a)
Lloyd, Josie **TZ**(127)
Lloyd, Kathleen **TZCBS**(15a)
Lloyd, Norman **TZCBS**(24b); **NG**(23b)
Lloyd, Suzanne **TZ**(9)
LoBianco, Tony **TZCBS**(5a)
Locher, Felix **TZ**(61)
Locke, Sondra **NG**(23b)
Lockwood, Gary **NG**(35)
Lofton, Christopher **TZCBS**(34b)
Lombardo, Coleby **TZCBS**(32a)
London, Frank **TZ**(52, 122)
Long, Frederick **TZCBS**(18a)
Long, Lisa **TZCBS**(3c)
Long, Richard **TZ**(92, 137)
Lorange, Steven **NG**(17a)
Lormer, Jon **TZ**(26, 48, 88, 109)
Losby, Donald **TZ**(55)
Love, Phyllis **TZ**(94)
Lovsky, Celia **TZ**(143)
Lowell, Tom **TZ**(102)
Luft, Lorna **TZCBS**(3b)
Lukas, Karl **NG**(19a)

Lukofsky, Marla **TZSYN**(18)
Lupino, Ida **TZ**(4) (also see CREATIVE PERSONNEL)
Lupino, Richard **TZ**(37)
Lurie, Allan **TZ**(6)
Lydon, James **TZ**(49)
Lynch, Kate **TZSYN**(11)
Lynch, Ken **TZ**(3)
Lynes, Kristi **TZCBS**(34a)
Lynley, Carol **NG**(25b)
Lynn, Denise **TZ**(150)
Lyon, Sue **NG**(8b)
Lyon, Terese **TZ**(21)
Lyons, Gene **TZ**(37)
Lyons, Robert F. **NG**(14a)
Lytton, Herbert **TZ**(144)
Macaulay, Charles **NG**(22b)
MacGill, Moyna **TZ**(94)
MacIntire, James **TZCBS**(30)
Macklin, David **TZ**(133)
MacKrell, Jim **TZCBS**(22a)
MacMichael, Florence **TZ**(33)
Macnee, Patrick **TZ**(10); **NG**(21c)
MacPherson, Rafe **TZSYN**(23)
MacReady, George **TZ**(135); **NG**(1a)
Madden, Tommy **TZCBS**(18b)
Madison, John **NG**(26a)
Maga, Mickey **TZ**(2)
Maharis, George **NG**(8c)
Mahoney, Maggie **TZ**(115)
Maier, Tom **TZCBS**(21b)
Mainprize, James **TZSYN**(18)
Malet, Arthur **NG**(3b, 19b)
Mallory, Wayne **TZ**(130)
Malmuth, Evan **TZCBS**(28a)
Malone, Nancy **TZ**(150)
Maloney, James **TZ**(30)
Mamakos, Peter **NG**(8c)
Mangano, Frank **TZCBS**(32a)
Mann, Jack **TZ**(76)
Mann, Larry D. **NG**(26a)
Mantegna, Joe **TZCBS**(33b)
Mantell, Joe **TZ**(39, 122)
Mantooth, Randolph **NG**(9c)
Manza, Ralph **TZ**(98); **NG**(35); **TZCBS**(18c)
March, Lori **TZ**(14)
Marcuse, Theodore **TZ**(89, 96)
Marden, Adrienne **TZ**(89, 101)
Maren, Jerry **TZCBS**(18b)
Margolis, Andrea **TZ**(48)

Marihugh, Tammy **TZ**(108)
Marin, Russ **TZCBS**(2a)
Marinaro, Ed **TZSYN**(30)
Marion, Sidney **TZ**(148)
Mark, Tamara **TZCBS**(33a)
Marley, John **TZ**(86, 127)
Marlowe, Nora **TZ**(49, 139)
Marly, Florence **TZ**(83)
Marmer, Lea **TZ**(97)
Maross, Joe **TZ**(14, 93)
Marr, Eddie **TZ**(9, 56)
Marringly, Hedley **NG**(6b)
Mars, Kenneth **TZCBS**(16c)
Marsh, Jean **TZ**(7)
Marsh, Linda **NG**(12a)
Marshall, E. G. **NG**(9a)
Marshall, Joan **TZ**(83)
Marshall, Sarah **TZ**(91)
Martin, Barney **TZCBS**(8c)
Martin, Buzz **TZ**(5)
Martin, Dewey **TZ**(15)
Martin, Greg **TZ**(121)
Martin, Jared **NG**(21b)
Martin, Nan **TZ**(117); **TZCBS**(5a, 25b)
Martin, Ross **TZ**(13, 108); **NG**(19b, 37)
Martin, Sandy **TZCBS**(4c)
Martin, Strother **TZ**(72)
Martinez, Alma **TZCBS**(2c)
Martinez, Joaquin **TZCBS**(3a)
Marvin, Lee **TZ**(72, 122)
Masak, Ron **TZ**(19)
Masset, Andrew **TZCBS**(5b, 25b)
Massey, Raymond **NG**(5b, 33)
Massey, Walter **TZSYN**(22)
Masters, Michael **NG**(38)
Masters, Natalie **TZ**(127)
Mather, Jack **TZSYN**(5)
Matheson, Murray **TZ**(79); **NG**(43); **TZMV**(2)
Matheson, Tim **NG**(21c)
Matteo, Mona **TZSYN**(10)
Matthews, Carmen **TZ**(56)
Maxwell, Frank **TZ**(23)
Maxwell, Jenny **TZ**(58)
May, Deborah **TZCBS**(23a)
Maynor, Asa **TZ**(123)
Mayo, Raymond **NG**(38)
Mayo, Virginia **NG**(15a)
Mayron, Melanie **TZSYN**(11)
Mazursky, Paul **TZ**(19, 97, 106)
McCabe, Gregory **TZ**(86)

McCall, Mitzi **TZ**(16); **TZCBS**(16c)
McCallion, James **NG**(15a)
McCallum, David **NG**(12a)
McCarter, Brooke **TZCBS**(33a)
McCarthy, Annette **TZCBS**(18c)
McCarthy, Kevin **TZ**(24); **TZMV**(3)
McCarty, Chris **TZCBS**(16b)
McClure, Doug **TZ**(3)
McClure, Rob **TZSYN**(8)
McClure, Tipp **TZ**(122)
McCord, Robert **TZ**(58, 59, 71, 115)
McCourt, Malachy **TZLC**(2)
McDonald, Christopher **TZCBS**(26b)
McDormand, Frances **TZCBS**(21a)
McDowall, Roddy **TZ**(25); **NG**(1a)
McGann, Marlon **TZSYN**(27)
McGeachie, Calum **TZSYN**(12)
McGiver, John **TZ**(120, 147)
McGonagle, Richard **TZCBS**(12a)
McGowan, Oliver **TZ**(11)
McGrath, Doug **TZMV**(1)
McGuire, Harp **TZ**(54)
McHattie, Stephen **TZSYN**(26)
McIntire, Carl **TZ**(27)
McIntire, John **TZ**(31)
McIver, Elliot **TZSYN**(20)
McKay, Allison **NG**(9d)
McKellar, Danica **TZCBS**(12a, 33b)
McLaughlin, Emily **TZ**(77)
McLean, William **TZ**(85)
McLeod, Jackie **TZSYN**(8)
McLiam, John **TZ**(68, 75, 110, 128)
McMahon, Horace **TZ**(33)
McMahon, Jenna **TZ**(37)
McMahon, Mary **TZ**(96)
McMurtry, John **NG**(40)
McNamara, Maggie **TZ**(133)
McNear, Howard **TZ**(95, 120)
McNeil, Duncan **TZCBS**(6b)
McQueen, B. J. **TZSYN**(29)
McRae, Frank **TZCBS**(10c)
McRaney, Gerald **NG**(26a)
McRobbie, Peter **TZLC**(2)
McVeagh, Eve **TZ**(86, 146)
Melichar, Jon **TZCBS**(18c)
Mell, Joe **TZ**(83)
Melton, Troy **TZ**(85)
Melvoin, Don **NG**(5a, 7b)
Melymick, Mark **TZSYN**(30)
Mendenhall, David **TZCBS**(6a)
Menick, Jon **TZCBS**(28c)

Merande, Dodo **TZ**(120)
Meredith, Burgess **TZ**(8, 55, 65, 111);
  NG(3b, 38); **TZMV**(P)
Merrill, Gary **TZ**(76)
Merrill, Dina **NG**(44a)
Metcalfe, Burt **TZ**(22)
Metropole, James **NG**(26c, 46)
Micale, Paul **NG**(37)
Michaels, Lori **TZCBS**(28a)
Michaels, Shawn **TZ**(153)
Middleton, Burr **TZCBS**(19a, 33a)
Mier, Gregory **TZCBS**(10b)
Migenes Johnson, Julia **TZCBS**(23b)
Migram, Michael **TZMV**(1)
Miles, Vera **TZ**(21)
Milland, Ray **NG**(8c)
Millar, Lee **TZ**(17)
Miller, Adele **TZCBS**(5a)
Miller, Barry **TZ**(21b)
Miller, Dick **TZMV**(3)
Miller, Mark **TZ**(114)
Miller, Michael **TZSYN**(26)
Miller, Tony **TZ**(144)
Milletaire, Carl **NG**(6b)
Millhollin, James **TZ**(34, 55, 114)
Mills, Brooke **NG**(22c)
Milner, Martin **TZ**(21)
Mims, William **TZ**(115); **NG**(8c)
Minardos, Nico **TZ**(97)
Minot, Muriel **TZCBS**(13a)
Mirren, Helen **TZCBS**(9a)
Mitchell, Bob **TZ**(115)
Mitchell, Cameron **NG**(22a, 38)
Mitchell, George **TZ**(26, 109, 133)
Mitchell, John Cameron **TZCBS**(24b)
Mitchum, John **TZ**(60, 152)
Mobley, Roger **NG**(38)
Moede, Titus **TZ**(84)
Moffat, Donald **NG**(18a); **TZCBS**(13c)
Monaco, Mimi **TZCBS**(22c)
Monette, Richard **TZSYN**(30)
Montgomery, Elizabeth **TZ**(66)
Montgomery, Michael **TZ**(5)
Moody, Ralph **TZ**(88); **NG**(3b)
Moon, Frank **TZCBS**(27a)
Mooney, Laura **TZMV**(2)
Moorehead, Agnes **TZ**(51); **NG**(4b, 9d)
Morales, Esai **TZSYN**(20)
Morgan, Alexandra **TZCBS**(2a)
Morgan, Harry **NG**(23c); **TZSYN**(1)
Morgan, Molly **TZCBS**(10c)

Morgan, Read TZ(12)
Mori, Jeanne TZCBS(17b)
Moriarty, Michael TZSYN(12)
Morick, David NG(17b); TZCBS(17a)
Morris, Garrett TZCBS(8c)
Morris, Greg TZ(130)
Morris, Howard TZ(114)
Morris, Iona TZCBS(2c)
Morris, Jeffrey TZ(130)
Morris, Kimberly Ann TZCBS(21b)
Morris, Virginia TZCBS(3b)
Morrison, Barbara TZ(101)
Morrow, Byron TZ(25)
Morrow, Jeff TZ(20); TZCBS(24a)
Morrow, Vic TZMV(1)
Morse, Barry TZ(87); TZSYN(5)
Morse, Robert NG(11c); TZCBS(5b)
Morsell, Fred TZCBS(7a)
Morton, Howard NG(2b)
Morton, Judy TZ(100)
Morton, Wayne TZCBS(13a)
Mosley, Roger E. NG(21c)
Moss, Ezekiel TZCBS(30)
Moultrie, Melissa TZCBS(10a)
Muehl, Brian TZCBS(13a)
Muellerleile, Marianne TZCBS(15c)
Mulkey, Chris TZCBS(32b)
Mullavey, Greg TZCBS(1b)
Mulligan, Richard TZCBS(13a, 29)
Mullikin, Bill TZ(28)
Mumy, Bill TZ(58, 73, 121); TZMV(3)
Munco, Howard TZCBS(19b)
Munday, Mary TZ(133)
Munro, Neil TZSYN(10)
Murdock, George TZ(98); NG(1c)
Murphy, Ben TZSYN(28)
Murtagh, Kate TZ(152)
Murukh TZCBS(1a)
Muse, Margaret NG(36)
Mustin, Burt TZ(47, 86)
Myers, Addison TZ(76)
Myhers, John TZCBS(5b)
Napier, Alan TZ(119); NG(16a, 28b, 32)
Naughton, David TZSYN(27)
Neal, Mavis TZ(30); NG(24b)
Neilsen, Lucinda TZSYN(15)
Nelkin, Stacey TZCBS(24a)
Nello, Tommy TZ(62)
Nelson, Barry TZ(150)
Nelson, Ed TZ(105); NG(29b)

Nelson, Harriet NG(36)
Nelson, Nels TZ(28)
Nelson, Ozzie NG(36)
Nemes, Scott TZMV(2)
Nesbitt, Paul TZ(100)
Nettleton, Lois TZ(75); NG(27a)
Neuman, Karen TZ(33)
Newlan, Paul TZ(153)
Newmar, Julie TZ(116)
Newton, John TZ(92)
Neyer Craven, Mimi TZCBS(2a)
Nicholas, Denise NG(21c)
Nichols, Barbara TZ(53)
Nichols, Lance TZCBS(9a)
Nicol, Alex TZ(99)
Nielsen, Leslie NG(8d, 13a)
Nigra, Christina TZMV(4)
Nimoy, Leonard TZ(80); NG(39) (also see CREATIVE PERSONNEL)
Nisbet, Stuart TZ(121); NG(34, 36)
Nissman, Michael TZCBS(10c)
Nix, Rosary NG(8a)
Noble, Trisha NG(16a)
Nolan, Jeanette TZ(84, 109); NG(2b, 10a)
Nono, Claire TZCBS(1b, 31)
Noonan, Kerry TZCBS(6b)
Normant, Elizabeth TZCBS(6a)
Norris, Karen TZ(150)
Nothnagel, Ian TZSYN(9)
Novak, John TZSYN(28)
Noven, Kip NG(31)
Nucci, Danny TZCBS(19a)
Nunez, Miguel TZCBS(7a)
Nusser, James NG(22c)
O'Brien, Myles TZCBS(24a)
O'Brien, Richard NG(17b)
O'Brien, Rory TZ(101)
O'Brien, Tom TZCBS(30)
O'Connell, Arthur NG(20b)
O'Connell, William TZ(101)
O'Connor, Glynnis TZCBS(27a)
O'Connor, Tim TZ(118)
O'Donnell, Gene NG(7b)
O'Hara, Patrick TZ(105); NG(23b)
O'Hara, Shirley TZ(60, 118)
O'Keefe, Raymond TZCBS(30)
O'Kelly, Don TZ(35)
O'Malley, J. Pat TZ(5, 31, 49, 56, 90, 136, 152)
O'Malley, Kathleen TZ(136)

O'Malley, Lillian **TZ**(56)
O'Moore, Patrick **TZ**(152); **NG**(24b)
O'Neal, Anne **TZ**(86)
O'Neal, Kevin **TZ**(102)
O'Neal, Patrick **TZ**(131); **NG**(11a)
O'Neill, Amy **TZCBS**(10a)
O'Neill, Chris **TZLC**(2)
O'Quinn, Terrance **TZCBS**(2c)
O'Regan, James **TZSYN**(2)
O'Sullivan, Colleen **TZ**(33)
Oakland, Simon **TZ**(60, 104)
Oates, Warren **TZ**(19, 130)
Ober, Philip **TZ**(141)
Oberon, Elan **TZCBS**(10c)
Obney, Jack Ross **TZCBS**(21b)
Ohta, Bennett **TZCBS**(14c)
Oliver, Barret **TZCBS**(18a)
Oliver, Susan **TZ**(25); **NG**(22c)
Olmstead, Nelson **TZ**(89)
Olsen, Richard K. **TZLC**(2)
Opatoshu, David **TZ**(105)
Osmond, Cliff **TZ**(97)
Ossetynski, Leonidas D. **NG**(22b)
Otis, Ted **TZ**(15)
Overholts, Jay **TZ**(2, 40, 53, 54, 56, 77, 85)
Overton, Frank **TZ**(5, 107)
Owen, Deirdre **TZ**(10)
Owen, Tudor **TZ**(112)
Packer, Doris **TZ**(100)
Page, Geraldine **NG**(26b, 28b, 40)
Palance, Jack **TZLC**(2)
Pall, Gloria **TZ**(11)
Palmer, Anthony **TZCBS**(14b)
Palmer, Tom **TZ**(44)
Pankin, Joy **TZCBS**(3a)
Paolone, Catherine **TZCBS**(23b)
Parker, Suzy **TZ**(137); **NG**(2b)
Parker, Warren **TZ**(78)
Parkes, Gerard **TZSYN**(3)
Parks, Trina **NG**(12a)
Parr, Jutta **TZ**(58)
Parr, Kate **TZSYN**(19)
Parsons, Jennifer **TZCBS**(6b)
Parsons, Milton **TZ**(78, 115); **NG**(19b)
Partlow, Richard **TZCBS**(24a)
Partridge, Sarah **TZCBS**(7a)
Pascal, Marianna **TZSYN**(!5)
Pasco, Nicholas **TZSYN**(22)
Pastorelli, Robert **TZCBS**(9a)
Pataki, Michael **TZ**(80)

Paton, Laurie **TZSYN**(29)
Patrick, Chris **NG**(21b)
Patrick, Dennis **TZCBS**(35b)
Patterson, Hank **TZ**(133, 154)
Patton, Dianna **TZCBS**(32b)
Paul, Don **TZCBS**(3b)
Paulin, Scott **TZCBS**(4c)
Payne, Julie **TZCBS**(4b)
Payne, Ron **TZSYN**(8)
Peaker, E. J. **NG**(15b)
Pearce, Alice **TZ**(56)
Pedi, Tom **NG**(11a)
Peel, Richard **TZ**(10)
Peets, Remus **TZMV**(1)
Pelto, Matt **NG**(3b, 7b, 23a)
Pender, Tony **TZLC**(2)
Penny, Joe **TZCBS**(30)
Penny, Sydney **TZCBS**(23b)
Pera, Radames **NG**(12b)
Perkins, Jack **TZ**(18)
Perrin, Vic **TZ**(25, 133)
Perry, Barbara **TZ**(31)
Perry, Joe **TZ**(29, 97)
Perry, Joseph **NG**(14a)
Perry, Steven **TZ**(27)
Persky, Lisa Jane **TZCBS**(25a)
Persoff, Nehemiah **TZ**(10)
Peters, Brock **NG**(21c)
Peters, Gerald S. **NG**(23b)
Peters, House, Jr. **TZ**(33)
Petersen, William L. **TZCBS**(21a)
Peterson, Arthur **TZ**(17)
Peterson, Hank **TZ**(86)
Peterson, Melinda **TZCBS**(19a)
Peterson, Nan **TZ**(5, 50, 140)
Peterson, Steve **TZCBS**(16b)
Petrie, George **TZ**(103); **TZCBS**(23a)
Pettet, Joanna **TZ**(4a, 17b, 29a, 31)
Petty, Lori **TZCBS**(22c)
Peugh, Willard **TZCBS**(2a)
Phillips, Barney **TZ**(19, 40, 64, 110)
Phillips, Ethan **TZCBS**(22b)
Phillips, Lee **TZ**(119, 143)
Phillips, Patricia **TZSYN**(30)
Phillips, Ruth **TZ**(143)
Phillips, Wendy **TZCBS**(10b)
Phipps, William **TZ**(19)
Piazza, Ben **TZCBS**(2c)
Pickard, John **TZ**(132)
Pickens, Slim **NG**(45)
Piddock, Jim **TZCBS**(22b)

Pine, Philip **TZ**(13, 117)
Pitlik, Noam **NG**(9a)
Platt, Alma **TZ**(96); **NG**(10a)
Platt, Ed **TZ**(59)
Pleasence, Donald **TZ**(102)
Pniewski, Mike **TZCBS**(18c)
Pogue, Ken **TZSYN**(25)
Poindexter, Lawrence **TZCBS**(18c)
Pointer, Priscilla **TZMV**(2); **TZLC**(1)
Polis, Joel **TZCBS**(10b)
Pollack, Sydney **TZ**(45)
Poon, Anna Maria **TZCBS**(9b)
Pope, Peggy **TZCBS**(16c)
Popwell, Albert **NG**(3c, 21c)
Porter, Debby **TZMV**(1)
Postil, Adam **TZCBS**(7a)
Potts, Annie **TZCBS**(2a)
Potts, Jonathon **TZSYN**(4)
Poule, Ezelle **TZ**(41, 88)
Powell, Ricky **NG**(20a)
Powers, Bruce **TZ**(31)
Prange, Laurie **NG**(14b)
Pratt, Robert **NG**(41)
Prescott, Robert **TZCBS**(16a)
Press, Laura **TZSYN**(17)
Presson, Jason **TZCBS**(10a)
Price, Vincent **NG**(9c, 30)
Prince, Michael **TZCBS**(13b)
Proctor, Philip **TZCBS**(6b)
Prohaska, Robert **NG**(18a)
Pruner, Karl **TZSYN**(13)
Purdy, Deanna **TZCBS**(2b)
Purdy, Kristi **TZCBS**(2b)
Pushman, Terence **NG**(6b, 28b)
Pyle, Denver **TZ**(138)
Quaid, Randy **NG**(23c)
Quick, Eldon **NG**(10a); **TZCBS**(21a)
Quigley, Gerry **TZSYN**(14)
Quinlan, Kathleen **TZMV**(3)
Quinn, Bill **NG**(12a, 22a); **TZMV**(2)
Raber, Adam **TZCBS**(2a, 33b)
Raffin, Deborah **TZSYN**(19)
Ragin, John **NG**(7b)
Railsback, Steve **TZCBS**(19b)
Raine, Jack **TZ**(141)
Rainey, Ford **NG**(12a)
Raino Edwards, Ella **TZCBS**(23a)
Ralston, Jane **TZCBS**(16c)
Rand, Edwin **TZ**(21)
Randall, Anne **NG**(21b)
Randall, Sue **TZ**(11, 140)

Randolph, John **NG**(7b)
Raven, Elsa **TZMV**(2)
Rawlins, Sam **TZ**(13)
Rawls, Hardy **TZCBS**(9a)
Ray, Anthony **TZ**(52)
Raybould, Harry **TZ**(18)
Raymond, Guy **TZ**(116)
Redd, Mary Robin **TZCBS**(16b)
Redford, Robert **TZ**(81)
Redican, Dan **TZSYN**(9)
Redmond, Marge **TZ**(120)
Reed, Walter **TZ**(43)
Reese, Tom **TZ**(75)
Reiner, Carl **NG**(15d)
Rennick, Nancy **TZ**(34, 54)
Repp, Stafford **TZ**(43, 72, 148)
Revill, Clive **TZCBS**(18b)
Rey, Alejandro **NG**(43)
Reynolds, Burt **TZ**(120)
Reynolds, Michael J. **TZSYN**(16)
Reynolds, Mike **TZCBS**(7b)
Reynolds, William **TZ**(19)
Rhodes, Barbara **NG**(40)
Ribbel, Tony **NG**(5a)
Ribisi, Vonni **TZCBS**(11a)
Rich, Michael **TZCBS**(10a)
Richard, Darryl **TZ**(102)
Richards, Evan **TZMV**(2)
Richards, Frank **TZ**(55)
Richards, Karla **TZCBS**(16b)
Richards, Paul **NG**(4a)
Richardson, Michael **NG**(34)
Richman, Josh **TZCBS**(7a)
Richman, Mark **TZ**(155)
Rickles, Don **TZ**(55)
Ricossa, Maria **TZSYN**(13)
Riegert, Peter **TZCBS**(11b)
Riley, Larry **TZCBS**(17b)
Riordan, Robert **TZ**(57)
Roach, Jennifer **TZCBS**(26a)
Robbins, Brian **TZCBS**(7a)
Robbins, Garry **TZSYN**(29)
Robelo, Mike **NG**(17b)
Roberts, Pernell **TZCBS**(22c)
Roberts, Rachel **NG**(4b)
Roberts, Roy **TZ**(124)
Roberts, Tony **NG**(20a)
Robertson, Cliff **TZ**(59, 98)
Robertson, George R. **TZSYN**(21)
Robertson, Rebecca **TZCBS**(16b)
Robins, Oliver **TZCBS**(15a)

Robinson, Andrew TZCBS(20a, 33c)
Robinson, Bartlett TZ(49, 89)
Robinson, Edward G. NG(20a)
Robson, Wayne TZSYN(29)
Rodgers, Enid TZCBS(13a)
Roland, Gilbert NG(25a)
Roll, Grant TZSYN(12)
Roman, Nina TZ(110)
Roman, Susan TZSYN(27)
Romero, Cesar NG(15b)
Romeyn, Jane TZ(65)
Rooney, Mickey TZ(125); NG(33)
Rooney, Wallace TZ(60, 99, 103)
Roope, Fay TZ(26)
Rosenthal, Alan TZSYN(6)
Ross, Ron TZCBS(16c)
Rossen, Carol TZ(49)
Roth, Gene TZ(62)
Roth, J. D. TZCBS(34a)
Rourke, Hayden TZ(52)
Rowan, Roy TZ(56)
Rubin, Jennifer TZCBS(35a)
Rucker, Dennis NG(21a)
Rue, Ed NG(44a)
Ruffino, Val TZ(71)
Ruggieri, Françoise NG(21b)
Rule, Janice TZ(29)
Rusch, Gloria TZCBS(3c)
Rush, Barbara NG(19a)
Rushakoff, Sid NG(5a)
Ruskin, Joseph TZ(38), NG(20a)
Russ, Tim TZCBS(3c, 34b)
Russell, BiNG TZ(67, 133)
Ryan, Eileen TZ(23)
Ryan, Fran NG(9d)
Ryder, Edward TZ(55)
Sabinson, Lee TZ(50)
Sage, David TZCBS(20a)
Sagoes, Ken TZCBS(13b)
Saint John, Morgan TZCBS(27a)
Sak, Bill TZCBS(27a)
Saldana, Theresa TZCBS(9a)
Salmi, Albert TZ(26, 80, 116); NG(25a)
Salsberg, Gerry TZSYN(7)
Sampson, Robert TZ(91)
Sand, Paul TZCBS(34a)
Sanders, Cynthia TZCBS(25a)
Sanders, Hugh TZ(10, 77, 116)
Sanderson, William TZSYN(9)
Sands, Lee TZ(17)
Santana, Jose TZCBS(15b)

Santos, Joe TZCBS(22c)
Sanvido, Guy TZSYN(20)
Sargent, Glenna NG(32)
Sargent, Joe TZ(53)
Sargent, William TZ(113, 132)
Sasson, Suzanne TZCBS(7a)
Savage, Fred TZCBS(26a)
Savalas, Telly TZ(126)
Sawyer, Toni TZCBS(23b)
Sax, Arline TZ(12, 53)
Saxon, John NG(27a)
Sayre, Jeffrey TZ(17)
Scally, James TZCBS(14b)
Scanlon, John G. TZCBS(14c)
Scannell, Kevin TZCBS(18c)
Scarber, Sam TZCBS(30)
Schaefer, Craig TZCBS(23b)
Schallert, William TZ(33); TZMV(3); TZCBS(23a)
Schenkkan, Robert TZCBS(22b)
Schildkraut, Joseph TZ(74, 96)
Schmidt, Georgia NG(5a); TZCBS(13a)
Schofield, John D. NG(24b)
Schrage, Lisa TZSYN(14)
Schreiber, Avery TZCBS(8a)
Schwab, Lonna TZMV(4)
Schwarz, Reiner TZSYN(18)
Scolari, Peter TZSYN(10)
Scott, Elliott TZCBS(23b)
Scott, Henry TZ(27, 104)
Scott, Jacqueline TZ(113)
Scott, Joe TZ(57)
Scott, Pippa TZ(45)
Scott, Simon TZ(18)
Scotti, Vito TZ(33, 97)
Scourby, Alexander TZ(18)
Sears, Djanet TZSYN(9)
Seay, James TZ(103)
Seel, Charles TZ(84); NG(10a)
Selberg, David TZCBS(26a)
Selby, Sarah TZ(148)
Selzer, Milton TZ(95, 145)
Selznick, Alvie TZCBS(28a)
Seymour, Carolyn TZCBS(5b)
Shackelford, Ted TZSYN(3)
Shanewise, Lenore TZ(86)
Shannon, Barbara NG(9c)
Shatner, William TZ(43, 123)
Shattuc, Norma TZ(101)
Shaw, Helen TZMV(2)

Shaw, Joseph **TZSYN**(5)
Shawn, Dick **TZCBS**(18c)
Shaye, Lin **TZCBS**(2c)
Sheiner, David **TZ**(104)
Shelley, Joshua **TZCBS**(18b)
Shelton, Jacques **TZ**(130)
Sherman, Orville **TZ**(84)
Shirley, Mercedes **TZ**(118)
Shoop, Pamela **NG**(28a)
Shutan, Jan **NG**(21b)
Sickner, Roy **TZ**(101)
Sikking, James B. **NG**(3c, 9a)
Silbley, Grey **TZLC**(1)
Silva, Henry **NG**(6c)
Silver, Johnny **NG**(3b)
Silvera, Frank **TZ**(92)
Simmons, Georgia **TZ**(156)
Simon, Robert F. **TZ**(112)
Simonett, Ted **TZSYN**(10)
Sinclair, Judy **TZSYN**(6)
Singer, Marc **TZSYN**(2)
Singleton, Doris **TZ**(124)
Singleton, Penny **TZ**(147)
Sirianni, E. A. **NG**(11d)
Skaggs, Jimmie F. **TZCBS**(19b)
Skerritt, Tom **TZCBS**(26a)
Skomarovsky, Vladimir **TZCBS**(21b)
Slaten, Max **TZ**(30)
Slattery, Kerry **TZCBS**(3b)
Sloane, Everett **TZ**(17)
Smith, Cedric **TZSYN**(1)
Smith, Charles Martin **TZCBS**(11a)
Smith, Cotter **TZCBS**(16b)
Smith, Ebbe Roe **TZCBS**(19b)
Smith, Howard **TZ**(30, 101)
Smith, Kent **NG**(26a, 42)
Smith, Lane **TZCBS**(20a)
Smith, LoriNG **TZ**(50, 114)
Smith, Marilyn **TZSYN**(13)
Smith, Patricia **TZ**(58)
Smith, William **TZCBS**(23a)
Snyder, Robert **TZ**(82)
Socher, Cheryl **TZMV**(2)
Sofaer, Abraham **TZ**(35)
Sokoloff, Vladimir **TZ**(48, 71, 97)
Solomon, Bruce **TZCBS**(15a)
Sondergaard, Gale **NG**(17a)
Sorci, Juliette **TZCBS**(33c)
Sorel, Louise **NG**(2a, 18a)
Soreny, Eva **TZ**(107)
Sorrells, Robert **TZ**(35)

Soule, Olan **TZ**(38, 148)
Spain, Artie **NG**(41)
Spain, Fay **NG**(33)
Spanier, Francis **NG**(12b)
Spear, Danny **TZCBS**(33a)
Spencer, Douglas **TZ**(55)
Spenser-Roth, Caprice **TZCBS**(28a)
Spiner, Brent **TZCBS**(19b)
Squire, Katherine **TZ**(82, 103)
Stafford, Tim **TZ**(156)
Stanger, Hugo **TZCBS**(13a)
Stanhope, Ted **TZ**(9)
Stanley, Kim **NG**(11a)
Stanwood, Michael **NG**(23a)
Stark, Don **TZCBS**(24b)
Steele, Barbara **NG**(28b)
Stehli, Edgar **TZ**(24)
Stein, Rod **NG**(18c)
Stephens, Harry **TZCBS**(26b)
Sterling, Patricia **NG**(30)
Sterling, Robert **TZ**(111)
Stern, Jenna **TZLC**(2)
Stevens, Inger **TZ**(16, 44)
Stevens, Marc **TZ**(86)
Stevens, Naomi **TZ**(21)
Stevens, Warren **TZ**(83); **TZCBS**(24a)
Stevenson, Robert J. **TZ**(75, 85)
Stewart, Malcom **TZSYN**(26)
Stewart, Peggy **TZ**(68)
Stock, Barbara **TZSYN**(5)
Stockwell, Dean **TZ**(80); **NG**(42); **TZSYN**(22)
Stokes, Ron **TZ**(144)
Stone, George E. **TZ**(78)
Stone, Harold J. **TZ**(67)
Stout, Paul **TZCBS**(13a)
Strangis, Judy **TZ**(120)
Stransky, Chuck **TZCBS**(19a)
Strasberg, Susan **NG**(14a, 43)
Stratford, Tracy **TZ**(91, 126)
Stratton, Chet **TZ**(63, 110)
Strickland, Amzie **TZ**(22); **TZCBS**(13b)
Strickler, Jerry **NG**(3c)
Stroll, Edson **TZ**(42, 96)
Strom, Diane **TZ**(56)
Strong, Leonard **TZ**(16)
Strudwick, Shepperd **TZ**(29)
Stuart, Barbara **TZ**(40)
Stuart, Maxine **TZ**(42)
Study, Lomax **TZ**(89)

Sturgis, Norman TZ(12)
Suarez, Eunice NG(3b)
Sudlow, Joan TZ(22)
Sues, Alan TZ(145)
Sullivan, Barry NG(1b, 38)
Sullivan, Jenny NG(21b)
Sullivan, John L. TZ(144)
Sullivan, Liam TZ(61, 102)
Summers, Hope NG(17a)
Summers, Jerry NG(22b)
Sunday, Mark TZ(12)
Surovy, Nicholas TZCBS(4a)
Sutton, Frank TZ(98)
Svanoe, Bill NG(11b)
Swan, Robert TZCBS(4c)
Swan, William TZ(135)
Swedberg, Heidi TZLC(1)
Swiegart, Charles TZCBS(13a)
Swingler, Richard TZMV(2)
Swoger, Harry TZ(83)
Szabo, Albert TZ(38)
Tabori, Kristoffer TZCBS(12a)
Taeger, Ralph TZ(140)
Taft, Sara TZ(108)
Tafur, Robert TZ(89)
Takei, George TZ(151)
Talbot, Stephen TZ(56, 90)
Taloe, Jack TZCBS(3b)
Tambor, Jeffrey TZCBS(9a, 28c)
Tannen, Charles TZ(89)
Tapscott, Mark TZ(76)
Tarbuck, Barbara TZCBS(11b)
Tate, Larenz TZCBS(13a)
Taylor, Anne NG(20a)
Taylor, Dub TZ(88)
Taylor, Ferris TZ(21)
Taylor, Mark TZCBS(20a)
Taylor, Rod TZ(11)
Taylor, Sue NG(14b)
Taylor, Tamara TZCBS(33b)
Taylor, Vaughn TZ(8, 76, 100, 117, 136)
Taylor, William B. TZMV(1)
Taylor Smith, Aileen TZSYN(8)
Teal, Ray TZ(111)
Tedrow, Irene TZ(5, 44)
Tennant, Victoria TZCBS(21b)
Terry, Robert NG(3b)
Thatcher, Torin NG(6b)
Thaxter, Phyllis TZ(99)
Therrien, Al TZSYN(22)

Thomas, James Edward TZCBS(25b)
Thomas, Richard NG(28b)
Thomas, Rosemarie TZCBS(3c)
Thomerson, Tim TZCBS(22a)
Thompson, Charles TZ(111)
Thompson, Elizabeth NG(37)
Thompson, Kevin TZCBS(18b)
Thompson, R. H. TZSYN(8)
Thorson, Russell NG(34)
Throckmorton, Nancy TZCBS(25a)
Thursby, David TZ(45)
Titus, Jim E. TZ(117)
Tobey, Kenneth NG(38); TZCBS(24a)
Tobin, Dan TZ(52)
Tochi, Brian TZCBS(9b)
Tompkins, ANGel NG(3a)
Tompkins, Joan NG(18a)
Tone, Franchot TZ(61)
Toth, Frank TZMV(4)
Touliatos, George TZSYN(30)
Towers, Marc TZ(17)
Townes, Harry TZ(13, 62); NG(23a)
Townsend, Dwight TZ(16)
Trent, Russell TZ(9)
Trinka, Paul NG(17b)
Tripp, Paul TZ(90)
Troscianiec, Hank TZLC(2)
Troupe, Tom NG(5b)
Truex, Barry TZ(86)
Truex, Ernest TZ(12, 86)
Trujillo, Thomas NG(24a)
Trundy, Natalie TZ(105)
Tucker, Forrest NG(16c)
Tucker, Wayne TZ(28)
Turley, Jim TZ(7, 58, 71, 85)
Turman, Glynn TZCBS(7b)
Turnbull, Ann TZSYN(8)
Turner, Arnold NG(10a)
Turner, Maria TZ(68)
Twomey, Anne TZCBS(12a)
Tyburn, Gene NG(8a)
Tyler, James TZ(143)
Tyrone, David NG(44a)
Udy, Helene TZCBS(2a)
Unger, Joe TZCBS(32b)
Utay, William TZCBS(16c)
Vahanian, Marc NG(15c)
Val, Marion NG(3b)
Valentine, Karen TZSYN(25)
Vallee, Rudy NG(11c)
Van, Alex TZLC(1)

Van, Frankie **TZ**(27); **NG**(35)
Van Ark, Joan **NG**(35)
Van Cleef, Lee **TZ**(72)
Van Dreelen, John **TZ**(149)
Van Evera, Warren **TZSYN**(5, 25)
Van Lynn, Vincent **NG**(27b)
Van Patten, Joyce **TZ**(119)
Van Patten, Vincent **NG**(15c)
Van Vleet, Richard **NG**(3c)
Van Zandt, Julie **TZ**(92)
Vandever, Michael **TZ**(19)
Vargas, Edmund **TZ**(97)
Verne, Karen **TZ**(74)
Vernon, Harvey **TZCBS**(4b)
Vernon, Jackie **NG**(5a)
Vinaccia, Gina Marie **TZCBS**(23b)
Vincent, Billy **TZ**(96)
Visitor, Nana **TZCBS**(9a)
Vogt, Lynn **TZSYN**(2)
Von Glatz, Ilse **TZSYN**(23)
Von Leer, Hunter **NG**(9c)
Von Radicki, Barbara **TZSYN**(27)
Von Scherler, Sasha **TZCBS**(9a)
Votrian, Ralph **TZ**(80)
Waggner, Lea **TZ**(22)
Wagner, Lindsay **NG**(15a, 48)
Wagrowski, Gregory **TZCBS**(19b)
Walcutt, John **TZCBS**(32b)
Walker, Bill **TZ**(145)
Walker, Isabelle **TZCBS**(1b)
Walker, Peter **TZ**(23)
Wallace, Helen **TZ**(88)
Wallace Stone, Dee **TZCBS**(4b)
Wallach, Katherine **TZCBS**(12a)
Wallis, Shani **NG**(6c)
Walls, Bud **NG**(9a)
Walsh, Gwynyth **TZSYN**(24)
Walsh, M. Emmet **TZCBS**(8c)
Walsh, Sydney **TZCBS**(3b)
Walsh, William **TZ**(22)
Ward, Elizabeth **TZCBS**(13a)
Ward, John **TZ**(118)
Ward, Jonathan **TZCBS**(10a)
Ward, Wally **TZCBS**(34a)
Warden, Jack **TZ**(7, 35)
Warner, Bob **TZSYN**(4)
Warner, Sandra **TZ**(28, 98)
Warren, Lesley Ann **NG**(41)
Warwick, Robert **TZ**(18)
Waterbury, Laura **TZCBS**(1b)
Waters, Sneezy **TZSYN**(28)

Watkins, Frank **TZ**(127)
Watson, Larry **NG**(3a, 15d, 22a, 25a, 32)
Waxman, Stanley **NG**(11d, 18b)
Wayne, David **TZ**(6); **NG**(15a)
Wayne, Fredd **TZ**(53, 67)
Weaver, Dennis **TZ**(62)
Weaver, Fritz **TZ**(14, 65); **NG**(13a); **TZCBS**(13c)
Webb, Bunty **TZSYN**(3)
Webber, Peggy **NG**(21a, 27a)
Webster, Mary **TZ**(32, 108)
Wedgeworth, Ann **TZCBS**(28a)
Weed, Adam **NG**(37)
Weinrib, Len **TZ**(110)
Weisser, Norbert **TZMV**(1)
Weissman, Jeffrey **TZMV**(4)
Weitz, Bruce **TZSYN**(23)
Welch, Nelson **TZCBS**(12a)
Wellman, James L. **TZ**(89)
Wells, David **TZCBS**(19b)
Wells, Jack **TZCBS**(6b)
Welsh, Kenneth **TZSYN**(11)
Wendt, George **TZCBS**(28c)
Wescoatt, Rusty **TZ**(31)
Wessel, Richard **TZ**(124)
West, Adam **NG**(10b)
West, Red **TZCBS**(25a)
Westcott, Helena **TZ**(134)
Westerfield, James **TZ**(55)
Weston, Amber Lea **TZSYN**(2)
Weston, Ellen **NG**(8a)
Weston, Jack **TZ**(22, 120)
Westwood, Patrick **TZ**(50)
Wheeler, Margaret **TZMV**(4)
Wheeler Duff, Susan **TZCBS**(11b)
Whipp, Joseph **TZCBS**(2a)
White, Christine **TZ**(57, 123)
White, Daniel **TZ**(48)
White, David **TZ**(23, 100)
White, Jesse **TZ**(78, 101)
White, Myrna **TZCBS**(6a, 25b)
White, Ruth **TZ**(117)
White, Will J. **TZ**(14, 89)
Whitman, Stuart **NG**(23a, 32)
Whitmore, James **TZ**(118)
Whitmore, Jr., James **TZCBS**(4c, 35b)
Whitney, Peter **NG**(26a)
Whyte, Patrick **TZ**(34)
Wilbanks, Don **TZ**(127)
Wilcox, Collin **TZ**(137)
Wilde, Cornel **NG**(26a)

Wilkerson, Guy **TZ**(43)
Willard, Ellen **TZ**(72)
Willes, Jean **TZ**(64)
Willette, Joann **TZCBS**(17a)
Williams, Adam **TZ**(16, 46)
Williams, Edy **TZ**(98)
Williams, John **TZ**(120); **NG**(6c, 29a)
Williams, Mack **TZ**(62)
Williams, Philip **TZSYN**(18)
Williams, Steven **TZMV**(1)
Williamson, Ermal **TZCBS**(16c)
Willis, Bruce **TZCBS**(1a)
Willis, Brynja **TZCBS**(2a)
Willock, Dave **TZ**(45)
Willows, Alec **TZSYN**(7)
Wills, Chill **NG**(3b)
Wilson, Brittany **TZCBS**(1b)
Wilson, Dick **TZ**(6), **TZ**(132)
Wilson, Patricia **TZCBS**(13a)
Wilson, Scott **TZCBS**(17b)
Wilson, Teddy **TZCBS**(13a)
Wilson, Thick **TZSYN**(29)
Windom, William **TZ**(79, 110); **NG**(7b, 29b)
Wingreen, Jason **TZ**(30, 75); **NG**(3c, 12b)
Winningham, Mare **TZCBS**(20b)
Winstead, Deborah **TZLC**(1)
Winters, Jonathan **TZ**(70)
Winwood, Estelle **TZ**(24)
Wiseman, Joseph **TZ**(82); **NG**(3a)
Witcher, Geoff **TZCBS**(25b, 33b)
Wolfe, Ian **TZ**(128); **NG**(26a)
Wolff, Frank **TZ**(32)
Woloshyn, Illya **TZSYN**(7)
Wood, Jeanne **TZ**(63)
Wood, Lana **NG**(28a)
Wood, Terri Lynn **TZCBS**(16b)
Wood, Ward **TZ**(146)
Workman, Lindsay **TZ**(112); **NG**(3b)
Worley, Jo Anne **NG**(16a)
Wright, Ben **TZ**(10, 74, 83)
Wright, Billie Joe **TZCBS**(27a)
Wright, Howard **TZ**(77, 144)
Wright, Susan **TZSYN**(29)
Wulff, Kai **TZMV**(1)
Wyenn, Than **TZ**(26); **NG**(6c)
Wyllie, Meg **TZ**(47)
Wynant, H.M. **TZ**(41)
Wynn, Ed **TZ**(2, 132)
Wynn, Keenan **TZ**(36)

Yagher, Jeff **TZCBS**(25a)
Yagi, James **TZ**(112)
Yeager, Biff **TZCBS**(11b)
Yeo, Leslie **TZSYN**(7)
Yñiguez, Richard **NG**(24a)
York, Dick **TZ**(19, 52)
Young, Carlton **TZ**(89)
Young, De De **NG**(41)
Young, Gig **TZ**(5)
Young, Victor Sen **NG**(33)
Young, William Allen **TZCBS**(32b)
Younger, Jack **TZ**(101)
Yuro, Robert **NG**(15a)
Zakarian, Ruth **TZCBS**(23b)
Zand, Michael **TZCBS**(25b)
Zarchen, John **TZCBS**(31)
Zaremba, John **TZ**(112)
Zarou, Elias **TZSYN**(27)
Zeller, Jean-François **TZ**(142)